COMPLETE
WRECK DIVING
A GUIDE TO DIVING WRECKS

by Henry Keatts and Brian Skerry

Disclaimer

Scuba diving is potentially hazardous. Practiced incorrectly or with incomplete planning and procedures, it can expose a person to considerable risks including serious injury or even death. It requires specialized training, equipment, and experience. This book is not intended as a substitute for the above or for the diver to abandon common sense in pursuit of diving activities which are beyond his abilities. This book is intended as a source of information on various aspects of wreck diving, not as a substitute for proper supervised training and experience. For training in wreck diving, contact a national certification agency. The reader is advised that all the elements of hazard and risk associated with scuba diving and wreck diving cannot be brought out within the scope of this text. The authors, publisher, and manufacturers presented in this book, are not liable for damage or injury including death which may result from any scuba diving activities, with respect to information contained herein.

Cover photo of the tug boat *Jay Scutti,* in 85 feet of water off Fort Lauderdale, Florida taken by Brian Skerry

First Printing 1995
Watersport Publishing, Inc., P.O. Box 83727, San Diego, CA 92138

Printed in the United States

International Standard Book Number ISBN: 0-922769-38-9

Library of Congress Catalog Card Number: 94-61789
Keatts, Professor Henry, Skerry, Brian
   Complete Wreck Diving
    A Guide To Diving Wrecks

COMPLETE
WRECK DIVING
A GUIDE TO DIVING WRECKS

by Henry Keatts and Brian Skerry

Watersport Publishing, Inc.
Post Office Box 83727 • San Diego, CA 92138

Dedication

To Marcia and Carole for their eternal understanding.

Table of Contents

Acknowledgements

The writing of this book is the result of many years of wreck diving and an association with a number of talented individuals who have shared in our quest to seek out the silent fleets beneath the sea. A debt of gratitude is extended to all who contributed to the final outcome.

We are especially grateful to Bill Carter, Jr. for his great assistance in so many areas of this book, with a specific focus on his expertise of wreck hunting. A special thanks also to Captains Eric and Lori Takakjian, Tom Mulloy, Steve Bielenda, Bill Palmer, and Joe Gallo for their continued support in getting us, on short notice, to so many wrecks. For his perspective as a wreck diving instructor, we thank David Morton, who assisted from the very beginning with practical, valuable information. Thanks also to George Farr for editorial assistance on portions of this text and to Admiralty lawyer Peter Hess for his explanations and interpretations of maritime law.

For wreck divers today, much of the way has been paved by early pioneers. We often have the luxury of knowing which methods will work and which ones will not. Brad Luther is truly one of these pioneers and we are grateful for the wealth of information he has shared with us.

For advising on some of the finer points of videotaping shipwrecks, a special thanks is in order to award winning filmmaker Nick Caloyianis, one of the few professional cameramen comfortable with any camera and any format. For his undying enthusiasm and willingness to always assist in underwater photographic pursuits, a heartfelt thanks to Mike Drainville—but get ready; we've got a lot more to do! While on the subject of underwater photographic pursuits, many thanks to Fred Dion of Underwater Photo-Tech for his outstanding technical support and for always keeping the cameras firing.

We wish to also thank the following people for their consultation and contributions: Bill Campbell, Arnie Carr and John Fish of Historical Maritime Research Group of New England, Jim Christley, Dave Clancy, Carlton Davidson, Mike deCamp, Elaine Gallo, Bill Quinn, Brad Sheard, Paul Sherman, Patrick Smith, Dr. Ruth Turner, David Warsen and Charles Zimmaro. The authors gratefully acknowledge the contributions and cooperation of the following organizations:

EG & G

Douglas Co. Historical Society

Museum of Comparative Zoology, Harvard University

National Archives

National Park Service

NOAA

Steamship Historical Society

U.S. Coast Guard

Henry Keatts extends special thanks to Viking Diving Division for use of their excellent diving suits, Poseidon for the use of their superior regulators and Beuchat for the use of their quality Aladin Pro dive computer.

Finally, a sincere thanks to Ken Loyst of Watersport Publishing, Inc. for his envisioning *Complete Wreck Diving* and to our wives Carole and Marcia for their undying patience.

Preface

Henry Keatts and I have had a grand time with wreck diving. In pursuit of wrecks, our adventures have taken us from the Revolutionary War on Lake George, New York, to the American Civil War off of Cape Hatteras, North Carolina. We have slept on the deck of a lobster boat in the waters that Papa Hemingway fished in the Dry Tortugas, and watched from our hotel room the fury of a hurricane tossing pleasure boats upon the beach of Block Island, Rhode Island. We have visited submarines, schooners, cutters and liners. We have relished our treasured recoveries and reflected on somber remains. We have traveled through time.

When Ken Loyst of Watersport Publishing, Inc. asked us to consider writing *Complete Wreck Diving,* we were both flattered and a bit reluctant. As a rule, we had always preferred to write about wreck diving history or our adventures and not about technique. As more thought was given to the request, we recognized the need for a comprehensive manual on wreck diving.

The recognition of this need was due, in part, to the many people who would often ask, "How do I get started in wreck diving?" at the end of our numerous speaking engagements. This was not an easy question to answer. There are many excellent wreck diving courses, but there are those that are incomplete as well. Suggesting a course, then, was no guarantee that the individual would truly learn to dive wrecks. We therefore had no definitive answer that would satisfy the person asking.

We realized that reviewing the fundamentals of wreck diving would benefit both the novice and the experienced diver. In the process, we too hoped to learn. Thus, we accepted the task. With the decision to write the book made, it was necessary to resolve how it should be put together. A great deal of thought went into

this decision, with the conclusion being: a manual that would treat the subject of wreck diving—"soup to nuts." We believed it should offer the reader who knows nothing about wreck diving a solid foundation to begin exploring wrecks. It was an answer to the question, "How do I get started in wreck diving?" It would explain how to find wrecks, how to equip oneself, how to actually dive the wrecks, and other pertinent information. Although it follows a logical sequence of progression, the book can also be used in a modular fashion. A diver that already knows how to dive wrecks might want to learn about how to conduct research or how to conserve artifacts. The diver can simply review these chapters without having read previous chapters. *Complete Wreck Diving* also approaches the subject from several perspectives, as there are often several methods that can be employed to accomplish one goal. We have attempted to offer methods ranging from one end of the spectrum to the other, with techniques that allow for enjoyable wreck diving even on a budget. It is our sincere hope that divers of all experience levels and of all means will find this text useful.

Brian Skerry, November 1993

Introduction

An interesting lot indeed, these wreck divers. We spend thousands of hours of preparation on repairing drysuits, charging lights, tuning regulators and checking lift bags for holes, winding hundreds of feet of line onto an ascent reel, adjusting weight belts and always checking manifolds for leaks. We awake at 3:00 a.m., drive for hours, carry truckloads of gear onto a dive boat and steam miles offshore in heavy seas to get to our destination. We sleep in the equivalent of a torpedo tube in a damp sleeping bag or, more often, do not sleep at all; but get up the next morning to dive anyway. We enter the water and swim with the weight of a suit of armor on our bodies to spend a brief twenty minutes on the bottom. We will jeopardize our financial security by taking off endless days from our jobs so that, if all goes well, we can return home that evening with a brass valve handle, "prized artifact" that we will spend an entire weekend during the winter, locked away in the basement, fashioning into a belt buckle. Those of us not interested in the "material wealth" of such riches, instead pursue wrecks to uncover archeological mysteries and will spend a lifetime carefully excavating a square yard of buried wreckage with ping pong paddles and dental picks to find missing pieces of a clay pot. We anxiously seek each other out since others never truly understand us, but do not talk too much lest we give away our treasured secrets. Ah yes—An interesting lot indeed.

For many, exploring shipwrecks is a passion. It consumes their every waking thought, and subconscious thought, too. It is a drug of sorts that many find themselves addicted to, always wanting more. The wreck diver's soul is rich with adventure. It is a gypsy soul, willing always to pick up and move on to the next shipwreck in search of "fortune and glory." We are wanderers; continually pursuing the adventure. It is the journey which we savor, not the destination.

Complete Wreck Diving is about this journey. It is designed to be a handbook used to guide the reader through the various stages of this trip. Wreck diving is a term used to describe everything from a leisurely swim over a sunken runabout in fifteen feet of lake water, to a complex mixed gas dive to a freighter in four hundred feet of water in the North Sea. This vast range of extremes within the same heading, makes it difficult, at best, to address every possible wreck diving scenario. *Complete Wreck Diving* was designed to address wreck diving. The principles of basic wreck diving are applicable whether diving in shallow or deep water. If a wreck diver wants to venture to great depths, then the diver must become proficient at deep diving. If the wreck diver wishes to choose enriched air or mixed gas as a breathing medium, then the diver must learn the intricacies of these specialties before employing them. The essentials of wreck diving, however, are what we have addressed. They do not change with different depths of water, nor are they useful only to the beginner. With a firm understanding of these essentials, a wreck diver can then branch out into more complex areas of diving if that is what he/she wishes.

Let the journey begin...

At-A-Glance

Chapter 1 – Why Dive Wrecks?

Designed to inspire. A brief explanation of the contribution wreck diving can make to our understanding of maritime history, not to mention the potential for adventure.

Chapter 2 – Getting Started: What You Should Know About Ships and Shipwrecks

To dive shipwrecks, it helps to understand them. Types of ships, how they sink, what happens to them after they sink and why these things are important.

Chapter 3 – Research

The backbone of wreck diving. How to get started, sources of information and research methodology.

Chapter 4 – Finding Your Wreck

Research might tell you where the wreck you seek is located, but you still need to get there, which is easier said than done. This chapter shows you how to plot an exact course to that virgin shipwreck.

Chapter 5 – The Physical Search

The ocean is a big place and finding even large shipwrecks can be like finding the proverbial needle in a haystack. This chapter contains the various methods of actually searching for a shipwreck.

Chapter 6 – Charter Boats

The alternative to finding your own shipwreck is to be taken to one by someone else. Charter boats for wreck divers are becoming more plentiful each year. Before venturing out to sea, it is a good idea to consider all the possibilities.

Chapter 7 – Gearing Up: Wreck Diving Equipment and Pre-Dive Preparation

This chapter discusses the importance of selecting the correct wreck diving gear, as well as emphasizing the uniqueness of the shipwreck environment. Equipment management, equally crucial, is also highlighted as is gaining comfortability and competency as a wreck diver.

Chapter 8 – Diving The Wreck

Tying in, shipwreck navigation, prevention and hazards are all explained in this chapter. Also emphasized are the geographical differences encountered in wreck diving in various locations.

Chapter 9 – Shipwreck Identification

Whether it is a shipwreck you have found or an unidentified wreck that has been dived for years, there are numerous methods that can be used to identify a sunken ship. This chapter examines the various clues shipwrecks offer the wreck diver to solve the mystery.

Chapter 10 – Artifacts

The thrill of recovering a prized relic from the deep is a dream that can easily come true for wreck divers. What are artifacts, how to find them, how to get them, how to conserve them and display ideas are explained in depth. Legal considerations are equally emphasized with up-to-date information.

Chapter 11 – Sunken Ships and Salty Shutters: Making Images of Shipwrecks

Returning from a dive with shipwreck images is a treasure quite unlike any other. The shipwreck environment is unique and places certain demands on the photographer and camera equipment. Gear selection as well as techniques are "focused" on in this chapter.

Diver silhouetted over the listing coning tower of the German submarine **U-352**.

Chapter 1

Why Dive Wrecks?

I rolled over in my bunk and opened my eyes realizing the dawn had finally arrived. It had been a night of restless sleep, but somehow I had managed to get a few hours of needed rest. At about the same time I realized that it was light outside, my stomach began to tighten in anticipation as I also remembered that today was the day, the day that Hank Keatts and I were to dive the U.S.S. Monitor.

For many months we had prepared for this day. Books on Civil War history had been read, builder's plans examined, legal requirements reviewed, dive profiles rehearsed, travel arrangements made and now, finally it was time to dive. Our friend and colleague Gary Gentile had endured much to organize this project. It was critical that everything from now on go well.

I parked my car in the lot at Oden Marina in Cape Hatteras, North Carolina and stepped out into the thick tropical air that hung like a damp blanket on my skin. Although it was still early, and the sky gray with overcast clouds, the heat and humidity bordered on oppressive. I popped the trunk and we began the familiar routine of countless trips between car and boat, loading the mountains of gear that would be needed for the dive. A light but steady breeze was blowing and the forecast called for the wind to increase as the day wore on. If we were going to do it, there was no time to waste. With all the gear stowed and secured, the engines of the Little Clam were fired up, lines cast upon the dock and we began steaming out of the harbor, leaving a now quiet Oden Marina in our wake.

Moving away from the beach where the water color is green and murky, we soon crossed over into the rich blue offshore waters of the Gulf Stream, indicating we were only minutes away from our target. As we approached what the boats LORAN told us was the place we wanted to be, we spied a large orange tuna float bobbing on the surface. In front of the orange float, tied to the same line, was a white plastic jug. The floats marked a mooring line that had been set a couple of days before. Since NOAA regulations did not allow anchoring into the wreck, a mooring had to be set up in order to dive. The mooring was to be placed one hundred feet away from the wreck, so there would be no contact with the Monitor. Regulations also forbade any vessel from anchoring within five hundred feet of the Monitor, so rather than simply tie-off to the mooring, we would have to be dropped up-current of the floats and drift to them. In studying the floats from our boat, it was easy to see we had our work cutout for us. A strong current was running, indicated by a "wake" rippling around the floats. Gentile informed us, however, that there were supposed to be two large orange tuna floats and one white jug, so we brought the boat in close and using a boat hook, pulled up the line. The other float was there all right, but had no buoyancy left since it had been bitten in half, by a shark most likely. At last, there might be some excitement after all!

The dive team this day would consist of seven individuals split into three groups, all who were quite anxious to get into the water. Ideally, there would be a still photographer, videographer, and model on the wreck at the same time. Keatts, myself, and Hank Garvin would make up one group; Gentile and Billy Deans another and Jon Hulburt, Greg Massi and Gene Peterson another. The plan called for Gentile and Deans to get in first, followed *closely by Garvin, Keatts and me. The third team would wait until we were all back on the boat before beginning their dive.*

As the boat circled the site, we stretched on wetsuits and hoisted heavy sets of double tanks onto our backs all while fighting to keep from falling in the three-foot seas that rocked us from gunwale to gunwale. Before donning his final pieces of gear, Keatts reached into his dive bag and pulled out a red, white and blue cloth flag. In the flag's center was the prestigious insignia of the Explorers Club. Their endorsement of this project had been requested and was willingly granted. In support, they awarded flag number 132, a flag that had been on several historic expeditions, to be carried to the site of the Monitor. *As a fellow in this famed organization, Keatts had taken possession of the esteemed banner for today's dive. Not having a pocket in which to place the flag, he handed it to me. I folded it carefully and tucked it inside the pocket of my buoyancy compensator. When the first two teams were ready and all systems were go, the captain headed the boat into the current away from the floats and gave the signal to hit the water. Keatts, Garvin and I followed Gentile and Deans by just a couple of minutes and began rapidly drifting towards the orange float. We kept our eyes trained on that precious float and steered our bodies like torpedoes directly at it. Should we miss grabbing the line, it would be all over. The boat would have to pick us up and the dive would be forfeited. In intervals separated by seconds, we each snagged the float in-turn, knowing that at the end of that line, awaited a piece of history that few had ever visited. Although the wreck lay in approximately two hundred and thirty feet of water, the mooring line was made nearly five hundred feet long, so as not to pullout the danforth anchor imbedded in the sandy bottom.*

Exhaling, I did a jackknife dive and began descending the line. Several feet ahead of me was Keatts. His action of pulling down the line first with his right hand then with his left, caused his body and bright yellow double tanks on his back to rock from side to side, nearly hypnotizing me as I followed closely behind. The strength of the current forced me to keep looking straight ahead, for a glance to the side might rip the mask from my face. After a seven minute descent down the line, we had reached the bottom and were given our first view of the legendary warship. To reach it, we had to swim nearly sixty feet away from the mooring line, but we had come too far not to go the distance. When we finally stopped our steady progression and paused for a moment, we were standing in the shadow of the unmistakable turret, now displaced in the stern and supporting the disintegrating hull resting on top of it. The only sound I could hear was that of my own breathing, as I gazed upon this surreal setting of the once proud ironclad now corroding in a twilight blue world. Fighting the urge to simply stare in awe, we both went to work. Pulling open the velcroed pocket on my compensator, I reached inside, pulled out the Explorers Club flag and handed it to Keatts. On this side of the wreck, we were in the lee of the current and we were able to carry out our task. With his back to the turret, he unfurled the flag, posing for me to photograph this impressive scene. As I stared intently through the viewfinder, I could hear the high pitched whine of an underwater propulsion vehicle in the distance. I looked to my right to see Billy Deans "flying" in on his Aquazepp, with its blazing headlight illuminating his path. To my left was Gentile, moving in for a closer view and behind me was Garvin. Visibility was perhaps thirty-five to forty feet; however all the commotion in this one area had disturbed the bottom silt, reducing visibility to about five feet. With the flag sequence complete, we split up trying to see as much as possible in the precious few minutes remaining. I swam past the remains of the armor belt, the heavily encrusted propeller and skeg to the starboard side of the ship where an intact glass lantern globe lie among the wreckage. Black sea bass swam in tight proximity as if protecting it as one of their young. The flash of my strobe brought daylight for an instant to this instrument of light that last felt the warm glow of a flame nearly a century and a half ago. Glancing at my bottom timer and pressure gauge, I reluctantly admitted to myself that it was time to go. I kicked past the stern of the wreck and made my way back towards the anchor line. The current that plagued us on the trip down the anchor line was now a lifting force, easing our bodies up the line and returning us to where we began. As I lifted off the bottom, I turned to watch the lunarlike landscape fade into the bluish haze, trying hard to memorize forever the image in my mind.

The one hundred plus minutes of decompression was a substantial penalty to pay for a brief eighteen minutes of bottom time, but I for one would never complain. As we drifted on a detachable float line that had been clipped to the main mooring line, five divers in the cobalt blue sea, our minds replayed the events that had just transpired. It was truly the experience of a lifetime.

Back at the house where project members were staying, the corks popped and the champagne flowed. We gathered around the television to watch the "dailies" of video footage shot on the wreck that day. The mood was festive and the sense of accomplishment could be felt as easily as the Hatteras heat. Sipping my champagne, I stepped outside onto the wooden sundeck and saw Keatts loading some gear inside the car. We had a long ride home ahead of us with plenty to talk about. A lot had been done, but there was a lot left to do. For now, however, nothing needed to be said. There would undoubtedly be many more wreck diving adventures, but at the moment, I was just looking forward to getting a restful night sleep.

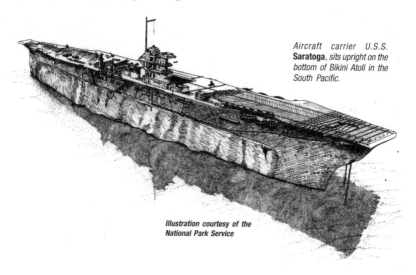

Aircraft carrier U.S.S. **Saratoga**, sits upright on the bottom of Bikini Atoll in the South Pacific.

Illustration courtesy of the National Park Service

Photo By Brian Skerry

An unexpected prize! Tom Mulloy displays a 73-pound silver ingot found on a shallow water shipwreck off the Massachusetts coast.

From the wooden timbers of a Basque whaling ship off Labrador, to an intact United States aircraft carrier in the lagoon at Bikini, or a Swedish warship's cannon-strewn debris field in Stockholm Harbor, the maritime history of mankind rests not only in dusty volumes of forgotten text, but in the sea itself.

Since the time that man first ventured forth upon the sea, he has left in his wake a tangible history, a history in the form of shipwrecks. It is a history that tells how our predecessors lived, worked and thought. It depicts the struggles, battles and conflict of bygone eras that today with the luxury of hindsight often seem so unimportant. It is a history of people who had epic courage and a thirst for adventure and knowledge. It is a history of ourselves.

As occupants of the second half of the twentieth century, we possess a unique opportunity to explore this tangible history firsthand. With the advent of scuba (self-contained underwater breathing apparatus), we have the freedom to visit our maritime legacy in the field and are not relegated to merely reading about it or viewing it behind glass in a museum. Unlike those before us who set sail upon the sea to learn more about their world, we set forth beneath it to learn about them. To dive on shipwrecks is to embark on a multi-faceted journey, a journey that begins with an innate human catalyst – curiosity.

Since the earliest days of mankind's evolution, the human species has demonstrated an undying curiosity of the world in which it lives. It could well be that curiosity was the impetus for man's evolutionary ancestors leaving the primordial sea in search of a new life on land. It is without question the driving force that returns man to the sea in search of his heritage.

Viewing the vanquished victims of war is a somber moment wreck divers often experience.

Diving shipwrecks, perhaps more so than most undersea pursuits, provides an outlet for this inquisitive nature we possess. New divers and seasoned veterans alike share a sense of wonder when visiting a wreck for the first time. We swim over the rusting hulls or rotting timbers anxiously shining our dive lights under fallen beams or into dark open hatchways, always searching, always hoping. During these submerged sojourns we seek souvenirs, images or knowledge with which we can return home richer than we left, richer by fulfillment of accomplishment, not monetary gain.

That is not to say that wreck divers are adverse to finding sunken treasure. It would be difficult to find a wreck diver (or any diver for that matter), who would not admit that the thought of swimming over a carpet of gold coins on a forgotten wreck gets their pulse racing. But there is more to shipwrecks than that. It is human nature to desire finding treasure. Just as some people keep a constant lookout for money dropped on a sidewalk or change overlooked in a pay phone. A diver settling down on a shipwreck sometimes considers the possibility of a lost fortune that he might be destined to find. There are accounts of divers who have stumbled onto sunken treasure; however, it is not very common. The "mother lodes" that receive such grand attention by the media are most often found by professional treasure hunters who have dedicated their lives to making these discoveries. Keep in mind,

*The tragic 1991 pre-Christmas sinking of the **Salem Express** claimed the lives of well over 500 people (purported closer to 820 lost). This Egyptian passenger ferry settled in 110 feet of water, 22 kilometers southeast of Safaga Port, Egypt.*

however, that for every success story we hear about, there are scores of those who were not as fortunate. This does not mean that we should abandon all hope. Remember that your chances of finding sunken treasure are considerably better swimming along an undersea ledge where ships have reportedly gone down than they would be standing on shore simply pondering what might be out there.

Earlier in this chapter, we touched on the fact that wreck diving affords a unique opportunity to explore history firsthand. This is not something to be taken lightly. Read about a steamship sinking and it might be interesting. See the steamer's helm in a museum and the event may become more realistic. Discover that steamer's helm for yourself on the wreck during a dive and you have actually experienced history. In fact, in a case like this one, you have become part of the history.

It may very well be that if people are not interested in history it is because history often seems so remote—one dimensional characters and events written on the pages of a textbook. To involve oneself in wreck diving is to become intimate with the past. When you uncover a wooden deadeye on a sunken schooner, you cannot help but wonder who touched it last. Diving a wreck is much like reading a novel by beginning on the last page. The preceding chapters which include the cast of characters and the drama that led to this tragic ending is what we seek, a detective story of sorts with potential clues awaiting each dive. We may think that we know a wreck's story: vessel A left port B and en route to destination C, collided with vessel D and sank. As you submerge yourself deeper into the story, however, you may begin to see more of the human side. You might find a piece of jewelry inscribed to a beloved son or uncover through research that the first mate who froze to death in a

Taking the first step to adventure, a well-equipped wreck diver strides into the sea.

lifeboat was supposed to be married in just a few weeks. These elements add a completely new dimension to diving shipwrecks, a dimension that allows you to not only explore in the present, but get closer to the past.

Voltaire, the eighteenth century French philosopher said, "History is but the register of human crimes and misfortunes." So it is with shipwrecks, except for those that were intentionally sunk as artificial reefs. They are the scenes of accidents or wartime conflict. The wrecks are the remains of others' misfortunes. Were it not for wreck divers who, by their endeavors, refuse to let these stories be forgotten, thousands of ships and thousands of souls would be lost to time and left to waste in a sea that has kept to a vow of silence. But the stories live on.

Throughout history it is rare to find evidence of a disaster left for future generations to examine. In 1937, the Hindenburg exploded into flames resulting in a fiery death for thirty-five passengers and crew; yet today, nothing of this once mighty airship remains. Legendary ocean liners such as the *Titanic* or the *Andrea Doria*, however, can be explored. We have little to examine from the lives of pioneers such as Lewis and Clark; yet a barge like the *Breadalbane*, belonging to pioneers from nearly the same era, lies intact beneath Canadian seas. During wartime it would be absurd to expect a fighter plane shot down in combat or a tank destroyed in ground battle to be left in place, but a ship is removed from view when it sinks. As wreck divers, we are privileged to swim through sunken aircraft cockpits, glide down the rusty corridor of a once noble warship and even view the remains of a sailor's ocean grave. Such experience adds knowledge and insight of a period; it is as close as one can get to having been there.

This kind of exploration can lead to encounters with those who actually were there. When this occurs, it transcends diving, crossing over into something much more important. In May of 1992, for instance, a group of wreck divers arranged an event that illus-

Photo by Brian Skerry

trates this unique aspect of diving shipwrecks. Fifty years before, the German submarine *U-352* was engaged in battle with the U.S. Coast Guard cutter *Icarus* off the North Carolina coast, a battle that would end with the U-boat being sunk, and thirteen of her crew killed in action. Half a century had passed and yet most people were unaware of the event. Through the efforts of divers, sparked by shipwrecks and the history they represent, eight of *U-352*'s survivors were brought from Germany to North Carolina to meet with members of the *Icarus* crew in an event

*Living a lesson in history. Wreck divers share an emotional ceremony with German survivors of the sunken **U-352** commemorating the 50th anniversary of the submarine's sinking, on a dive boat over the site.*

Photo by Brian Skerry

Examining anchor chains, this wreck diver finds a link to the past.

that was to culminate with a journey to the site of the sunken sub. Fifty years to the day after the sinking occurred, a dive boat was anchored over the site with divers and U-boat veterans alike commemorating the anniversary with a special ceremony. All that could be read about the men of World War II simply could not compare to an experience like this. Standing next to these genial men on the deck of a rolling and pitching dive boat anchored over their former submarine was a very special moment indeed. To see them now in their sixties or seventies, dressed in tweed sportcoats and dress slacks, with tears welling up in their eyes as the names of their lost shipmates were read, was a lesson in history those on that dive boat will not soon forget.

With the rigors of everyday life, many adults believe that the wonder and dreams of childhood years are but a pleasant distant memory. The "expeditions" into the nearby forest in search of rare flora or fauna, finding the source of a winding backyard stream, or a summer's afternoon excursion for fossils in a neighborhood sandpit are only fleeting recollections that occasionally creep into their conscious thoughts. But wonder is not dead. Discovery and adventure need not only be for a child's imagination, or a scientist, or an astronaut. It is surely alive and well and living in every wreck diver. Though it is a romantic notion to imagine oneself traipsing off to exotic locales in search of lost ships and maritime relics, it is equally as romantic to do these things in the course of a weekend having driven no further than to the closest beach.

In an age when even space travel receives only a passing mention on the evening news, it would seem that significant exploration by the average individual has long since passed. With wreck diving, however, it is as close as the nearest body of water. Although it may not be readily evident to the vast majority of the population, shipwrecks are within reach of nearly everyone. The wreck diver can find a Polish destroyer in a Norwegian fiord or a Russian submarine victim off the coast of Poland. There are Spanish galleons to be explored in Ireland, East Indiamen in western Australia and ferry boats in the Red Sea. But we need not only look towards saltwater. In the United States, for example, a diver can visit sunken submarines without ever seeing the ocean. Within the murky currents of the Patuxent River off Solomons, Maryland lies the remains of the American submarine *S-49*, and just a few miles away in the Potomac River off Piney Point, will be found the German submarine *U-1105*. These are only a small few of the countless sites that exist throughout the world. Shipwrecks are everywhere—and therein lies adventure.

Visit the home of most any serious wreck diver and you will often be visiting a maritime museum of sorts. Well-preserved nautical artifacts displayed in the family room, along with photographs of ships above and below, are common sights in addition to wellkept files of shipwreck vital statistics. The accumulation of these things is not the result of government grants or the fieldwork of Ph.D.'s. They are the results of average people with an above average thirst for adventure. People who by vocation are construction workers, accountants, doctors or teachers, but by avocation are explorers. Columbus, Magellan and John Franklin are just a few of the famed explorers who set sail for very practical reasons, though it must have taken more than a sense of duty to strike out into the unknown. It is this quality, a desire of discovery and adventure, that the wreck diver shares with all explorers. It is also true that in addition to the adventure that comes from diving wrecks, the *wreck hunter* has the potential to significantly contribute to our knowledge of maritime history. With thousands of ships still awaiting discovery, opportunity abounds.

In September 1991, a group of divers on a charter boat located a previously unknown German U-boat off the coast of New Jersey. Although there was not supposed by be a submarine in the area, their methodical exploration of unknown sites led to a discovery that will rewrite history books, a discovery made on a Labor Day weekend by people who simply opted for a day at sea rather than the backyard barbecue.

There are probably as many reasons to dive on shipwrecks as there are shipwrecks to dive on, which is much of the allure. Whether you intend to only occasionally view a tropical shipwreck while on vacation or pursue our sunken past with a passion, we think you might find yourself paraphrasing the words of Egyptologists who gazed into the tomb of Tutankamen and said, "We have seen wonderful things."

As you set forth on this journey be prepared for the spell that will befall you when you return to the surface with that first rust stain on your wetsuit. For many it is a spell that lasts a lifetime.

illustration © by James L. Christley

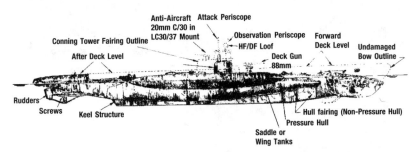

Starboard Elevation indicating the level of detorioration/damage

The **U-352** *was sunk in action during World War II. The German submarine, in 115 feet of water off North Carolina, is a popular dive site.*

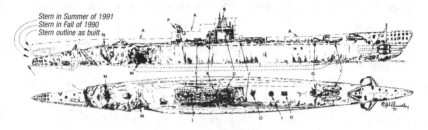

A. Outline of original superstructure
B. Periscopes
C. Air Flask
D. Conning Tower
E. Torpedo Tubes
F. Air Flasks
G. Forward Torpedo Loading Hatch
H. Battery Access Hatch
I. Forward Personnel Access Hatch
J. Snorkel Induction Mast
K. Air Induction Mast
L. After Induction Standpipe Cluster
M. Damage Hole in Aft Starboard Side of Engine Room
N. Damage Hole in Overhead of Stern Room
O. Damage Hole in Overhead of Forward Crew's Quarters
P. Breech and Mount of Aft Anti-Aircraft Gun

illustration © by James L. Christley

The **U-853** was sunk in action druing World War II. The German submarine, in 130 feet of water off Rhode Island, like all warships sunk in action are deemed to have never been abandoned by the sovereign power.

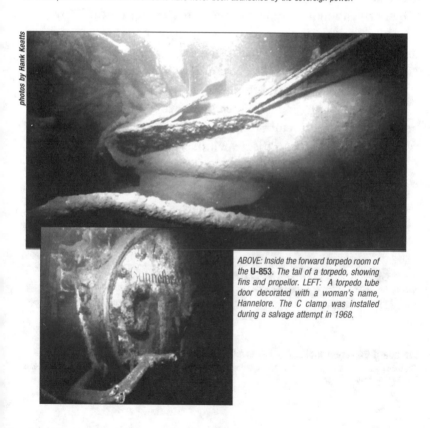

photos by Hank Keatts

ABOVE: Inside the forward torpedo room of the **U-853**. The tail of a torpedo, showing fins and propellor. LEFT: A torpedo tube door decorated with a woman's name, Hannelore. The C clamp was installed during a salvage attempt in 1968.

Chapter 2

Getting Started
What You Should Know About Ships and Shipwrecks

photo courtesy of the United States Coast Guard

*In the shadow of the Brooklyn Bridge, the bow of the tanker **Empress Bay** slowly sinks in New York City's East River following a fiery collision with the Swedish freighter **Nebraska** in the early morning hours of June 25, 1958. A knowledge of ships is paramount for safe and productive wreck diving.*

A large bronze screw-propellor on the U.S. submarine **Bass** *off of Block Island, Rhode Island, immediately tells divers they are in the stern; however, on most wrecks, orientation is not quite as easy.*

Anatomy of a Ship

For us to properly understand shipwrecks, we must first understand ships. In the way that a serious reef diver is able to recognize the many species of fish inhabiting a particular region, as well as know something about their behavior, so should the wreck diver know something about their quarry. There is no need to become an authority on the building of ships, but the success and enjoyment of wreck diving will be greatly enhanced by knowing something of their design. As will be discussed in a later chapter, part of the safety in wreck diving comes from knowing where you are at all times. It is quite easy to become disoriented on an unfamiliar wreck, particularly if you have little knowledge of its design. Should your goal be to recover artifacts, you will need to give serious thought as to what you are likely to find and where you are likely to find it before ever getting in the water. Your chances are poor, for instance, of locating a porthole on most submarines. And, if you hope to recover the bridge telegraph on a sunken freighter, it will help tremendously to first be able to find the bridge. Even the most redumentary knowledge of ships will prove extremely helpful in the pursuit of finding and diving shipwrecks.

Since earliest time man has constructed floating crafts capable of carrying him seaward. In the centuries that followed these first voyages, the development of shipbuilding evolved into a science. Regardless of how advanced or primitive a vessel is, however, there are certain elements that are common to all ships. The most basic of these elements is the hull, which is the main structure of any vessel. It is the frame or body of the ship and the section in contact with the water. The shape of a vessel's hull is influenced by a number of variables, including material used in construction, means of propulsion, and the purpose of the vessel. The most significant is the latter, the vessel's intended use. A ship designed to carry coal along a coastal route will be put together quite differently than one designed to carry passengers overseas. Although ships are often built with very specific uses in mind, hulls generally fall into one of two categories: round or long. The round hull is most commonly used for ships designed to carry cargo, whereas the long hull is built primarily for speed. The other sections of a vessel are much more specific; they cannot be so easily categorized. Their variables have

Ships built for speed favor a long sleek hull design.

changed drastically over time, resulting in a vast array of designs a wreck diver may encounter. For the purposes of wreck diving, a general knowledge of ship types, propulsion and how these things fit into the chronology of maritime history, will provide dimension to the sport, far beyond making dives on objects that otherwise have no identity.

Types of Vessels

This brief introduction does not attempt to deal with the extraordinary variety of types of small craft.

It is easy to speculate that water separating one land mass from another stirred early man's interest in crossing from one shore to the other. He could swim if the distance was short enough. If not, a bobbing tree trunk could be straddled then several lashed together, followed by hollowing them out for crew, passengers, and cargo. Propulsion, first by current and paddling, was improved with rigid, flat blades forced through the water by occupants of the craft.

Sailing Ships

When someone realized that the wind could be harnessed to do the job better, animal skins, woven sheets, or the like, mounted on sticks above the boat, allowed wind to push it without manual effort. That worked, but only so long as the wind blew toward the destination. Boatmen either rowed their way back or waited for a favorable change of wind direction. As boats became larger and faster over the centuries, trade and transportation increased.

The problem of sailing against the wind continued to plague mariners until Norwegian ships added a steering oar that was operated with a tiller off the right stern side of their boats. That "steer-board" came to be known as "starboard," the term that still refers to the right side of any vessel.

Several important changes occurred in ship design between about 1200 A.D. and the advent of the great age of sail that extended from 1460 till 1860. The most important development in ship design during the period was substitution of the steering oar with a wooden rudder hung from the sternpost by means of pintles (pivot pins) and gudgeons (sockets). The rudder was pivoted laterally to change the course

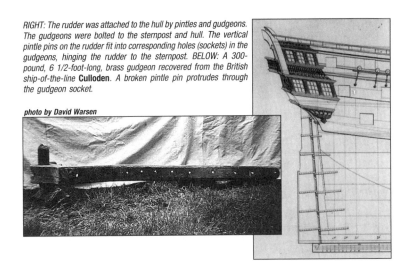

RIGHT: The rudder was attached to the hull by pintles and gudgeons. The gudgeons were bolted to the sternpost and hull. The vertical pintle pins on the rudder fit into corresponding holes (sockets) in the gudgeons, hinging the rudder to the sternpost. BELOW: A 300-pound, 6 1/2-foot-long, brass gudgeon recovered from the British ship-of-the-line **Culloden**. A broken pintle pin protrudes through the gudgeon socket.

photo by David Warsen

of a vessel. With the rudder, perverse winds could be harnessed to improve ship performance. The unknown inventor is believed to have been a shipwright in one of the lowland European countries on the North Sea, possibly Holland. This revolutionary development led to deeper hulls, hull shape changes, and vastly improved rigging. Masts were added and sails were changed in size, shape, and location on the vessel. The "steering wheel" was introduced in 1703.

Large ships were built with 14-inch x 14-inch beams that ran athwartships, or at right angles to the fore and aft lines, supporting the decks and holding the frame together. They were not one piece; a tapered joint in the middle was held together by three or four iron fastenings. The keel, a 20-inch-square beam about 150 feet long, was made from six or seven tree trunks. The wooden hull of such a ship would have about 13 miles of watertight seams and 3,000 feet of timber for the masts and yards (spars).

Square-rigged ships were propelled by acres of sails on giant masts constructed of wood, iron, or steel. The principal masts often were 200 feet from keel to truck (the top). The rigging was designed to secure the masts and yards from the ferocity of sea and wind. Wind forces transferred by the sails via the masts to the hull with the aid of the rigging were sufficient to drive an 8,000-ton ship and cargo at speeds up to 17 knots through heavy seas.

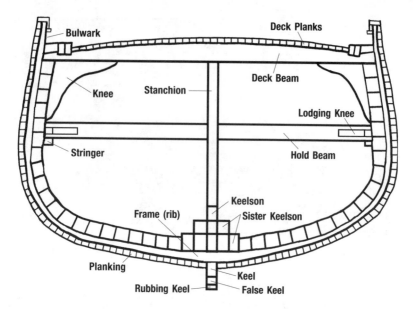

A cross-section of a wooden ship illustrating some of the basic components.

Masts and yards had to be able to withstand storms, even hurricanes, while canvas could blow away. All large sailing ships carried considerable stores of sails.

Masts began as single, trimmed trees in the Middle East. In the 13th century Marco Polo returned from China with the idea of multimasted ships. Europeans and Americans added masts built in sections and added more and more yards (spars) across them. Such ships were called square-riggers and are easily identifiable; schooners carried only fore and aft sails set between a fixed boom (a lower yard). Schooners evolved into ships with four, five, six, and even seven masts, each carrying only two sails, both set between a lower boom and hoisting gaff. They were equipped with simplified mechanization and required less manpower.

The development of masts, yards, and rigging was slow at first, and vessels were confined to fair weather areas. As technology advanced, the Trade Winds were gradually exploited for trans-Atlantic travel; then, the more rigorous and dangerous sailing routes such as 'round Cape Horn were challenged.

The deployment of cannon on ships gradually brought about a distinction between merchant ships and warships. However, in the

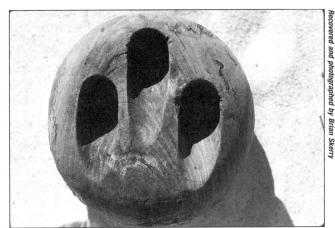

Sought after by wreck divers, the deadeye was a common fixture on early sailing ships.

late 18th century many merchant ships were heavily armed, and often a line of dummy gun ports was painted at the lower-deck level to create the appearance of a 64-gun warship.

The chief structural difference between the two types lay in the shape of the hull. Warships were built with fine underwater lines to give them better sailing qualities. Speed and maneuverability, however, were less important to a merchant ship than the amount of cargo that could be carried on a given keel length.

Warships

Viking warships changed to cope with an inherent defensive weakness; their low midships freeboard made them vulnerable to easy boarding by the enemy. Housings called "castles" were raised on the bow and stern as final retreats for defense against boarding invaders. The structure in the bow was the "forecastle," later abbreviated to fo'c'sle, the forward part of a vessel designated for crew's quarters. That high bow and high stern profile influenced ship design until 1860. The Spanish galleon is a familiar example of that contour.

An important event in the development of warships was the introduction of gunpowder. The explosive was first used in land warfare in Italy in 1326, and the first guns were issued to ships in England about 15 years later. They were hand guns, but gradually heavy cast iron cannon were added to increase the destructive power of warships.

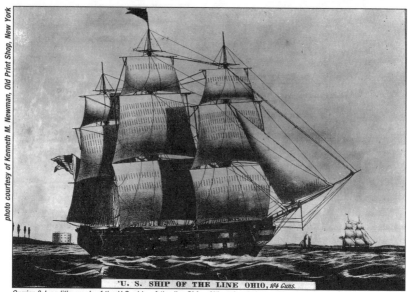

'U. S. SHIP OF THE LINE OHIO, *104 Guns.*

Currier & Ives lithograph of the U.S. ship-of-the-line **Ohio**. Although rated as a 74-gun warship, she carried up to 104 cannons.

As they became larger, naval warfare tactics changed. The greatest damage could be inflicted from a ship by standing off and delivering broadsides against an enemy. In a fleet engagement British warships of like firepower formed a battle line, stem to stern, windward of the enemy for maneuverability and freedom from the drifting smoke of cannon fire. The combined broadside of such a formation concentrated the maximum volume of fire on the foe.

Warships of the British Royal Navy with 20 guns or more were rated on a scale based on their armament. Those of 64 or more guns were designated "ships-of-the-line" or "line-of-battle ships," from which the term battleship was derived. They were the ships large enough to have a place in the line of battle. They had earlier been referred to as "capital ships," a term that still refers to larger warships.

The British rating system changed between 1677 and 1792 from including only "ships-of-the-line" to six rates with 33 variations of number and size of guns. First and second rate ships were those of 90 to 110 guns (battleships). Third rate carried 64 to 80 guns (cruisers). Fourth or common rate carried 50 to 74 guns (also cruisers). Fifth rate, with 32 to 40 guns (frigates) were used as commerce raiders. Sixth rate, 16 to 22 guns (sloops) served as couriers and escorts. The crews ranged from 195 on a 125-foot sixth rate sloop to 720 on a 290-foot first rate "ship-of-the-line."

The naval cannon, a muzzle-loader on a wooden carriage, underwent rapid technological changes during the second half of the 19th century. The result was a larger, long-range, breech-loading gun. High-explosive shells replaced the round, solid shot of the older cannon. The advance in armament led to the use of iron and later steel as a replacement for wood as the material of which ships were constructed. The high penetrative capability of the new shells resulted in even thicker steel armor to protect ships against them.

During the 18th century, the sterns of warships had open galleries or walkways, but near the end of the century, sterns were closed in and windows were added. In the early part of the 19th century the elaborate basket-work beak head under the bowsprit was gradually replaced by the much more practical round bow. The era of the beautiful wooden sailing ships was almost over. Composite construction, timber cladding on an iron frame, became the preferred design. In the latter half of the 19th century the timber cladding was replaced by iron plates. The last major warship action under sail was the Battle of Navarino in 1827 in which a combined British-French-Russian fleet defeated a Turco-Egyptian fleet during the Greek War of Independence.

The last span of the graceful sailing ship era was left to American merchant vessels, the fast sailing, slender-hulled clipper ships. The steam age rapidly altered hull design because boilers, engines, and associated paddle-boxes or screw had to be accommodated.

Steamships

The steam engine revolutionized transportation on land with steam locomotives, and on water with steamships. James Watt, a Scottish inventor, patented improvements on the existing steam engine in 1769, and England was the first to adapt it for commercial use. But, the American, Robert Fulton was first to make it a maritime success. Fulton's famous steamboat *North River*, commonly called *Clermont*, was launched in 1807 and operated on the Hudson River between

Fultons first steamboat, the **Clermont.**

New York and Albany. The first trip was the beginning of an epoch in transportation 20 years before the advent of railroads. It stimulated rapid steamboat development in the United States.

In only a few years, large numbers of steamships were successfully operating on Long Island Sound, Chesapeake and Delaware Bays, the Mississippi River Basin, freshwater lakes, and other inland waters. From those beginnings steamships progressed to the Atlantic and Pacific Oceans; the first steamship crossing of the Atlantic, or any ocean, was made by the *Savannah* in 1819. During her 29-day voyage from Savannah, Georgia to Liverpool, she used her steam engine on 12 different days to test it in all kinds of wind and weather. Most of the time she was under sail, using her steam engine only to supplement the action of wind.

During the slow transition from sail to steam, shipbuilders shied away from reliance solely on steam power. The transAtlantic passenger liner **Oregon**, *built in 1883, was fitted with four, full-rigged masts and sails in case her single-screw propulsion system failed. The Cunard steamer was rammed and sunk off Long Island, New York, in 1886 in 130 feet of water.*

The technical development of American steamboats was so marked, and the economic results so significant, that many Europeans came to the United States to learn the new technology. However, steamship passengers during the 1820s were often apprehensive of the revolutionary form of transportation. Boiler explosions were not uncommon. In the United States 52 such mishaps occurred in one year, with 256 people dead and 104 injured. Such incidents often sent the vessel to the bottom.

Early transAtlantic steamers used wooden paddle wheels for propulsion, but in the late 1830s the screw-propellor was developed by Francis Smith and John Ericsson (who later designed and built the U.S.S. *Monitor* during the Civil War), each working independently. The *Great Britain*, launched in 1843, was the first major iron-hulled vessel and the first such vessel to be propeller-driven.

The availability of cheap iron plate in the mid-1860s increased the use of the metal for ship hull construction. Improved steelmaking processes made mass production of cheap steel possible, and it was adopted for ship construction in the 1880s.

A dive on a steamboat is a visit to a bygone era. It was a period of tremendous importance in the growth of the young United States and the entire world.

The Long Island Sound side-wheeler passenger-steamer **Larchmont** *was rammed by a schooner in 1907 off Rhode Island, and sank in 140 feet of water.*

Steam engines were gradually replaced by oil-fired internal combustion engines. The introduction of small gasoline and kerosene engines for marine propulsion occurred in the last quarter of the 19th century. During the first two decades of the 20th century, gasoline and kerosene gradually replaced steam in small commercial craft.

The use of oil engines in ships developed rapidly after introduction of the diesel engine around 1910. The development of geared-

The wreck of the side-wheeler passenger-steamer **Winfield Scott** *is located in the Channel Island National Park & Marine Sanctuary (California), in about 30 feet of water.*

turbine propeller drive and the introduction of oil-burning boilers early in the 20th century were important enhancements. Modern ships employ the turbine-electric drive as well as geared turbines.

A diver's view of the steamer **Larchmont**'s huge paddle-wheel as it stands today.

Iron, and later steel, replaced wood in the construction of ship hulls, and steam replaced sail as the means of propulsion. The change was gradual, emerging from sailing ships with steam auxiliary power to steamships with sail auxiliary power to propulsion by steam alone. The gradual changes make it difficult to date a wreck simply because of its hull material or its means of propulsion.

The freshwater and ocean bottoms are littered with the remains of vessels from each period. Wreck divers frequently recover artifacts from them. A basic knowledge of ship construction and rigging is important to recognize and understand the functional importance and historical significance of the artifacts.

Fastenings

In the late 18th century, all European and American ships were built in much the same way. Though some people were already dreaming of ships built of iron, wood remained the only hull material for another half century.

A large amount of wood was needed for even a small ship, but the quantity required for a large one was prodigious. The H.M.S. *Royal George*, built in 1756, was the British Royal Navy's largest ship-of-the-line during the American Revolution. The warship required the timber of 5,739 1/2 full-grown trees in its construction. Those trees growing 30 feet apart would have covered almost 150 acres of forest.

Note the axe marks near the end of this 10-1/4" drift pin from the U.S.S. **Ohio**. The raised metal produced by the cuts would better secure the pin in its predrilled hole. The head of the pins were flattened or rounded as the pin was driven into the hole by sledge hammer. Most drift pins are longer than the one shown here.

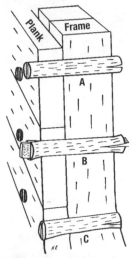

A. Trunnels were driven through pre-drilled untapered holes. **B.** The two ends are cross-wedged perpendicularly to the run of the grain. **C.** The ends are cut off.

Wooden ships were fastened together by metal drift pins, spikes, and nails. They were first made of iron, but later of non-corroding copper, then new alloys were used. Other joins were made with long wooden pegs called "trunnels" or "treenails."

Hull fastenings and rigging gear are frequent finds on shipwrecks. The metal used in nails will usually date a fastening to a period within 50 years of its manufacture. Iron nails were most often used to fasten planks to timbers above the waterline until 1783. At that time copper-zinc alloy nails were used on warships and better constructed merchant vessels. In the mid-1800s new alloys were introduced and nails, spikes, bolts, and "drift" pins were made from various bronzes.

Spikes are large, chisel-pointed nails 6 to 12 inches long, usually with square heads. Drift pins are metal rods, usually substantially longer than spikes; they were used to reinforce the ship's structural members. The term drift pin comes from the process of beating them into pre-drilled holes, called drifting.

Copper or bronze fastenings are often found only in the bow of a merchant ship, while iron fastenings are usually found in the midships and stern. Copper and the new alloys do not oxidize as quickly as iron, and the bow has to bear the force of the sea as a vessel cuts through the waves. Bronze spikes, for a typical example, will be found only in the bow of the sailing vessel *Montana*, which sank off Block Island, Rhode Island in 1907. A diver can find such bronze fastenings even if

TOP PHOTO: David Morton and Pat Williams inspect a piece of wreckage that washed ashore on Fire Island, New York, in February 1993. Note the trunnels projecting from the wooden ribs. ABOVE LEFT: The piece of wreckage is about 25 feet of the ship's bow. The ends of planks were fastened to the ribs with two brass spikes. ABOVE RIGHT: the outer end of one trunnel securing a plank to a rib. The end has been wedged in a triangular pattern; thin pieces of wood are still within the cuts.

photos by Henry Keatts

they are buried to the head in a plank. They are covered with green patina, a thin layer of corrosion that appears on copper or alloys such as bronze, as a result of oxidation.

In areas where greater flexibility was needed, treenails or trunnels (large wooden dowels) held planking and timber together. They would swell with moisture, thus making a firm fitting. The

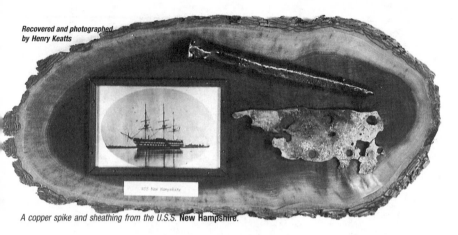

A copper spike and sheathing from the U.S.S. New Hampshire.

fastenings were staggered alternately to prevent a split in the plank's line of grain.

Until the late 1700s wooden vessels were at the mercy of ship-worms. Infestations of the bivalve mollusks below the waterline frequently abbreviated the life of wooden-hulled ships. The application of steam power to rolling mills made copper plating readily available. The entire British battle fleet was copper sheathed during the American Revolution. Sheathing a vessel, simply meant attaching this thin layer of copper to the ship's hull. At the beginning of the 19th century better constructed merchant ships were protected in the same manner. Copper sheathing in contact with the head of an iron fastening destroyed the iron by galvanic action, so copper-zinc alloy fastenings were substituted for iron ones below the water line.

Small copper nails used to fasten the sheathing to the hull, and fragments of copper sheathing are frequently found by divers. Pieces of sheathing from the United States ship-of-the-line *New Hampshire* in 10 to 40 feet of water in Massachusetts Bay are of both industrial and historical interest. Many of the copper fastenings and much of the sheathing used in construction of the *New Hampshire* and the U.S.S. *Ohio* were forged at the Paul Revere Foundry. It was Paul Revere who invented the world's first metal rolling press for the production of sheet metal. The process not only produced great quantities of sheet metal in large sizes, but the sheets were of uniform thickness. Revere received a contract for a large quantity of copper drift pins, spikes, sheathing, and sheathing nails from the United States Navy in 1816. The keels for both warships were laid in 1817. A ship-of-the-line needed about 17 tons of copper just for sheathing and nails to fasten it to the hull.

Small copper nails found on wrecks that sank before the late 18th century were probably from lead patches that were used on weakened parts of the hull or from lead fittings such as scuppers.

Today, the few remaining square-rigged sailing ships, the super tankers, and the battleships that we see went through a laborious evolution. An evolution that is far from over.

Causes of Shipwrecks

Despite the fact that shipbuilding has evolved into a rather sophisticated science, man has yet to design a ship that cannot sink (which, for wreck divers, is probably a good thing). Certainly no one designs a ship with the intention of having it end up on the ocean floor, but, as history has shown us, a fair number will inevitably wind up there. Advances in the field of hull design from the use of strategically placed, watertight compartments, to the development of double hulls (not to mention equally impressive improvements in navigational

Photo courtesy of the U.S. Coast Guard

*The 574-foot freighter **Republica de Columbia** lists to starboard with the bow of the 520-foot U.S. containership **Transhawaii,** pierced through her engine room portside, east of Cape Hatteras, North Carolina on September 14, 1972. Though ships have navigational equipment, collisions still occur.*

techniques and marine electronics) have drastically reduced the number of sinkings but have by no means eliminated them completely.

Knowing how a ship sank is a strategic piece of the puzzle in locating lost ships. This knowledge is also helpful for the diver trying to unravel what it is they are looking at on the bottom. Throughout the centuries ships have reached their final harbor beneath the waves for a wide variety of reasons. Collisions have always been a primary cause of shipwrecks, but even within this single heading are numerous subheadings. A collision might be caused by carelessness, pilot error, fog or too much rum. It may have been high winds or snow or even severe currents that were responsible for putting two ships on a collision course. Understanding as much as possible about what caused the ship to sink can prove extremely useful to the serious wreck diver. On the wreck of the Shell Oil tanker *Pinthis*, which sank in 1930 in Cape Cod Bay, for example, veteran diver Bill Carter located the ship's steam whistle buried in the gravel bottom to the side of the main wreckage by theorizing what happened when the tanker sank. The wreck now lies nearly completely capsized or "turned turtle" on the bottom in approximately one-hundred feet of water. She was rammed by a steamer in the bow area of her starboard side and sank quickly. On frequent prior dives, Carter had seen pieces of debris lying on the bottom to the side of the wreck. He knew that most ships that are rammed, sink by coming to rest on the side of the collision because air is trapped on the opposite side. But, the *Pinthis* was

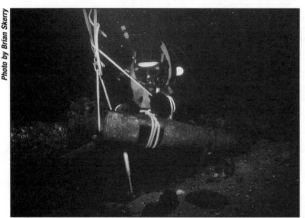

Rusty Carter attaches lines and a liftbag to a large steam whistle found on the tanker **Pinthis** *by his father Bill. Knowlege of events surrounding a ship's sinking can greatly benefit the artifact hunting diver.*

The American schooner **John Rommell, Jr.** *ashore at Provincetown, Massachusetts, badly iced up and a total loss in February 1875.*

full of oil cargo when rammed, leading him to conclude that the ship was pushed over by the collision, and the weight of the oil continued the momentum of the impact, rolling her over to come to rest on her port side.

The vessel probably would have landed on the bottom completely upside down but for two factors. The deck house and su-

Henry Keatts examines the now silent, encrusted breeches, of U.S.S. **Wilkes Barre**'s 40mm guns off Key West, Florida.

perstructure, as well as the buoyancy of the oil, prevented that from happening. Lying on her port side, the steam whistle, which was attached to the smokestack, would have stuck out somewhat perpendicular to the bottom. Over time, the oil leaked out giving more weight to the hull and the weaker superstructure collapsed allowing the wreck to end up in the position we see today. These series of events allowed the steam whistle to be left on the bottom next to the wreck instead of directly under the wreck which would have been the case had the tanker simply capsized immediately upon sinking. A diver knowing something about a ship's demise, then, truly has an advantage.

Collisions are only one of the many ways that a ship can become a wreck. Striking submerged objects, foundering, stranding, and explosion have equally taken their toll throughout the years. Storms have always been and remain today a sailor's constant adversary. Fire, a tragic and often fatal nightmare aboard ship, was particularly hazardous on wooden ships such as the numerous sailing vessels or steamers in operation prior to the mid-19th century. At the opposite end of the spectrum from fire is ice which was also an ever present hazard in northern latitudes, forming heavily on ships, adding weight and throwing off a vessel's center of balance.

Another major contributor of shipwrecks that litter the sea has been war. Shortly after man began to sail, he learned that military control of the seas gave him supreme advantages over his adversaries. The result of these conflicts are warships from nearly every era in man's history. They are decorated not with banners, flags or ensigns, but with marine organisms. They are inhabited now by schools of fish instead of fighting sailors as they decay in silent testimony of what once was important.

As we begin to combine our knowledge of a type of ship with how it sank, we can theorize as to the drama that unfolded in those final moments. Did the passengers on board the liner have time to gather their belongings? Did the purser manage to remove valuables from the safe, or did the liner sink in minutes, amidst a frenzy of panic? Answers to such questions fill in the gaps and contribute to this undersea detective story of wreck diving.

Evolution of a Shipwreck

The sailor cast adrift from his sinking ship looks on its final plunge under the sea as the end of his ship's story. For the wreck diver however, it is only the beginning. The sinking ship leaves behind no trace, with its tracks being quickly covered by the next wave on a journey to a new life below, a life in which the ship will continue to evolve until finally it is no more. For the undersea world is a dynamic environment and has a drastic effect on anything that occupies its briny realm. Another significant factor then, in the story of a shipwreck, is to understand the processes that continue to take place after the ship sinks.

Despite the images portrayed by many feature films, shipwrecks rarely look very much like the ships they once were. Left to the devices of Mother Ocean, the once proud ship begins to lose its stature. The phrase "time capsule" is often used to describe a sunken ship and, although this may adequately describe a site where artifacts can be recovered and knowledge can be learned, it should not always connote a well-preserved wreck. Shipwrecks are not static. They will continue to decay. Even wrecks that occur in fresh water will also decay, albeit at a significantly slower rate than those in the sea. Given enough data, divers or wreck hunters can reasonably predict the condition a wreck will be in when it is found.

A panel of fir wood recovered from the Santa Barbara Channel in California. The panel shows the severe damage caused by shipworms.

The variables that will determine the present condition of a wreck are numerous, with factors combining together to create countless scenarios. Rather than attempt to describe the multitude of possibilities, we will instead identify some of the major agents and show examples of how they can interact resulting in a particular type of wreck site. What we are really examining are the biological, chemical and geological effects on sunken ships. One of the first variables to consider is the material used in the ship's construction. The evolution of shipbuilding saw the use of a variety of materials over the years. For the purposes of this text, we will limit our examination to the most common of materials used, the first being wood. Both hardwoods and soft woods were used to build ships and, when a ship of wood is sent to Davey Jones' locker, it is not only *Lloyds' Bell but the dinner bell as well that rings.

Riding the tides and currents of the world's oceans are wood boring animals that love dining on wooden shipwrecks. The animals are of two major types: shipworms and gribbles. Contrary to its name, the shipworm is actually a bivalve mollusk of which there are 13 known genera with *Bankia* and *Teredo* being the most common. Having a wormlike body, the mollusk uses its two shells as boring tools. After boring a hole in the wood, the animal works its way in, feeding on plankton and wood. The tunnels they produce are coated with a calcareous lining that the animal secretes.

Certain species are capable of grinding a burrow up to six feet long. Centuries of shipbuilders have employed everything from applications of pitch and tar to copper sheathing to metal based

---

*Lloyds of London, one of the oldest and largest insurers of world shipping, rings a bell each time a vessel it insured sinks.

paints to prevent these slithering foes from sinking their ships by eating their way through the bottom. Once a wooden ship has been sunk, however, it belongs to these ravenous denizens of the deep and the munching begins.

Tom Mulloy surveys a newly discovered wooden wreck in Cape Cod Bay, suspected to be the **Windsor,** a schooner barge which sank in 1946. Only sections of the hull remain.

Although found in all oceans, shipworms have a low tolerance for extreme temperatures and lack of salinity; therefore, vessels sinking in Polar or Arctic seas have a considerably better chance of surviving as intact shipwrecks for longer periods of time. In temperate or tropical oceans, the rate of disintegration in shipwrecks is accelerated due in part to the ideal conditions for shipworm breeding.

The second major category of wood borers is the gribble (*Limnoria lignorum*) or termite of the sea. Gribbles are actually arthropod crustaceans, similar to lobster, shrimps and crabs. Their main diet is the fungi filaments of the wet wood, and in the process of ingesting the fungus, they create many small tunnels within the wood. The gribble is not nearly as deep a diver as the shipworm, having a depth range of generally no more than 60 feet. Thus, a shipwreck lying in 60 feet of water or less has to contend with both gribbles and shipworms, nibbling on her knees and gnawing on her catheads. Soft woods such as pine are particularly vulnerable to the ravages of borers while hardwoods, especially grades with high contents of tannin, like teak, are somewhat more durable.

Although studies have been conducted over the years as to how quickly marine borers can reduce a shipwreck to nothing more than wood chips, the numerous variables involved preclude giving exact time frames. We do know that in the proper environment it does not take very long. Dr. Ruth Turner of Harvard University, the world's leading authority on marine borers, has conducted exhaustive research in this area which has included the placing of wooden panels on known shipwreck sites to be monitored over time for evidence of decay. One such experiment involved placing white pine panels, eight inches long, four inches wide, and one inch thick, on the S.S. *Central America* off South Carolina in 8,500 feet of water. When examined after only two years, the panels were so badly eaten that they could easily be broken in two by hand. According to Dr. Turner, shallow water wrecks would be exposed to even greater populations of wood borers, destroying the ship at an even more rapid rate.

With this knowledge it is safe to assume that if a wreck hunter was searching for a wooden schooner that sank in the mid-1800s on a rocky ledge in one-hundred feet of water, expectations of finding very much of the ship itself would be low at best. It would of course be possible to locate various parts of the ship or cargo, but in the environment outlined above, little of the true vessel would remain.

When diving on an old wooden wreck, it is common to see peculiar wedge-shaped or triangular pieces of wood among the debris. In the middle of these pieces you will usually find a spike or some other type of ship's fastenings made of copper or bronze. In these cases the metallic salts from the fitting have leached out into the surrounding wood forcing the wood borers to stop when they get to the contaminated wood. If there is one thing that leaves a bad taste in the mouth of a wood borer it is anything metallic. The same would be true of a porthole found lying in the sand with pieces of wood still screwed to it. Perhaps part of a wooden bridge or deck house, it would have fallen free when the surrounding structure was consumed, although remnants of the wood remain attached to it, uneatable to the munching menaces.

About the only chance a wreck diver has of seeing large sections of an old saltwater wooden wreck, short of diving in the

Canadian Arctic, is for the wreck to have been buried below the sea floor. Wood borers require the flow of seawater for oxygen to sustain life and, therefore, cannot attack a wreck that has been buried beneath sediment.

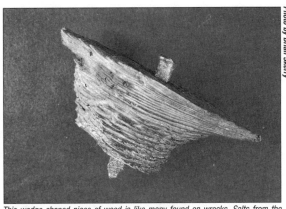

This wedge shaped piece of wood is like many found on wrecks. Salts from the copper spike in the center have leached out contaminating the wood to marine borers.

Oftentimes a wooden wreck will become infested with shipworms and gribbles only to eventually break up and become covered by sand, killing the wood borers and retarding the decaying process. Should the ship someday become uncovered, divers may be rewarded by viewing sections of a vessel that would otherwise have been lost forever.

When attempting to understand the "evolution" of a shipwreck, it is important to recognize the weak points of a particular ship's design and how they also contribute to the breakdown process. Wooden and metal ships are designed quite differently and will decay differently with or without the presence of marine borers. A good example of this is to observe a wooden sailing ship's cargo and how it contributes to the breakup and decay of the wreck. Since it is the keel that is the backbone and has all the strength in a wooden ship, cargo (be it silver bars or Roman amphora) is designed to be loaded over this section. When the ship sinks with even a slight list to one side, the cargo will shift over time coming to rest on the inside of the hull planking. This section of the hull being weaker and never designed to tolerate that kind of weight will eventually give way, allowing the cargo to spill out. This process may take a fair amount of time during which the ship will continue to list more dramatically to the side that the cargo has shifted to, resulting in the ultimate breakup of the ship.

Deterioration of a Wooden Shipwreck

illustration by James L. Christley

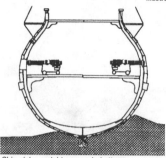

Ship sinks upright on sandy bottom.

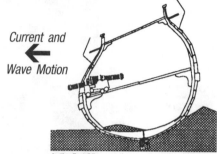

Current and Wave Motion ←

In the first 25 years, the structure of the ship starts to fail as marine organisms start their destructive work.

Within 50 years the cargo has probably shifted to the low side of the ship and started to be distributed along the bottom. Heavy weighted items add to the structural collapse.

Current and Wave Motion ←

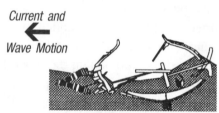

Deterioration continues to destroy the structure of the ship. The speed of the breakup depends on the area in which the ship sank. In deep cold water the action is very slow and it may take several hundred years to reach this point. In shallow tropical water, this may be the condition in only 20 years.

Current and Wave Motion ←

After the ship parts have been completely buried in sand and silt, the disintegration slows and the remains may last thousands of years.

As always, there are exceptions, and one wreck in particular comes to mind. Several years ago, Brian Skerry was exploring an area known as the "dumping ground" off Boston, Massachusetts, where ships were frequently scuttled over a period of many years. He dived on a site that looked promising based on a sonar record that showed a target rising high off the ocean bottom. Two wrecks were known to have been scuttled in this area of the dumping ground; an old wooden freighter named *Coyote,* and a steel- hulled Navy Eagle Boat. Since the *Coyote* was scuttled in 1932 and had been underwater for in excess of fifty years, it seemed unlikely it would be intact and sitting upright on the bottom. The safe bet was that the Eagle Boat had been found at last. When Brian descended the anchor line, however, to his disbelief, what he saw stretched out before him was a large wooden ship, intact, sitting upright on the bottom. The thinner, weaker decks had collapsed leaving a V-shaped hull remaining. A closer examination of the wreck combined with additional research revealed that the *Coyote* was built using iron strapping to support the wooden planks. Many shipbuilders did not fully trust iron when it became available as material to use. They often cautiously built composite vessels that incorporated the use of both wood and iron.

Iron shipbuilding became widespread around 1830 with steel taking over around 1870. Early on, these ships were riveted together, eventually rivets were replaced by welded joints. The use of these materials changed the entire make-up of ships. No longer was the keel the only strong point of a vessel. Metal ships could now be built as a girder with decks as strong as the bottom. Modern era ships made of these materials will also succumb to the decaying action of the sea once they have sunk, but the processes are quite different than those evident in wooden wrecks.

The sea, because of its salinity, is a highly corrosive environment to most metals used in shipbuilding. Iron, for example, corrodes ten times faster in seawater than in air. The corrosion of a metal shipwreck is actually a very complex process with multiple reactions taking place. Perhaps the most significant is the electrochemical process that begins when a metal ship sinks in the ocean and continues until the vessel is no more. This process can best be described as a large galvanic cell that is created from dissimilar metals being immersed in an electrolyte (salt water). An electric current is produced between the metals causing the least noble metal to dissolve (ionization). This process will continue between all the various metals of a shipwreck until nothing is left. Even if only an iron hull remains, the ionization will continue between less noble, or weaker sections of the same metal.

A perfect porthole lies in place on the wreck of the **Horatio Hall** *off Chatham, Massachusetts. Although the steamer sank in 1909, the porthole survived in pristine condition due to the cathodic protection of the iron hull to which it was fastened.*

Artifact collectors see examples of this often in very practical terms. If a brass porthole were thrown into the sea, it would soon begin to "de-zincify," which is to say that the zinc in the brass would dissolve because it is less noble than the surrounding metals which make up brass. Why is it then, that often a diver can remove a brass porthole from an old iron-hulled wreck, screws and all, in nearly perfect condition? It is because the iron was the sacrificial metal in this situation. It provides cathodic protection to the more noble brass, allowing the diver to unscrew the porthole quite easily (other corrosive elements may keep it from being easily unscrewed however!).

This electrochemical corrosion tends to be more severe along areas of stress such as bends or dents in the metal (of which ship-wrecks have many) causing these areas to decay first. Naturally thinner portions of the ship, like decking, would be the first sections to disappear. It should be emphasized that the higher the salinity content, the higher the rate of corrosion. Although the tendency is to think that fresh water wrecks are spared of this fate, they are not. Even fresh water lakes have the presence of some chlorides (salts) and the ionization process will take place, though at a significantly slower rate.

Temperature also influences the equation, with higher temperatures yielding higher corrosive rates. Working alongside the galvanic cell effect are other deterioration elements including anaerobic corrosion, caused by sulfate reducing bacteria, as well as localized changes in Ph factors. It is unnecessary for wreck divers to examine any of these processes in great detail. An awareness of corrosive actions, the effect of temperature and salinity and which sections will corrode first, will provide the diver with a solid background for explaining the condition of a metal wreck.

Geography of the area in which a ship sank is the next major variable that affects the evolution of a shipwreck. Generally speaking, wrecks that occur in shallow water are prone to a much shorter existence than those sinking in deeper water. Regardless of a ship's material, if it runs aground on a coral reef in Bermuda, it will be pounded by the waves into rubble in short order. A diver is therefore more likely to find an intact wreck in deeper water or at least deep enough to be free of the punishing action of the surf. Additional geographical elements include the type of bottom and prevailing currents in an area. An "active bottom" can have a dramatic effect on a shipwreck that happens to land right in its midst. For example, consider a large steel freighter that sinks on a bottom of fine white sand. The area is constantly raked by strong currents and the ship has settled perpendicular to the current. In all probability, over time, the current will "wash out" the sand from underneath the bow and stern causing the ship to gradually settle down lower into the bottom. If the washed out areas are severe enough, the stress put on the midship section could break the ship in two. The current will likely continue to deposit sand against the side of the hull eventually reaching the deck level and even possibly burying the center of the deck itself. This unremitting process, combined with an occasional storm which might deposit even more sand over the wreck, could completely bury the ship. A combination of sand and strong currents will also chip away at a ship, buffeting it like a sandblaster—each tide carrying away more and more of what was there. This is only one possible scenario. Countless others exist, but it is important to at least be aware of the major

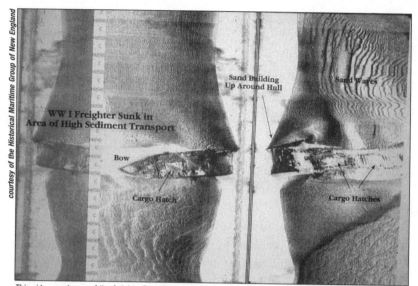

Sand Building
Up Around Hull

Sand Waves

WW I Freighter Sunk in
Area of High Sediment Transport

Bow

Cargo Hatch

Cargo Hatches

*This side scan image of the freighter **Port Hunter,** which sank in 1918, shows enormous amounts of sand building up along the wreck's starboard hull amidships. The sand in the bow area however, is being washed out due to the swift currents that rake this region. (white area in center is track of side scan)*

variables within the heading of geography that will determine what a diver will find.

Historical and Archeological Significance of Fresh Water

Up to this point we have only briefly touched upon shipwrecks that lie in fresh water. Since freshwater wrecks offer some of the most significant contributions to our knowledge of maritime history, not to mention some of the greatest wreck sites that can be seen anywhere, we present the following as a brief glimpse into an area with a rich maritime legacy, the Great Lakes.

The Great Lakes were formed during the retreat of the Pleistocene glaciers. They contain 40% of North America's surface fresh water. Lake Superior is not only the largest and deepest of the Great Lakes; its 31,820 square miles make it the largest lake in the Western Hemisphere. The vast expanses of water that make up the five Great Lakes hold their share of shipwrecks.

Wooden-hull wrecks, which seem more like a "real" shipwreck to the romantic eye, are in excellent preservation due to

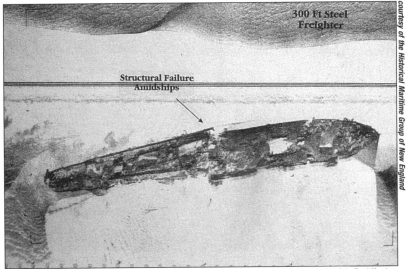

300 Ft Steel
Freighter

Structural Failure
Amidships

This follow-up side scan image shows that the washing out of the sand beneath the bow and stern of the **Port Hunter**, has led to the cracking of the hull amidships.

submergence in cold, fresh water. Wood borers, such as ship-worms, are marine animals and are not a threat to these histori-cal vessels. A prime example is the 165-foot wooden sailing ship *Cornelia B. Windgate*, lost in a winter storm in December 1875 and located a few years ago by side scan sonar. The wreck sits upright on the bottom in 190 feet of cold dark water, with little visible damage. The standing rigging was chain, so the masts still stand tall. As a measure of the excellent preservation in those cold Lake Huron waters (off Rockport, Michigan), the ship's name is so sharply clear on the bow that the tool marks are still apparent.

Oxidation decompression of metal occurs at a slower rate in cold, fresh water than in salt water. As examples, metal-hulled shipwrecks in Michigan's Isle Royale National Park (Lake Supe-rior) exhibit excellent preservation. .

The passenger-freighter *America*

One of the most popular dive sites at Isle Royale is the passen-ger-freighter *America*. She was one of the smallest passenger ships on the Great Lakes when she was launched in 1898 at the Wyan-

The **Cumberland,** *the 204.5-foot-long, wooden-hulled side-wheeler, struck Rock of Ages Reef off Isle Royale in 1877.*

dotte, Michigan yard of the Detroit Dry Dock Company. The steel-hulled steamer was 164.5 feet long, with a 31-foot beam, 11-foot depth, 486 tons, and was powered by triple expansion engines. Dunbar and McMillan Company, of Michigan City, put her into service for excursions between Chicago and Michigan City, and occasionally into Lakes Erie and Huron.

In 1903, the Booth Packing Company purchased the *America* to provide service between Duluth and all north shore points for its United States and Dominion Transportation Company. The little steamer was lengthened in 1911 to accommodate more passengers and cargo. An additional 19 feet was added to her length and her tonnage was doubled to 937 tons. She was described as palatial in promotional material, and in many respects she was. Elaborate facilities provided dining, drinking, and gambling to satisfy the tastes of her Great Lakes passengers.

In her 30 years of service on the Lakes, the *America* was involved in 11 accidents. If that seems like an unusually high number of incidents, it should be noted that the vessel traveled the dangerous waters of Lake Superior in all kinds of weather, frequently without navigational aids, and maintained tight schedules, with more dockings than most vessels.

Photo courtesy of the Douglas County Historical Society, Superior, Wisconsin.

The passenger-freighter ship **America**.

Sinking

Captain Edward E. Smith headed the *America* out into Lake Superior from Isle Royale's Washington Harbor in the early morning hours of June 7, 1928. At 3 a.m. the vessel was only about a half mile out of her dock when she trembled with a series of shocks as her bow plowed into a reef in the North Gap Channel. There was no confusion as passengers and crew assembled on deck. All five of the ship's lifeboats were lowered and all aboard were taken to Washington Harbor, only a half mile away.

Captain Smith, who was on the bridge at the time of the accident, had turned the conn over to his first mate John Wick, only five minutes earlier. The captain was on the last boat to leave the ship.

By 4:30 a.m. the 30-year-old steamer was totally underwater, except for a part of her bow and superstructure that stubbornly projected above the surface.

The wreck now lies in the North Gap of Washington Harbor, Isle Royale, about 200 feet off Thompson Island. The depth ranges from five feet in the bow to approximately 80 feet in the stern. The National Park Service maintains a two point mooring on the bow.

The wreck's general appearance is impressive; it seems that the whole ship is rising from the depths to sail again. Visibility is 30 or

The **America**'s bow points skyward after running aground.

more feet, and the remains are easily seen from the surface. From May 15 to October 1, a white buoy with a blue stripe attached to the bow in two feet of water marks the site.

The ship is tilted at a 45-degree angle, with a 30-degree list to port. There is much to see on the old wreck. The midship and stern are intact, including the engine room, galley, main salon, and some cabins. The forward deck houses are gone, but the holds are open. The ship's 700 horsepower T-3 engine still shines, giving the im-

A diver inspects the **America**'s well preserved purser's office.

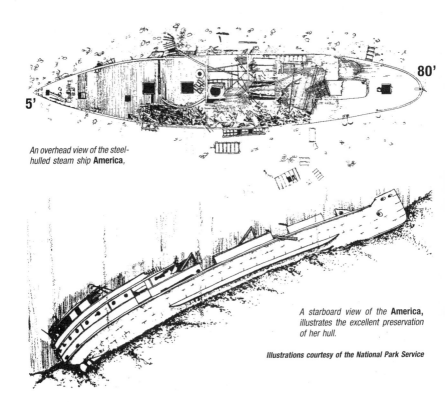

An overhead view of the steel-hulled steam ship **America,**

A starboard view of the **America,** illustrates the excellent preservation of her hull.

Illustrations courtesy of the National Park Service

pression that someone is kept busy on a regular schedule of keeping it polished.

Divers can penetrate nearly every area of the wreck, but passageways and cabins are narrow and dark, with hanging cables that make the dive even more dangerous. Even slight movement raises thick clouds of sediment within the wreck. A silt-filled storeroom near the galley has been labeled the "forbidden" room since a 1976 diving fatality. To reduce its hazard, the door to the room was removed. That increased the size of the opening, but it is still dangerous, and is not a place to stretch a diver's air supply.

A hatchway in the rear of the engine room on deck 2, opens into a companionway that goes out to the side of the ship, then toward the stern. The companionway leads to the dining area. The ship can be exited from the dining room through a cargo door. Dropping to the bottom off the stern of the ship provides an awesome view that includes the prop, and the rudder turned hard to starboard. It almost seems that the rudder is all that keeps the ship from sliding further into the channel.

The *America* has been referred to as the "happy" ship, a ship with a smile on her bow. That smile stayed above water for two years after the rest of the vessel sank. Now it is part of the algae-covered remains of a once happy ship that is known as one of the most popular dive sites on Isle Royale.

The bulk carrier *Chester A. Congdon*

Chester A. Congdon was built in South Chicago in 1907 by the Chicago Steam Boat Company. The steel-hulled ship was 532 feet in length, with a beam of 56.2 feet and displaced 6,530 tons. In 1918, the steamer was in bound from Thunder Bay in a dense fog, when she struck Canoe Rocks, a shoal that now bears her name, on the northwest side of Isle Royale. Salvagers removed part of her cargo of 380,000 bushels of Canadian wheat, but the ship's back was broken and she was declared a total loss. At the time, the *Congdon* was the largest ship to have been lost in the Great Lakes.

The wreck is in four major sections on both sides of the shoal. Depth ranges from 20 to 180 feet of water. The bow, with the pilothouse intact, is on the south side of the reef with a buoy attached at the stern in 70 feet. The bow sitting upright in 110 feet of water is an impressive sight.

The **Chester A. Congdon** *with a broken back.*

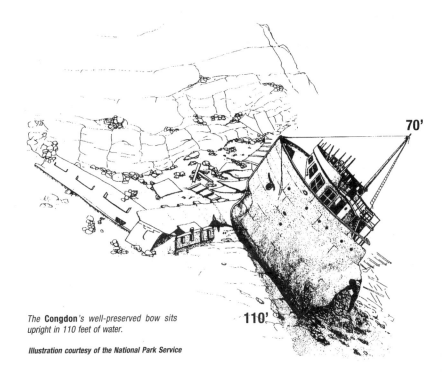

70'

110'

The **Congdon**'s well-preserved bow sits upright in 110 feet of water.

Illustration courtesy of the National Park Service

The bulk carrier *Emperor*

The ship's name denotes its position in the wreck diving community. In 1911, when the bulk carrier was launched, she was the largest ship ever built in Canada. The steel-hulled steamer was 525 feet long, with a beam of 56 feet and displaced 7,031 tons. At the time of her sinking, at 4:45 a.m., June 4, 1947, she was owned by the Canada Steamship Lines of Montreal. The *Emperor* had struck Congdon Shoals (Canoe Rocks), like the *Congdon* 30 years before. But unlike the *Congdon*, weather was not a factor in the disaster, the *Emperor*'s first mate had fallen asleep in a chair.

The good visibility and the virtually intact ship creates a photographer's paradise. A buoy is attached to the bow stem in 25 feet of water; the wreck gradually descends to the stern resting in 170 feet of water. A buoy attached to the deck in the stern is at 100 feet.

25'

170'

*The **Emperor**'s first mate had fallen asleep in a chair, resulting in the grounding of the largest ship ever built in Canada.*

Reminder

Isle Royale shipwrecks are in a National Park, and Federal law prohibits the removal or disturbance in any manner of underwater cultural sites and associated artifacts, this includes shipwrecks or remains of ships, as well as other antiquities on the bottom lands of waters in Isle Royale National Park. Penalties include prison sentences and fines up to $10,000. Rewards up to $500 may be paid to anyone who furnishes information that leads to conviction of a criminal violation.

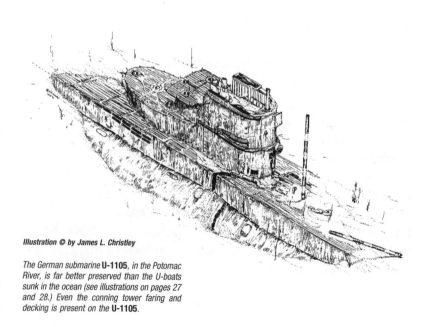

*The German submarine **U-1105**, in the Potomac River, is far better preserved than the U-boats sunk in the ocean (see illustrations on pages 27 and 28.) Even the conning tower faring and decking is present on the **U-1105**.*

Non-Environmental Effects On Shipwrecks

A final consideration in the evolution of a shipwreck is non-environmental effects, such as the destruction of shipwrecks by man. Although a ship may sink, it is not necessarily beyond the reach of further damage through the action of humans. When ships sink, they are often a hazard to navigation and must either be removed or cleared for the safe passage of other shipping traffic. Various means may be employed with the most common being either explosives or wire dragging. These methods will often clear the pas-

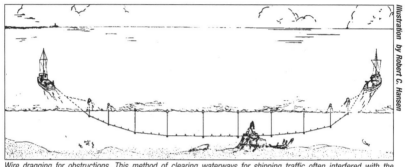

Illustration by Robert C. Hansen

Wire dragging for obstructions. This method of clearing waterways for shipping traffic often interfered with the "natural" evolution of a shipwreck.

sage to a certain depth of water, still leaving wreckage below. Any diver attempting to piece together the clues in the "detective story" of a shipwreck should be sure to check records regarding this common means of dealing with wrecks.

As we mentioned earlier in this chapter, several of the effects on shipwrecks described (and others not described) can work together creating many possible outcomes. If a freighter that was constructed with an iron hull and wooden deckhouses was torpedoed in 1943, burned and sank in 60 feet of water in an area of sandy shoal type bottom with three knot currents at mid tide, what do you think you would find today? Was it wire dragged? Blown up as a hazard? Where might you find the bell? Would the wreck even be exposed? Obviously, the more blanks you can fill in the better off you will be. Time spent learning about the type of vessel, how it sank, and the region in which it sank is never wasted. As we will see further in the next chapter, gaining this knowledge is the essence and backbone of productive wreck diving.

Side scan sonar printout of the tanker **Poling Brothers #2.** The 77-year-old ship, launched in 1863, sank in Long Island Sound in 1940. The wreck is in 65 feet of water.

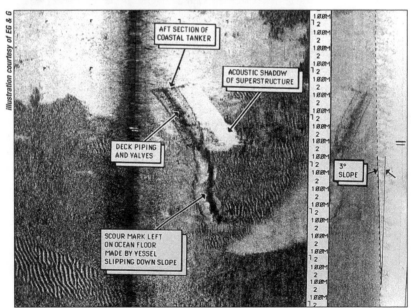

AFT SECTION OF COASTAL TANKER

ACOUSTIC SHADOW OF SUPERSTRUCTURE

DECK PIPING AND VALVES

3° SLOPE

SCOUR MARK LEFT ON OCEAN FLOOR MADE BY VESSEL SLIPPING DOWN SLOPE

The coastal tanker **Chester A. Poling** broke in two during a storm in 1977, and sank off Gloucester, Massachusetts in 95 feet of water. Huge seas produced by the 'Blizzard of 1978' moved the stern section into deeper water, leaving a scour mark on the bottom, readily apparent on this side scan sonar printout.

Chapter 3

Research

To be able to dive a shipwreck, we must first find a shipwreck. Finding a shipwreck to dive on can be accomplished in several ways. Perhaps the easiest is for someone else to take you to one or to tell you where one can be found. The alternative is to find one for yourself. This is the dream of any wreck diver and not as difficult as it might seem. There are virtually thousands of wrecks yet to be discovered, so there is no time like the present to begin. The place to begin is with research.

The beginning point of research will depend on how you wish to approach the task of finding a wreck. For example, you may have heard the name of a particular wreck and decide that is the one you want to find. In a case like this, you will need to find out as much as possible about that ship. Some of the information that will help you to find such a ship includes when it sank, how it sank, the exact date of the sinking, and the general region in which it sank. All of those questions can be answered by a variety of sources depending on the specific wreck. If the wreck you seek is anywhere close to land, a local newspaper might have written a story about it. To find that story, you will need to know the date of sinking. The date of sinking might be found from a source like Lloyds Register, published by Lloyds' of London, which can be found in most major libraries. If the wreck was sunk in wartime, you may be able to ascertain her location by studying deck logs of the vessel that sank her. You may not know of any specific wreck, but have an interest in a certain type of vessel such as steamships. In a case like this, it might be best to begin by looking through newspapers of that era to see which steamships sank. Once you have found a likely candidate, you can begin gathering as much information as possible to narrow down the area in which you will physically search for the wreck.

Regardless of which approach you take, when beginning as a wreck hunter, there is one proven method of increasing your odds of success. This method is to select a wreck which sank close to shore, preferably by striking a submerged object. If a wreck sank within sight of shore, there will usually be a fair amount of information available on its location. If it struck a submerged object, such as a ledge, a diver should easily be able to locate and search that ledge today. Wrecks that sank far offshore will naturally be more difficult targets.

Remember, even if you are not especially interested in finding an unknown shipwreck, research can prove invaluable when diving known wrecks. You might be interested in knowing what type of cargo a vessel carried or locating the room in which the safe was kept. In the way that studying ship construction adds a great deal to a wreck diver's knowledge, so too does any type of research. In addition to the obvious advantages of obtaining photographs or builder's plans that can be examined, or uncovering noteworthy information about the ship itself, research can offer even more. When conducting research, one often comes to learn about the individuals involved. The human beings that experienced this tragedy and the conditions of their lives can add so much to the complete story. Why did that 24-year-old submarine commander fire the torpedo in the last days of the war and would he have done so if he was 44 instead? What made that freighter captain order the helmsman to turn directly into the path of the oncoming steamer? Questions that

Newspapers are one of the best sources to consult initially, in the research quest.

will perhaps never be answered, but in asking them, we become closer to the event and more understanding of wrecks as something other than just decaying hulks on the ocean floor.

Thorough research will always reward the diligent individual willing to put in the time. There are countless sources from which information can be gained and one source will lead to another. Many long hours may be spent in libraries and archives before you ever set sail to begin a search at sea, but the time spent will be well worth the effort.

The Paper Trail

We suggest that research begin with documents and charts in archives, libraries and museum collections. Documents describing a particular wreck and sometimes charts giving the location of the wreck site may be available. Local historical societies contain excellent shipwreck information, often with files on individual wrecks. The pamphlet files and manuscript collections can be an important source. A maritime disaster would be given much more coverage in a local paper than in a metropolitan journal such as the **New York Times.**

Major metropolitan libraries such as the New York Public Library and the Boston Public Library contain considerable information on shipwrecks. Ask a Reference Librarian for assistance. Three excellent sources are **The List of Merchant Vessels of the United States, The Life Saving Service Reports, 1876-1914, and Lloyd's Register of Wreck Returns.**

The list of merchant vessels, published annually since 1868, contains a "Vessels Lost" section. However, it is also necessary to check the "Value of Shipping" section, because some of the listed vessels were salvaged.

The annual reports of **Life Saving Stations** list shipwrecks and describe rescue attempts. When locations are given in such reports, the bearings are "Magnetic Bearings," taken with rather crude range-finders.

Lloyd's Register was published quarterly or annually from 1870 to the present. The volumes list the owner, tonnage, dimensions, and a description of the vessel. It also lists vessels lost, broken up, or abandoned.

Lighthouse service records possess information similar to **Life Saving Station** records. The several volumes of **Bancroft's Works** deal with the histories of California (five volumes), Oregon, Washington, and the Northwest, and list the locations of many wrecks.

Another valuable source in large libraries is the microfilm copies of contemporary newspapers. The number of lives lost or the value of the cargo would usually determine the amount of coverage given to the disaster. Eyewitness accounts and interesting anecdotes regarding the disaster add to the basic information previously gathered.

The newspaper files should be checked for one or two years after a disaster for salvage operations and actions that might have decreased the wreck's threat as a navigational hazard.

Many large libraries have the **New York Times** on microfilm from 1851 to the present. When using a library's set of indexes for the **New York Times**, shipwreck information may be found in several sections, depending upon the year. A few examples:

Accidents - Boats	Marine Affairs	Shipping
Accidents - Shipping	Marine Intelligence	Shipping Board
Accidents - Submarines	Military Affairs	U.S. Navy
Insurance - Marine	Naval Affairs	

Marine Disasters

Libraries, such as the New York Public Library, the world's largest research and circulation library, possess old coast and geodetic maps that may offer information in regard to shipwrecks.

Records of the British Admiralty, in the Public Record Office, contain reports by captains and flag officers on the loss of Royal Navy vessels. Records of courts martial on captains tell the story of their lost warships. Letters and journals often give details of the loss of a ship. Similar records are in the Archives Nationales de France and the archives at Seville and Samancas in Spain. Records pertaining to the United States Navy are in the collections of the Naval Historical Center (Washington Navy Yard), the National Archives, and the Manuscripts Division of the Library of Congress. Documents relating to private shipping are also found in the National Archives, the Library of Congress, the manuscript collections of marine museums, libraries, and historical societies. All usually have photograph collections as well.

During the Depression, the W.P.A. (Works Progress Administration) hired writers to compile Customs Records into readable book form. Some locations of shipwrecks they have listed are not found elsewhere.

An important source of information that is often overlooked is the local fisherman. A trawler captain who snags a valuable net on a shipwreck records the loran numbers of the event so that he will avoid that obstruction in the future. A diver receiving such information should bear in mind that the snagged net was a few hundred feet behind the fishing vessel when the loran numbers were recorded. They represent the boat's location at the time, not the obstruction's.

It is far more interesting to explore a wreck when you are familiar with its history: when, how, and why it sank. Research is also important to become familiar with a ship's construction. That information will add a new dimension of interest in the exploration of its remains and will be an aid in searching for artifacts. Deck plans of the U.S. armored cruiser *San Diego* purchased from the National Archives will provide information indicating where the ship's magazines, guns, and armory were located.

National Oceanic & Atmospheric Administration

By the beginning of the 19th century, the American sailing fleet had reached an accelerated level of activity accompanied by substantial economic growth, but America was still virtually dependent upon Europe for many material needs. In 1807, in an effort to enhance the safety of transAtlantic crossings, President Thomas Jefferson founded the Federal Government's first scientific agency, the Office of Charting and Geodetic Survey. Jefferson selected Ferdinand Rudolph Hassler, a Swiss geodesist and recent immigrant to the United States, to head this agency.

Lacking both equipment and trained assistants, Hassler sailed to England for the charting instruments he needed. The War of 1812 left him stranded in Europe, but in 1816 he returned and began work around New York Harbor. Hassler was unskilled in politics, which led to problems with Congress, and after only two seasons the agency was given over to the Navy. When the Navy proved unable to chart the coast accurately, the civilian Coast and Geodetic Survey was established in 1832 under Hassler's direction.

Hassler divided his task into three categories: geodesy, the branch of applied mathematics that measures the shape, area, and curvature of a major expanse of land; topography, which defines the surface configuration of an area; and hydrography, which measures and maps the earth's surface waters as an aid to navigation. The strategies arrived at by Hassler and his colleagues continue in use as part of the nation's system of primary triangulation, in which the relative distance between two or more points is measured by a triangle or series of triangles in a navigational survey.

The agency is now known as the National Ocean Service, a component of NOAA, the National Oceanic and Atmospheric Administration. NOAA is a federal agency that was formed in 1970. Included under its direction are the National Weather Service, the National Environmental Satellite Data and Information Service, the Office of Oceanic and Atmospheric Research, and the National Marine Fisheries Service.

NOAA participates in the lives of nearly all Americans by providing weather forecasts to the general public and by issuing warnings of natural disasters such as hurricanes, floods, and tornadoes. Collectively NOAA works in a variety of ways from mapping and charting world-wide ocean waters to predicting atmospheric conditions, and protecting marine life and its environment. It also provides nautical and aeronautical charts and geodetic surveys.

Three NOAA vessels, the *Whiting*, the *Rude*, and the *Heck* are presently exploring the ocean floor for shipwrecks. To facilitate their search, each ship is equipped with an underwater side scan sonar. The device, towed behind a vessel, resembles a small torpedo; it can detect any object on the ocean floor up to one hundred meters on either side of the ship. A second sonar device then ascertains the precise depth, and often divers descend to examine the wrecks. The information gathered is registered on NOAA's newest charts, making it available to the diving and boating public.

Nautical Charts

Navigational charts published by NOAA indicate wrecks by the customary wreck symbol for sunken vessels that are considered hazardous to navigation. In addition, all known wrecks, including those not dangerous to navigation, are symbolized on the charts to the 300-fathom curve.

Nautical charts are an important research tool in determining the position of a shipwreck. Some wrecks are a serious threat to

FIGURE 3-1
Visible stranded shipwreck as depicted on a nautical chart.

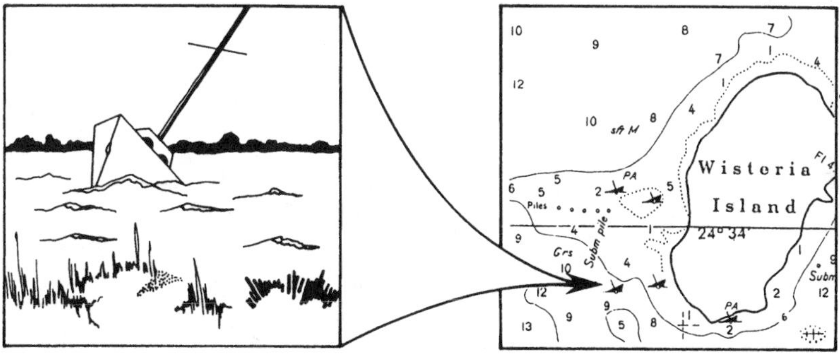

FIGURE 3-2 Sunken (submerged) Shipwreck Symbols

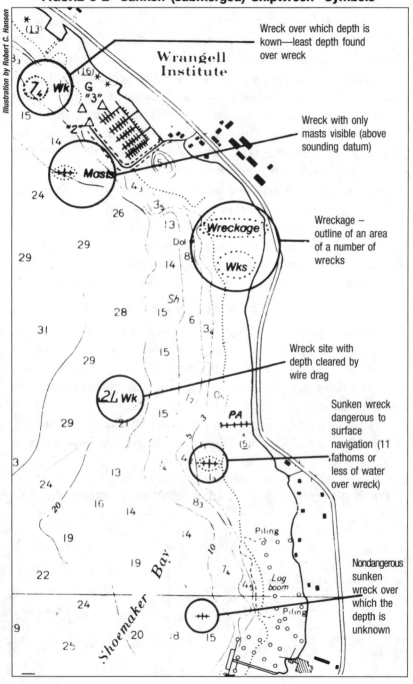

Wreck over which depth is kown—least depth found over wreck

Wreck with only masts visible (above sounding datum)

Wreckage – outline of an area of a number of wrecks

Wreck site with depth cleared by wire drag

Sunken wreck dangerous to surface navigation (11 fathoms or less of water over wreck)

Nondangerous sunken wreck over which the depth is unknown

Illustration by Robert C. Hansen

Wrangell Institute

Shoemaker Bay

navigation, and several different symbols are used on nautical charts to indicate their locations. Two basic types of symbols are used for wrecks—visibile and sunken. Visible wrecks are most frequently depicted on charts as shown in Figure 3-1 on page 75.

There are a variety of symbols used to depict submerged wrecks, as shown in **Figure 3-2** on the opposite page. Submerged wrecks considered dangerous to navigation are those with 66 feet or less of water over them; they are distinguished from non-dangerous wrecks by blue tint within a dotted circle. Additional information may be the known least depth or the depth to which a wire drag has cleared the site without hanging on wreckage. A clearance depth does not necessarily rule out the existence of a wreck, but only that the wire drag may not have been deep enough to hang on the wreckage. Details relating to the origin of a symbol are often contained in the National Ocean Service charting and surveying files.

The presence or absence of wreck symbols may change between charts of different scale, as shown in **Figure 3-3**. To obtain the most information about a wreck, it is important to use the largest scale chart. The scale of each nautical chart is shown by a ratio number. While more area is shown on charts with relatively small ratios, e.g. 1:200,000, more detail of an area is shown on charts with relatively large ratios, e.g. 1:40,000.

FIGURE 3-3

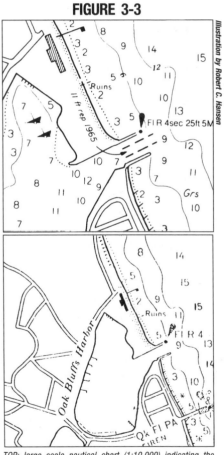

Illustration by Robert C. Hansen

TOP: large scale nautical chart (1:10,000) indicating the approximate position of two visible wrecks. ABOVE: nautical chart of the same area at a smaller scale (1:20,000) where symbols are not used.

Nautical charts of local areas are usually available at marine supply stores and marinas. They usually also carry catalogs of charts for other areas. A catalog illustrating nautical charts may be obtained free of charge for each coastal section by writing the National Ocean Survey, Distribution Division (C44), Riverdale, Maryland 20840. The four coastal sections are:

Chart Catalog 1 — United States, Atlantic and Gulf coasts; including Puerto Rico and the U.S. Virgin Islands

Chart Catalog 2 — United States, Pacific coasts; including Hawaii, Guam and the Samoan Islands

Chart Catalog 3 — United States, Alaska; including the Aleutian Islands

Chart Catalog 4 — United States, Great Lakes and adjacent waterways

Nautical charts and maps of United States rivers may be obtained from the U.S. Army Corps of Engineers regional offices:

VICKSBURG DISTRICT
P.O. Box 60
Vicksburg, Mississippi 39180
(601) 634-5000

OHIO RIVER DIVISION
P.O. Box 1159
Cincinnati, Ohio 45201
(513) 684-3002

CHICAGO DISTRICT
219 South Dearborn Street
Chicago, Illinois 60604
(312) 353-6400

MOBILE DISTRICT
P.O. Box 2288
Mobile, Alabama 36628
(205) 690-2511

OMAHA DISTRICT
6014 U.S. Post Office & Courthouse
Omaha, Nebraska 68102
(402) 221-3900

Charts of the Tennessee River and tributaries may be obtained from the Tennessee Valley Authority, Maps and Engineering Section, 416 Union Ave., Knoxville, TN 37902 (615) 632-2921

AWOIS

In 1981, The National Ocean Service implemented the Automated Wreck and Obstruction Information System (AWOIS) to assist in planning hydrographic survey operations and to catalog and store a substantial volume of reports of wrecks and obstructions that are considered navigational hazards within U.S. coastal waters. In 1988, AWOIS was converted from a UNIVAC mainframe computer to a personal computer based system using a licensed dBASE III plus software package. The basic format for each AWOIS record is intact but has been streamlined and expanded to include new information. Today, about 12,000 reports that have been received include unverified accounts of vessel casualties, as well as chronological history. All items have a position in latitude and longitude, position accuracy code, and chart number. As part of the hydrographic survey planning process, the records are reviewed and those wrecks or obstructions that require additional field investigation are assigned to specific field units. The results eventually become part of the AWOIS file so that a permanent record of a wreck or obstruction is always available.

Besides functioning as a survey planning tool, AWOIS is of potential value to various users outside the National Ocean Service. The historical record of selected wrecks, the accessibility of information in a sorted format, and its reasonable cost make AWOIS an important information source for divers. The information is an important supplement to other sources. However, AWOIS has limitations that should be considered by potential users. Most notably, it is not a comprehensive record of wrecks in any particular area. Historical research is constantly being conducted to improve the quality of the file, but it will never completely address every known or reported wreck. The emphasis is constantly placed on wrecks which may be a hazard to navigation.

Loran-C numbers are rarely reported in historical records and, because the National Ocean Service has not routinely recorded loran numbers at all wreck sites, that type of positioning data is not generally available from AWOIS. However, due to the popular demand for loran numbers, an effort is now being made for the file to reflect loran numbers. Users of AWOIS are encouraged to submit Loran-C numbers on wrecks to the National Ocean Service, whenever possible.

AWOIS listings can be obtained for a fee by writing: National Ocean Service, Hydrographic Surveys Branch (N/CG241), SSMC3, Silver Springs, Maryland 20910. The person requesting the information should provide the geographic limits of the desired area in latitude and longitude, or vessel names. Additional assistance for specific information is also available at a nominal fee.

FIGURE 3-5 An Example of an AWOIS File

```
                       NATIONAL OCEAN SERVICE
           AUTOMATED WRECK AND OBSTRUCTION INFORMATION SYSTEM
                            JUNE 18, 1985


                         REG                             GP SVY CARTO
     NAME      QUADRANT    #     LATITUDE    LONGITUDE  AREA AC ST  CODE CHART
---------------------  -------  ------------  -------------  ----  --  ---  ----- -----


---------------------  -------  ------------  -------------  ----  --  ---  ----- -----
01650
SAN DIEGO              1  0000000 40/32/25.62  073/02/30.64   C   33  *3  0100 12300

   HISTORY
     NM30/18--OBSTRUCTION BUOY HS, 2ND CLASS NUN, WAS ESTAB. JULY 19 IN 15 FMS
       ABOUT 50 YARDS WEST OF OBSTR, OVER WHICH THERE IS 6.5 FMS OF WATER;
       SHINNECOCK BAY LH BEARS 52 DEG (M), FIRE ISLAND LH BEARS 297 DEG (M), LONE
       HILL CG STATION BEARS 339 DEG (M).
     NM31/18--OBSTRUCTION GAS BUOY HS ESTAB. JULY 27 IN PLACE OF OBSTRUCTION BUOY
       HS, THEN DISCONTINUED.
     NM44/19--BUOY DISCONTINUED OCT. 21, THE WK HAVING DISAPPEARED (CHARTS CARRIED
       NO WK SYMBOL AT THIS TIME)
     NM30/18--SEE ABOVE (NON-DANGEROUS WK APPLIED TO CHART IN 1955 AFTER
       RE-EVALUATING NM)
     H6189/36--NOT FOUND, NO INVESTIGATION.
     CL347/58--1957 NAVY WK LIST: TWO WKS LISTED: NO.115, SAN DIEGO AT POSITION
       40-33-15N, 73-01-20W AND UNKNOWN AT POSITION 40-33N, 73-00-30W (BOTH CHARTED
       AS NON-DANGEROUS, THE UNKNOWN IS ASSUMED TO BE THE SAN DIEGO BASED ON THE
       REFERENCE TO AN NM DATED 10/30/19 AS THE SOURCE. ALTHOUGH NO NM IS DATED
       SUCH NM44/19 IS DATED 11/1/19 AND PERTAINS TO THE SAN DIEGO)
     CL351/59--PRIVATE LETTER: ALTHOUGH PART OF LTR IS MISSING AUTHOR APPARENTLY
       INDICATES THAT WKS CHARTED AT POS.40-33N, 73-00-30W AND 40-33-15N, 73-01-20W
       ARE NOT CORRECT AND A WK SHOULD BE CHARTED AT 40-32-25N, 73-02-35W, (A WK IS
       ADDED AS RECOMMENDED BUT NC WKS ARE REMOVED AS RECOMMENDED)
     H9577/75--OPR-517, PSR 5: PSR REQUIRED INVESTIGATION OF 2 BARGES REPORTED SUNK
       HERE THRU LNM34/74, LNM35/74 LNM38/74: WK FOUND ON MAINSCHEME, DIVERS
       IDENTIFY AS A 500 FT L VESSEL, LYING INTACT KEEL UP IN 90 FT OF WATER,
       ORIENTATION IS BOW NORTH, STERN SOUTH AND LETTERS EG VISIBLE ON STERN, LD IS
       53 FT (MLW) AT POS.40-32-25.62N, 73-02-30.64W.

   DESCRIPTION
      16      SOURCE DOCUMENT COPYRIGHTED
      20      SOURCE DOCUMENT COPYRIGHTED
     ****  NAVY--SHIPS HISTORY BRANCH: SAN DIEGO IS FORMER ARMORED CRUISER
       CALIFORNIA, NO.6: 503 FT L, 69.5 FT W, TWIN SCREW RAMMING TYPE BOW,
       RAISED ARMOR BELT AT WATERLINE, NAME ON STERN: SUNK BY CONTACT MINE LAYED
       BY GERMAN SUB, U-156, RECORD DOES NOT INDICATE POINT OF HULL RUPTURE BUT
       THOUGHT TO BE NEAR BOW ON PORT SIDE SINCE VESSEL LISTED TO PORT; WK
       PROBABLY STILL CONTAINS LIVE ORDNANCE AND TORPEDOES, ALSO HUMAN REMAINS,
       THERE IS NO RECORD OF SALVAGE BY NAVY AND WK HAS NOT BEEN ABANDONED,
       ADDITIONAL DESCRIPTION IN DICTIONARY OF AMERICAN NAVAL FIGHTING SHIPS,
       VOLUME 2, PG 13.
     ****  UNDERSEA SYSTEMS, INC, BOB SHOUROT: WK IS LOCATED AT LORAN C POSITION
       9930-Y-50643, 9930-Z-69873,RATES ARE 1982 OBSERVED AND WITHOUT CORRECTION
       PLOT ON CHART 12353, 13TH ED, AT POS.40-32-35N, 73-02-43W,
       WK IS UPSIDE DOWN AND ORIENTED BOW 20 DEG STERN 200 DEG 10 FM LD.
       POPULAR DIVE W/EASY ACCESS INTO HULL, DIVERS HAVE OBSERVED A SCOW SUNK
       ON STARBOARD SIDE OF WK, THOUGHT TO BE THE WK REPORTED THRU LNM34,35, 38
       AND 54 OF 1974, MR SHOUROT SAYS OWNER OF SCOW WAS ATTEMPTING TO ILLEGALLY
       REMOVE A PROPELLOR WHEN IT SANK AND SUBSEQUENTLY REPORTED A SECOND
       SINKING TO CONCEAL HIS ORIGINAL ACTIVITY, SHOUROT IS SURE THAT ONLY
       ONE SCOW EXISTS IN THIS AREA.

   SURVEY REQUIREMENTS
   INFORMATION
```

The type of data available from the AWOIS is shown in **Figure 3-5,** the record of the U.S. armored cruiser *San Diego,* a casualty of a German mine laid by *U-156* during World War I.

United States Coasts Pilots, Tide Tables, Tidal Current Tables, Tidal Current Charts and other publications are also available from NOAA.

The Twentieth Century has given rise to a remarkable advancement in scientific technology. Instruments are now available that Ferdinand Hassler probably never dreamed of, and yet his work lives on.

Charts of Foreign Waters

Nautical charts of foreign waters produced by and available from the Defense Mapping Agency Hydrographic/Topographic Center appear in nine regional catalogs:

1. United States and Canada
2. Central and South America and Antarctica
3. Western Europe, Iceland, Greenland, and the Arctic
4. Scandinavia, Baltic, and Russia
5. Western Africa and the Mediterranean
6. Indian Ocean
7. Australia, Indonesia, and New Zealand
8. Oceana
9. East Asia

The catalogs may be ordered for a fee from the Defense Mapping Agency, Office of Distribution Services, Attention DOA, 6500 Brooks Lane, Washington, D.C. 20315-0010. The telephone number is (800) 826-0342. The region 1 catalog also lists charts produced by the National Ocean Survey. NOS charts should be ordered directly from the NOS Distribution Branch.

Worldwide charts published by the British Admiralty, are available by writing to Hydrographer of the Navy, Hydrographic Dept., Ministry of Defence, Taunton, Somerset, TA1 2DN, England. For a fee you can purchase the British Admiralty chart catalog of worldwide charts, Publication NP- 131.

Nautical charts of Canadian waters may be obtained from the Dominion Hydrographer, Canadian Hydrographic Service, with offices in both eastern (P.O. Box 8080, Ottawa, Ontario, K1G 3H6 [613] 998-4931) and western (P.O. Box 6000, Sydney, B.C. V8L 4B2 [604] 656-8358) regions.

Library of Congress

The Library of Congress cannot undertake to satisfy all reference requests. Inquiries from Members of Congress receive first consideration, service to Government agencies comes next, and reference work for other inquirers is provided to the extent that the Library finds it possible to do so. However, inquiries which presumably can be satisfied by town, county, or State library resources are ordinarily answered with the suggestion that those libraries be consulted. **When a correspondent has utilized his local and regional resources and still requires aid**, the Library will, so far as the pressure of public business permits, provide limited reference service not otherwise available to the inquirer.

The National Ocean Survey published a series of wreck charts during World War II, indicating shipwrecks and their characteristics. At the close of hostilities, the charts were removed from circulation and are out of print. Only a permanent file set may be viewed at the Library of Congress.

Also, during World War II, the Defense Mapping Agency Hydrographic Center (formerly the U.S. Naval Oceanographic Office) published a series of wreck charts and a "Wreck Information List" for the coastal waters of the United States. Like the NOS wreck charts, they too are out of print. However, the Library of Congress can provide photographic reproductions of both the charts and sections of the list. Complete price and ordering information will be furnished upon request.

The Prints and Photographs Division is an archival collection for research. It does not function like a commercial agency which customarily sends out photographs on approval. There is no detailed catalog of their collections, and they do not prepare lengthy descriptive lists in response to inquiries. Requests for specific photographs limited to ten items every six months, can be handled by mail. Accurate information on the vessel is essential. The address is the Library of Congress, Washington D.C. 20540.

An interesting pamphlet produced by the Library of Congress in 1973 is entitled **A Descriptive List of Treasure Maps and Charts in the Library of Congress** (No. 030-004-0001204). It is a bibliography and affords the user information on treasure maps, atlases, and books, but is not intended for serious shipwreck research. Information on ordering the pamphlet is available from the Superintendent of Documents, U.S. Government Printing Office, Washington, D.C. 20402-9329. The telephone number is (202) 783-3238.

National Archives and Records Service

The National Archives is the official repository for permanent records of the United States Government that are no longer required for current operational purposes. There are several divisions within the National Archives that possess records about shipwrecks. The staff of the National Archives will conduct a limited search of the records if requested by mail. However, details such as the vessel's name, homeport, and the approximate date and locality of the disaster must be provided. Serious researchers can make advance arrangements with the staff for examination of the official records.

The Civil Archives Division, Legislative, Judicial and Fiscal Branch, has records relating to shipwrecks from about 1875 to 1940.

A leaflet entitled "Reference Report: Information about records and printed sources containing data about shipwrecks" is a compilation of data of United States Government records and private concerns in the permanent files of the National Archives. The leaflet covers Annual Reports of the Life-Saving Service (1876-1914); Annual Reports of the U.S. Coast Guard (1915-1931); newspaper articles; "The Lytle List", U.S. merchant steam vessels from 1807-1868; "Wreck Report of the Great Lakes 1886-1891"; wreck information of New England, Middle Atlantic coast, Florida and Pacific coastal areas; and casualty records for various years.

A group of three charts of the Great Lakes published by the U.S. Weather Bureau bearing the dates 1886-1891, 1886-1893, and 1894, are available as photostat copies from the National Archives, Cartographic Archives Division. A "Wreck Chart List" is available on request.

The Industrial and Social Branch, Civil Archives Division, has custody of the records of the U.S. Steamship Inspection Service. The **Annual Reports** (1881-1934) contain valuable information on shipwrecks.

The Military Archives Division is responsible for the safekeeping of the records of the U.S. Navy. Ship plans, including virtually all for ships built prior to World War II, are available. Requests should be limited to no more than one or two ships at a time. Current U.S. Navy ship plans, including those for many ships built during World War II, are available from the Navy Publications & Printing Service, Washington Navy Yard, Bldg. 157, Washington, D.C. 20374.

The Still Pictures Branch maintains most official Navy photography taken from about 1920 to January 1, 1958, including pictorial coverage of World War II and the Korean Conflict. It also holds files on merchant vessels.

Information from the National Archives' various Branches and Divisions may be obtained by writing the National Archives, 6th and Pennsylvania Ave., NW, Washington, D.C. 20408. The general information telephone number is (202) 501-5402.

United States Coast Guard

If you wish to research materials controlled by the Coast Guard, you must make an appointment through the Public Affairs Staff (G-CP), U.S. Coast Guard, 2100 2nd St., SW, Washington, D.C. 20593-0001. In accordance with federal law, their historical photographs are retired to the National Archives, whose address is above. Thousand's of photographs were retired to the National Archives in the 1950's. Upon delivery, the Archive's staff selected a small portion of the photographs that they felt were representative of the era, and destroyed the rest. Those still in their possession may be purchased through the Public Affairs Staff (202) 267-1587, (1960s to present). Coast Guard Casualty Reports may be obtained up to ten years after the incident from (202) 267-1424. Information may also be available from The U.S. Coast Guard Academy Library, New London, CT 06320.

Washington Navy Yard

There's a secret city in Washington, D.C., walled off and mysterious, yet open to the public. It was first a shipyard, then an arsenal where craftsmen forged naval guns. Now the forges are cold and it's simply the Washington Navy Yard. But the grounds and buildings, some dating back past the yard's founding in 1799, are largely unchanged, preserved by tradition and designation as a national historic landmark.

The Navy Yard is a fascinating compound of old streets and alleys where, as you walk the streets, you can imagine President Lincoln strolling with Admiral Dahlgren, discussing a new naval gun design.

There are outdoor displays of ships and cannon and two buildings that house the Marine Corps Museum and the Navy Museum.

Navy Museum

The Navy Museum (Building 70) is filled with dusty treasures; it offers an endless and engaging array of Navy history. There are large and small ship models, and a submarine room where you can sound the dive klaxon and inspect the Anacostia River through working periscopes. There is a piece of steel mounted on a wall that was removed from the sunken U.S. submarine *S-5* during the rescue of her crew. Today, that S-class submarine, off the Delaware Capes, is visited by divers.

Although such displays provide divers with a greater insight into the wrecks they visit, two other buildings in the compound offer the serious researcher an almost overwhelming abundance of information.

Navy Department Library

In 1800, President John Adams wrote to the first Secretary of the Navy, Benjamin Stoddert, requesting the Secretary "to employ some of his clerks in preparing a catalogue of books for the use of his office. It ought to consist of all the best writings in Dutch, Spanish, French, and especially English, upon the theory and practice of naval architecture, navigation, gunnery, hydraulics, hydrostatics, and all branches of mathematics subservient to the profession of the sea. The lives of all the admirals, English, French, Dutch, or any other nation, who have distinguished themselves by the boldness and success of their navigation, or their gallantry and skill in naval combats."

Of the books purchased before 1820, a number are still in the Library. Successive generations of librarians have continued to advance the coverage of naval literature with the latest treatises by experts in each subject as well as acquiring additional retrospective materials to broaden the base of the Navy's library. It is the most highly concentrated and most accessible collection of literature on the United States Navy and naval sciences.

There are about 140,000 volumes in the array of subjects of interest to the Navy in its general collection. In addition, some 10,000 rolls of microfilm cover a variety of material, published and unpublished. Hundreds of periodicals are received annually. Approximately 5,000 volumes are contained in a rare book collection. Many are very rare, all are very valuable. The earliest imprint is the Pomponius Mela *Iulius Solinus Itinerarium Antonini Aug. Vibius Sequester,* Florence, 1526. There are numerous titles printed in the 16th and 17th centuries. The bulk of the collection contains 18th century or later imprints.

The Library's address is Washington Navy Yard, Building 44, First Floor, Washington, D.C. 20374. The telephone number is (202) 433-4132.

Naval Historical Center

The Naval Historical Center (Building 57) has several divisions that possess information on the loss of U.S. naval vessels. The best place to start is the Operational Archives Branch (Third Floor). If they do not have the information you seek they will direct you to the appropriate branch. The telephone number is (202) 433-3170. The Ships' Histories Branch (First Floor) has the history of every U.S. Navy vessel. The telephone number is (202) 433-2585. The Curator Branch, Photographic Section has a wealth of photographs relating to U.S. Naval history. The telephone number is (202) 433-2765.

Submarine Force Library & Museum

Originally established as "The Submarine Library" by the Electric Boat Division of General Dynamics Corp. in 1955, it soon gained respect for its archival and research value. In April 1964, the entire holdings were donated to the Navy and relocated to the Naval Submarine Base New London at Groton, Connecticut. The name "Submarine Force Library & Museum" was formally adopted in 1969.

The Library & Museum is governed by a Joint COMSUBLANT/COMSUBPAC Instruction and is locally administered as a division of the submarine base. Historical guidance is provided by the Curator of the Navy through the Naval Historical Center. That makes the museum the official repository of submarine-related artifacts and information for the Submarine Force.

Today, the Submarine Force Library & Museum is an official U.S. Navy museum; its collection of submarine literature, artifacts, and memorabilia is unique. The lore which traces the submarine idea back to the days of ancient Greece is collected within its exhibit rooms.

The library collection contains over 10,000 volumes of submarine literature, including bound copies of Submarine War Patrol Reports. Histories of each U.S. submarine, biographies of submarine officers and information on submarines of foreign countries are also included. Perhaps the most valuable papers are those of John P. Holland, the designer and builder of the U.S. Navy's first submarine, and those of Simon Lake, another early submarine pioneer. Photographs and submarine plans are also available.

The Library is open to researchers and the interested public on weekdays by appointment. The Library welcomes reference letters and questions, and will provide accurate and annotated answers on all phases of submarine history and development. The address is Box 571, Naval Submarine Base New London, Groton, Connecticut 06349-5000. The telephone number is (203) 449-4276.

Smithsonian Institution

The files of the Museum of American History contain records on "early" explorations and shipwrecks as well as contemporary steamships. The staff will respond to requests by mail, with limited searches, but specific details of the ship and disaster must be provided.

Ship plans of naval vessels are available from the Naval History Division, Museum of History & Technology. Ship plans of commercial vessels may be obtained from the Transportation Division of the Museum.

The National Air and Space Museum, Information Management Division, has custody of all U.S. Army Air Service original photograph negatives. Among those of interest to divers are the complete 1921 and 1923 bombing trials, during which U.S. Army planes sank three battleships (*Ostfriesland, Virginia, and New Jersey*) and other naval vessels (including German U-boats) off the Virginia Capes in 250 to 380 feet of water.

Information may be obtained with a request in writing to the appropriate museum and division at the Smithsonian Institution, Washington, D.C. 20560.

U.S. Naval Institute

The Naval Institute, a private professional association, was established in 1873 for the advancement of professional, literary, and scientific knowledge in the naval and maritime services, and the advancement of the knowledge of sea power.

Naval Institute publications include the *Proceedings*, a monthly professional magazine; the *Naval Review*, an annual analysis of current naval issues; *Naval History*, a magazine published quarterly on that subject; professional, scientific, and historical books. Also included in its services are ship and aircraft photos.

The U.S. Naval Institute Library holds approximately 3,000 books and the complete index to *Proceedings*. The Institute currently houses one of the world's largest private collections of naval and maritime photographs. Out of the collection of 275,000 photographs and slides, dating back to 1883, there are approximately 35,000 ship and aircraft photos which are available for purchase. Send photo requests to the Photo Librarian, U.S. Naval Institute, Annapolis, Maryland 21402 or phone (301) 268-6110.

Steamship Historical Society of America

The Steamship Historical Society of America, Inc., is a tax exempt educational organization established in 1935 to bring together amateur and professional historians interested in the history of steam navigation.

The Society maintains one of the largest libraries in North America devoted exclusively to steamboat and steamship history. This professionally staffed facility is located in the University of Baltimore Library. Its growing collection includes many books, periodicals, special reports, pamphlets, brochures, menus, correspondence, records, drawings, postcards, and photographs. The extensive photographic collection totals approximately 70,000 ship prints, about 35,000 negatives, and approximately 30,000 printed postcards.

Society members are encouraged to use the library facilities for their research and enjoyment. Copies of any pictures not restricted may be purchased either by mail or in person. Address mail to: Librarian, SSHSA Collection, University of Baltimore Library, 1420 Maryland Ave., Baltimore, Maryland 21201.

Society membership applications may be obtained from SSHSA, 345 Blackstone Blvd., H.C. Hall Bldg., Providence, Rhode Island 02906.

Marine Museums

The major marine museums have research libraries in addition to their educational and fascinating maritime history displays. But it is even more important that they combine their wealth of documentary material with expertise in the area.

American Merchant Marine Museum

The American Merchant Marine Museum was established at the United States Merchant Marine Academy in 1979. The Museum is unique, for it concentrates on American shipping as it evolved since the end of the Civil War, placing strong emphasis on the modern merchant marine. The Museum does not have a library, but the Academy's Library is one of the best in the country. The Academy is located on Steamboat Road, Kings Point, New York 11024. The Library's telephone number is (516) 773-5000.

The Mariners' Museum

The Mariners' Museum, Newport News, VA 23606, has many unique educational and cultural displays, such as the "History of the Sailing Ship." Other exhibits include figureheads, scale models, arms, paintings, maritime decorative arts, and over 100 boats from around the world. An extensive 67,000-volume library also houses rare books and over 150,000 photos and films used by scholars from around the world. For further information contact the Public Relations Officer (804) 595-0368.

Mystic Seaport

Mystic Seaport's G.W. Blunt White Library is a research library specializing in American maritime history, the collections now number 40,000 printed volumes and periodicals; 400,000 pieces and 2,500 volumes of manuscript material, and 4,000 maps and charts. Since the collections are so extensive, the Library is an excellent place to begin research on American maritime subjects.

The Library, located on Greenmanville Ave., Mystic, CT 06355 (203) 572-0711 ext. 261, is open to those who, have a serious interest in maritime history. The Museum admission fee is waived for those wishing only to use the Library. The Library does participate in the American Library Association inter-library loan program, and the public will be assisted by the Library staff in initiating such loans.

The Mystic Seaport Museum holds the largest single collection of marine photographs in the world. Although the collection of more than one million prints and negatives emphasizes yachting, it also contains material relating to commercial maritime activities.

Inquiries about the collection should be directed to Manager of the Rosenfeld Collection, Mystic Seaport Museum, Mystic, Connecticut 06355.

* For additional Shipwreck Research Information, turn to Appendix A and B.

Research Methodology At Work

The following example demonstrates the effectiveness of research techniques in locating a previously undiscovered shipwreck. Uwe Lovas of Fredericksburg, Virginia, his brother Ron, and a friend Alan Russel, found the German submarine *U-701* on August 27, 1989. The U-boat had been sunk off Cape Hatteras during World War II by a United States Army bomber piloted by Lt. Harry Kane.

The search for the U-boat began in 1986. Some weekends were spent diving and collecting current data off Cape Hatteras, and vacation days were used for research. All documents about the *U-701* available at the Naval Historical Center and the National Archives in Washington D.C. were scrutinized. They included Lt. Kane's report of the sinking and interrogations of German survivors by the Office of Naval Intelligence—interesting reading that provided several leads. The most important deduction reached was that the submarine had to be in shallow water, probably no more than 150 feet. Kapitänleutnant Horst Degen and over 30 of his men escaped from the submarine. Uwe found it hard to believe that so many men without re-breather gear or life jackets would have survived an ascent of more than 150 feet. Horst Degen referred to the U-boat being in water 200 or 300 feet deep during his interrogation by the United States Naval personnel. Uwe preferred to believe that Degen had been trying to mislead the interrogators about his U-boat's true depth, hoping to discourage any thoughts of their finding it. The 150-foot water depth limit (for a free ascent) was based solely on Lovas' personal experience.

Convinced that the *U-701* was lost in water less than 150 feet deep, Uwe searched for additional data to help locate the wreck. The fact that the current carried the men away from the wreck site so quickly was an important clue. Possibly the search could be narrowed by focusing on areas less than 150 feet deep that were influenced by strong current. The lack of visual references in Kane's report of the sinking was disconcerting; he had made not a single reference to a buoy or wreck landmark. Uwe assumed that Kane would have reported such visual references if he had seen any, although he had already developed a distrust of Kane's information based on the widely divergent sinking locations reported.

To confirm his assumptions, Uwe checked the logs of several ships (at the National Archives, Military Reference Branch) that had escorted convoys past Cape Hatteras that day. All reported good surface visibility, typically seven to nine miles. There were clouds, mostly over the Gulf Stream; that is how Kane was able to surprise the lookouts on the U-boat. But when he dropped below the cloud layer, nearby buoys or shipwrecks should have been visible.

Uwe examined several declassified United States Navy wreck charts at the Library of Congress. They were printed in the first half of 1942 and showed several buoys and shipwrecks in the Cape Hatteras area that Kane might have seen. Diamond Shoals Light Buoy, anchored in 180 feet of water, was the most important buoy in the region. It was installed in place of the Diamond Shoals Lightship just after the start of World War II. Passing east of the buoy would clear the hazardous shoals. In the vicinity of the buoy were several visible wrecks. The *Australia*, the *Kassandra Louloudis*, the *Empire Thrush* and the *City of Atlanta* all had some part of the vessel showing above the water.

Since Harry Kane did not report sighting any buoys or wrecks, Uwe concluded that he must have sunk the *U-701* several miles north or southwest of Diamond Shoals Light Buoy. After the sinking, Kane tried to get a passing Panamanian ship to follow him to the U-boat's drifting crew, but the vessel's captain failed to comply. Kane spotted three Coast Guard cutters in the distance, flew over, and made the same request. the C.G. cutter *472* acknowledged the request and followed to the spot where Kane told them the U-boat had been sunk, but no survivors were located.

Uwe accepted that as a good lead. If he could establish the positions of the ships Kane saw shortly after the sinking, it would narrow the search significantly. "What a break!" he recalled saying to himself. Maybe not. He had no idea which direction Kane flew to intercept the Panamanian ship, or even later, the cutters. One might surmise that the Panamanian ship was traveling the "inside route," hugging the coast as close as safely possible. Failing to get the ship to follow him, Kane had returned to the *U-701* survivors when he spotted the cutters. The Panamanian ship was unidentified, even after exhaustive research by Uwe.

Uwe had better success with the Coast Guard cutters C.G.C. -*408, -472,* and -*480.* They had been ordered to escort the steamer *Georgeanna* from Norfolk, Virginia, to a safe anchorage off Cape Lookout, North Carolina. He visited the National Archives, Military Reference Branch to review the logs of each vessel. Unfortunately, the deck log for the lead vessel, C.G.C.-*480,* was missing. The logs for the other cutters were missing complete navigation data, so he was unable to reconstruct the exact course taken by the small convoy. Despite that disappointment, the logs proved that the *U-701* had been sunk above Diamond Shoals Light Buoy.

C.G.C.-*472* had been diverted from the convoy at 1510 hours, but the *Georgeanna* and her remaining escorts continued southbound on course and passed Diamond Shoals Light Buoy at 1730 hours. In the log of C.G.C.-*472*, at 1510 hours she followed Kane's bomber "out to sea," suggesting that the *U-701* was sunk east of the convoy's track. The search area had been reduced.

Reviewing the facts of the sinking led to the following conclusions, in order of importance.

1. The *U-701* was probably lost in shallow water, possibly less than 150 feet deep.
2. The U-boat was sunk north of Diamond Shoals Light Buoy.
3. The wreck was in an area of strong currents.
4. Since Harry Kane did not see any wrecks or buoys, the *U-701* was sunk well to the north of Diamond Shoals.
5. The U-boat was heading to the northwest when she was sunk.

Despite progress in reducing the search area, the hunt for the *U-701* was to be a formidable task. Well over ten square miles of water would have to be searched. The southern boundary for the search grid included a wreck believed to be the *Merak*, sunk during World War I. After perusing the National Ocean Service's AWOIS (Automated Wreck and Obstruction Information System) printout, Uwe felt the area near the *Merak* held some promise. There were a number of sonar contacts close to the *Merak* wreck symbol. Although it is possible that all were on the *Merak*, and errors in position led to their listing as separate wrecks, there was a chance that one of them might have been the *U-701*.

The upper boundary of the grid was a few miles north of the wreck of the *Ciltvaria*. It seemed to be a logical, well thought out search grid that was defined by use of all of the data. However, Uwe concluded that there was no way to reliably search such a large amount of water using only a bottom sounder.

Uwe explained, "Let me try to illustrate the magnitude of the search we were facing. Typically, when searching for a shipwreck, you steer a course along one of the loran TD (time difference) lines. There are two commonly used ones in the Cape Hatteras area that are aligned roughly north-south and east-west. Using the highest resolution or accuracy a loran receiver offers, the north-south lines are spaced about 55 yards apart while the east-west line is about 22 yards. We wanted to use the north-south TD line in our search. It would be easier to steer a straight course heading into the current. Also, we would need to run fewer lanes because of the wider lane spacing.

"Lt. Kane had reported that the *U-701* had been heading to the northwest when she was sunk, the U-boat would be almost perpendicular to north-south search lanes. Because the line spacing was so wide, about 55 yards, we 'only' had to run roughly 36 lanes for each square mile. The formula is nautical miles divided by lane spacing plus one. Be sure to use common units, i.e. yards. This equals over 36 nautical miles for every square mile of water searched. Now multiply that by over ten square miles. The wide line spacing of 55 yards, or 165 feet meant that, at best, we would have two search lanes pass over the U-boat's 218-foot length. The scenario was even worse if we chose to run east-west lines.

"With a line spacing of only 22 yards or 66 feet, using the east-west TD lines would have provided us with a tighter search grid. However, there were a staggering 91 lanes to be run for every square mile of water covered. To incorporate the entire search area would have forced us to travel close to 1,000 nautical miles. The futility of searching the east-west TD lines is fully understood when you realize that the U-boat was probably lying parallel to the east-west lines. Since the U-boat is at most only 25 feet wide, it is quite possible that the wreck would lie between the 66-foot wide search lanes, and thus go undetected. Bottom sonar only sees what is directly below the boat. Also, steering precise lanes with the Gulf Stream's strong current at your beam is extremely difficult."

The search group had no delusions about their limitations. After weighing the time, expense, and limited prospects of success using a grid search with bottom sonar, they had to abandon a search of the entire area. Uwe decided that they would approach the problem of finding the *U-701* from two different directions. First, a limited search of the area near the *Merak* using a system of grids. Second, investigate some trawl hang loran numbers in the area, through the book **Hangs and Obstructions to Trawl Fishing**, hoping someone had unwittingly discovered the U-boat.

The book contained well over 100 Loran numbers for trawl hangs in the Cape Hatteras area. However, few were in their search area. A number of trawl hangs outside the boundaries of the search area were selected on the premise that even if the U-boat wasn't there, another wreck might be.

In 1986, although the *U-701* remained undiscovered, time spent investigating the trawl hang loran numbers proved to be productive; one in five turned out to be a new wreck, at least new to Uwe's group. He stated, "many boat captains are credited with having located a particular wreck despite the fact they were given the loran numbers to the site by a fisherman." Only a small portion of the search grid, the area near the *Merak*, had been covered by the end of the year.

In April of 1987 Uwe purchased a copy of **Dive Into History: U-Boats**, by Henry Keatts and George Farr. Correspondence by the authors with the *U-701*'s captain, Horst Degen, and the bomber's pilot, Harry Kane, provided a number of additional facts surrounding the sinking of the U-boat.

Most amazing was the disclosure that immediately before the sinking, Degen saw the funnel and mastheads of a wreck against a distant shore through binoculars. Kane never reported sighting any wrecks. That led Uwe to conclude that any information provided by Harry Kane concerning the location of the *U-701* would be worthless; he was probably lost after sinking the U-boat. Degen's report of seeing a wreck was believable, but his claim of observing a distant shoreline could have been an illusion. After reviewing the Eastern Sea Frontier diary at the Naval Historical Center, Operation Archives Branch for the first six months of the war, Uwe compiled a list of vessels with masts and/or funnels above the water. Only one ship sunk in the vicinity of Cape Hatteras fitted that description, the British vessel *Empire Thrush*.

A review of a photograph of the sunken *Empire Thrush* at the National Archives, Still Picture Branch convinced Uwe that Kapitänleutnant Degen could have seen the wreck. The top of the wheelhouse was barely underwater, and two masts and her funnel were standing far above the water's surface. Records at the Naval Historical Center, Operational Archives Branch listed three different locations for the wreck, all near Diamond Shoals.

Despite Harry Kane's statement that he felt the *U-701* was sunk 24 miles east of Avon, North Carolina, it was now obvious that the U-boat was lost much further to the south. No torpedoed ships were recorded as sunk east of Avon. Kane had been corresponding with Degen since 1980, trying to pinpoint the U-boat's loca-

Wreck of the **Empire Thrush** shortly after being sunk. Note masts and funnel sticking out of the water.

tion, and he knew that Degen had seen a wreck just before the attack. The contradiction between Degen's and Kane's stories is pointed out by Keatts and Farr.

In **Dive Into History: U-Boats**, Degen recalled that his U-boat had touched bottom in 195 feet of water. Uwe would not allow himself to believe the submarine was resting in water that deep. The fact that the crew had escaped "after she struck the sea floor" left no question in his mind that the wreck was in dive-able water depth. The new information called for revision of Uwe's list of conclusions.

1. The *U-701* was probably lost in shallow water, possibly less than 150 feet deep and no deeper than 200 feet.
2. The U-boat was sunk north of Diamond Shoals Light Buoy.
3. The *U-701* was located some distance to the east of the wreck of the *Empire Thrush.*
4. The wreck of the *U-701* was in an area of strong currents.
5. The U-boat was heading to the northwest when she was sunk.

The size of the area to be searched was reduced. Additionally, it was moved closer to Diamond Shoals. The eastern boundary of the search area now included water depth to 200 feet. Uwe did not believe the wreck was in water that deep, but it would have been folly to exclude it.

The key to finding the *U-701* was the wreck of the *Empire Thrush.* Locating it would reduce the search area down to a few square miles. A sonar search for the U-boat would then become reasonable.

It was time for Uwe to return to the Naval Historical Center. Records relating to the sinking of the *Empire Thrush* revealed that the freighter was built in 1919 in New Jersey for the United States Maritime Commission. She was 395 feet long with a beam of 51 feet. She was turned over to the British in May 1941 under the Lend-Lease Act.

In April 1942, the *Empire Thrush* was enroute from Tampa, Florida, to Halifax, Nova Scotia with a cargo of rock phosphate, citrus concentrate, TNT and gunpowder. On the morning of April 14, shortly after passing the Diamond Shoals Light Buoy, she was torpedoed and sunk by *U-203*.

Uwe searched for the loran numbers for the *Empire Thrush* to no avail. In fact, he could find nobody who knew, or would admit to knowing, the location of the wreck. There was always the possibility that it had been salvaged, but there was no supporting evidence. Because a shipwreck almost 400 feet long does not just "disappear," a grid search for the freighter would be made at all three of the United States Navy coordinates listed in the records at the Naval Historical Center. Locating the *Empire Thrush* would be a real challenge of the group's expertise in finding shipwrecks. Unless they could find the freighter, they had little chance of locating the much smaller U-boat.

Uwe and his group failed to locate either the *Empire Thrush* or the *U-701* in 1987; it was disappointing to spend so much time searching and come up empty handed. The search area would have to be expanded, and more research was needed to pinpoint the wreck's location. Despite the failures of 1987, all were firmly convinced that they would find the U-boat. What had started as a casual effort became an obsession. The Keatts-Farr book had provided the catalyst, confirming some facts surrounding the sinking and adding important new ones.

Near the end of 1987 Uwe spoke with Harry Kane by telephone. Kane was surprisingly helpful considering all the phone calls he probably received from people asking about the *U-701*. Eventually, Uwe felt comfortable enough to ask if Kane might have gotten lost at some point during his flight. Uwe will always remember Harry Kane's surprisingly candid response.

"He started by telling me how inexperienced a pilot he was. After the attack on the U-boat he spotted a ship far off to the west, and proceeded to fly toward it. Kane asked the vessel to follow him to the sinking site but the ship didn't do so. Kane then told me that he miscalculated the reciprocal course to return to the *U-701* survivors. Kane's plane was traveling in the wrong direction. Unable to find the drifting German survivors, Kane spotted the approaching southbound convoy and was able to get the C.G.C.-*472* to follow him back to where he hoped the survivors would be. Kane searched for a while longer until his fuel reserves forced him to depart.

"Kane told me how excited he was after the attack and that he didn't realize his error in navigation until much later in the flight. At that point it was impossible to correct. Haze limited visibility to seven miles, so he was unable to sight any fixed landmarks. Even immediately after the attack on the *U-701*, he never knew his plane's exact position. I asked him if he had noticed any wrecks nearby at the time of the sinking and he said no. Thanking him for his help, I told Kane I would call him if we found the U-boat."

No further information concerning the location of the *Empire Thrush* was found at the Naval Historical Center or the National Archives. The search would have to continue at all three positions listed in the Navy records. Each location was evaluated by the likely accuracy of the coordinates and was searched according to its probability ranking.

In May 1988, the search resumed. Several disappointing grid searches were made for the freighter. Despite the failure, it was not time wasted; each area searched was marked off on the charts, and the areas remaining became smaller and smaller.

Searching grids is very boring and searchers must maintain vigilance. On arrival at the site, marker buoys are dropped at each corner of the box to be searched. The box is searched by dividing it into a series of lanes. It is much like mowing a very large lawn. After searching a few lanes, boredom sets the stage for inattention. A few lapses in concentration could result in failing to see a wreck on sonar as the boat passes over. In addition, it is important to

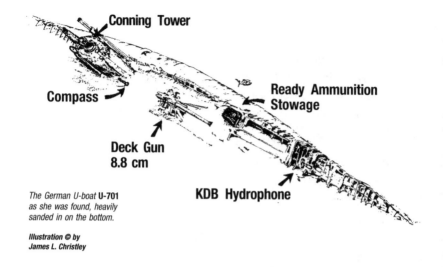

Conning Tower

Compass

Deck Gun 8.8 cm

Ready Ammunition Stowage

KDB Hydrophone

The German U-boat **U-701** *as she was found, heavily sanded in on the bottom.*

Illustration © by James L. Christley

watch the ocean surface for sea turtles, fish, and other indications of the presence of a wreck.

An accident with the boat and trailer, while returning from Cape Hatteras ended the searches for the 1988 dive season. However, during the layoff, Uwe built a magnetometer that was used in May 1989, to locate a wreck that was believed to be the *Empire Thrush,* but its position differed from the location given in official records. Only after locating the *U-701* was it confirmed that the group had indeed found the *Empire Thrush.*

Uwe returned to the Naval Historical Center, Operational Archives Branch to study the logs of the United States Navy blimp *K-8.* He had read in **Dive Into History: U-Boats**, that the blimp had located the German survivors, by this time only seven men, 50 hours after the sinking, at 36-18 N, 73-32 W, about 110 miles offshore.

On August 27, 1989, combining the location of the unconfirmed *Empire Thrush* wreck with the navigation information in the log of the rescue craft, Uwe Lovas and his small band of persistent searchers enjoyed the thrill of diving to the wreck of the *U-701,* in 110 feet of water.

Uwe's success can be attributed to his strict adherence to the following methodology:

1. Exhaustive research
2. Scientific organization of known data
3. Assessment of probabilities
4. Rejection of misleading clues
5. Setting action priorities
6. Launching vigilant searches

Research Is Rewarding

As was the case with Uwe Lovas and the *U-701*, research can be rewarding. However, as Uwe found, it is sometimes confusing and requires additional research. Another example of the need for diligent research is illustrated by the coastal tanker *Poling Brothers #2* which was sunk in Long Island Sound in 1940 in about 65 feet of water. The tanker has a steel hull, but when we researched the vessel we noted that she was launched in 1863. All merchant ships were built with wooden hulls at that time. That led us to question the wreck's identification. Further research revealed that the old ship indeed had been launched as a wooden-hulled vessel. But in 1926, the 63-year-old tanker's hull was covered with steel plates.

Researching shipwrecks is indeed rewarding. Whether or not you find a virgin wreck, the information you gather on known wrecks will make future dives more rewarding.

Chapter 4

Finding Your Wreck

Chart Work

With your research now completed (if research can ever truly be completed) it may seem as though it is time to load the gear onto the boat, fire up the engines and get to that wreck as soon as possible. The sea is vast, however, and there are no road signs; so before you alert the media about having found that virgin wreck, a bit more work is in order.

If the purpose of your research is to aid in locating a wreck, then the hours, weeks, months and maybe years spent, are for one primary reason—to pick a spot in the ocean where you now think the wreck will be found. Hopefully you will have learned many other facts while conducting your research that will prove valuable once you have found the wreck; but for now the goal is to get there. Based on all of the data, you should study a nautical chart of the region in which you will be searching and let X mark the spot. In other words, place a mark on the chart where you believe the wreck to lie. You should first take the time to familiarize yourself with reading a nautical chart. Gain an understanding of how to interpret the various symbols and nomenclature. There are a num-

PILOTING BOOKS

1. *Piloting, Seamanship and Small Boat Handling*, by Charles F. Chapman
2. *American Practical Navigator*, by Nathanial Bowditch
3. *Navigation and Nautical Astronomy*, by Commander Benjamin Dutton USN

ber of excellent books available on piloting, any of which would be a wise investment for the individual interested in locating shipwrecks. In these sources you will not only learn how to navigate by today's standards, but how mariners of the past navigated as well. This may seem like a superfluous point, but in attempting to solve the maritime detective story you are working on, it may in fact be crucial.

When attempting to place the X on the chart where you think the wreck is located, you should do so by staying as close as possible to primary information. Try to recreate the methods used by those who recorded the original data. If you were simply given loran coordinates for a wreck by a fisherman, then by all means use a loran. But if the research gave you other means of recording the wreck's position, it will be to your benefit to use the most original data. The best way to illustrate this is to give an example of an actual shipwreck discovery.

In 1980, the wreck of the steamer *Kiowa* was located in Boston Harbor. The steamer had sunk in 1903 and, through research, a re-

FIGURE 4-1

KIOWA

NOTICE TO MARINERS

3: (73) 1904 – MASSACHUSETTS – BOSTON HARBOR ENTRANCE – WRECK OF STEAMER *KIOWA* MARKED BY BELL BUOY – Referring to Notice to Mariners No. 2 (31) of 1904, the Lighthouse Inspector of the Second District gives further notice dated January 8, 1904, that a bell buoy, painted red and black in horizontal stripes has been placed in 42 feet at mean low water 125 feet N. 10° E. true (NNE. mag.) from the bow of the sunken steamer *Kiowa* entrance to Boston Harbor on the following bearings:

Hardin Ledge spindle, S. 34° E. true (S. by E. 7/8 E. mag.) Point Allerton Bar Beacon, S. 60° W. true (WSW 1/2 W. mag.) Boston Lighthouse, N. 73° W. true (NW by W1/4W. Wly mag.)

port of **Notice to Mariners** was found, giving the position of a bell buoy that was placed one-hundred and twenty-five feet from the bow of the wreck. Though the buoy was long since gone, with the bearings listed, its 1904 position could be ascertained. From there it should only be one-hundred and twenty-five feet to the missing wreck. (See **Figure 4-1**)

FIGURE 4-2

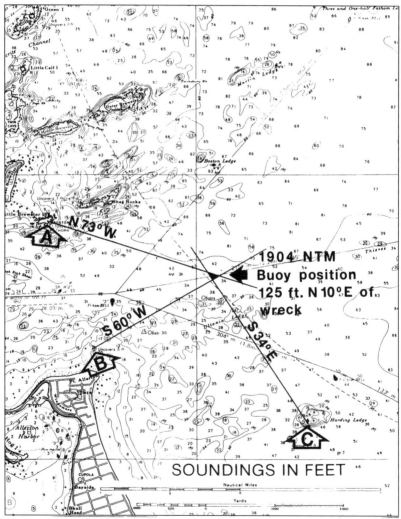

Using the information given in the report from **Notice To Mariners,** *three lines are drawn on the chart creating a search triangle for the wreck of the* **Kiowa**.

To follow the directions we must first understand them. Bearings in 1904 were expressed in different terms than they would be today. S.34°E. true actually means 146° true (34° east of south). By calculating the three given bearings, we arrive at a spot that should be near the wreck. When the three positions were actually drawn on the chart, a triangular search area was shown. (See **Figure 4-2**) Within that search area, the *Kiowa* was indeed found!

Depending on the research, countless factors may be involved in arriving at a presumed location. Nothing should be overlooked and attention to detail and to original methods is imperative. Remember also that the location of objects used as reference points in original recordings, may be in different locations today. If, for instance, a lighthouse was given as a reference point for locating a wreck years ago, be sure that the lighthouse is in exactly the same position today. This also applies to sea level changes, river and inlet changes or the filling in of harbors. A place, due to changes such as those mentioned above, may not be anywhere close to the original location. Every potential scenario must be considered in an effort to pinpoint the search area.

Placing the X on the chart or designating a search area is only the first phase of chart work. The second phase is ensuring that you can get to that spot easily. In order to reduce the chances of drifting aimlessly around in the boat looking for the right place to drop the anchor, it is necessary to identify as many methods as possible for reaching the desired target. Using just a few basic and inexpensive instruments, the wreck hunter should be able to record at least three major and different methods of reaching the wreck. These three methods are: visual ranges, compass or magnetic bearings and sextant or horizontal angles; all of which should be recorded *before* venturing out to sea in search of the wreck.

It should be re-emphasized, that the beginning wreck diver or, in this case, the beginning wreck locator, should concentrate initial efforts on shipwrecks that have sunk within sight of land. Wrecks of this category provide the searcher with many more resources that can be used to locate the ship. When attempting to locate wrecks far offshore, we must generally rely on more sophisticated pieces of equipment and there is *usually* less information to go on.

The first method for reaching the desired location is to obtain visual ranges from the chart. There are two types of visual ranges, direct lineup and spatial, and both should be recorded when possible. To obtain direct line visual ranges you will need to study the chart to find two objects on land that will line up when you are positioned over the desired target. The greater the distance between the two fixed objects the better, since they will provide more precise positioning because they will "move" quickly when you move and will *only* line up properly when you are over the target. The objects you choose can be just about anything that will be visible when you are in the search area (anything that does not move - buoys will not work!). You might find that from the potential wreck site a straight line can be drawn which will intersect the edge of a distant cliff and a more distant water tower or perhaps a lighthouse with a radio antenna. When recording visual ranges, or any type of bearing, it is important to record at least two completely different sets of ranges as close to ninety degrees apart as possible. The reason for having at least two ranges or bearings is to have at least two intersecting lines of position which will intersect only over the wreck site. The reason for choosing ranges far apart or as close to ninety degrees as possible, is to create a more precise angle of intersection. It is also a lot easier to line up sets of ranges that are not close together when you are pitching and yawing around in a boat. The trick is to line up one of the ranges and then move closer to it or farther away from it until the other range lines up. When both ranges line up you should be over the desired site. (See **Figure 4-3**)

If direct line ranges are not clearly evident, it is possible to use the same principle with a slightly different twist. Spatial ranges work in a similar way; however, instead of lining up fixed objects by direct line of sight, you spatially relate fixed objects that lie on a horizontal plane. Although on a horizontal plane, at least two of the objects must be at varying distances from you. For example, looking at the chart, you realize that from the wreck site you should be able to see two separate towers and a cupola at different distances but on a horizontal plane.

FIGURE 4-3

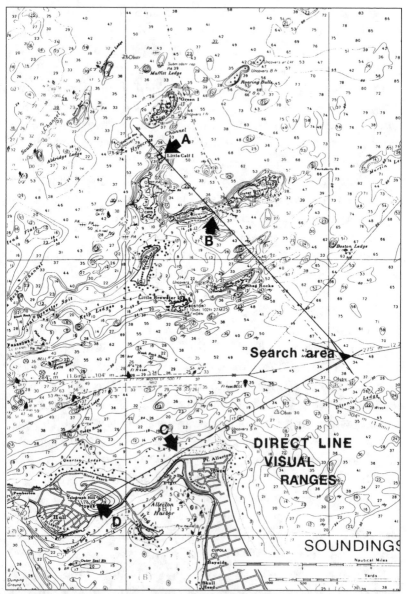

One method of reaching the precise search area for the Kiowa, is to calculate direct line visual ranges from the chart. In this example, two lines, that will intersect over the search area, are drawn lining up objects on shore that can be seen when at sea. The bottom range lines up the tower at Telegraph Hill (D) with the edge of the Point Allerton cliff (C). The top range lines up the eastern edge of Little Calf Island (A), with the eastern edge of Middle Brewster Island (B).

In **Figure 4-4**, the Pt. Allerton tower is just right of center between the Telegraph Hill tower and the cupola. If it is in that position on the chart, it will be in that position when you are at sea, over the desired area.

The spatial ranging method may require a bit of time staring at a chart to find suitable ranges, but once found, they will be very

FIGURE 4-4

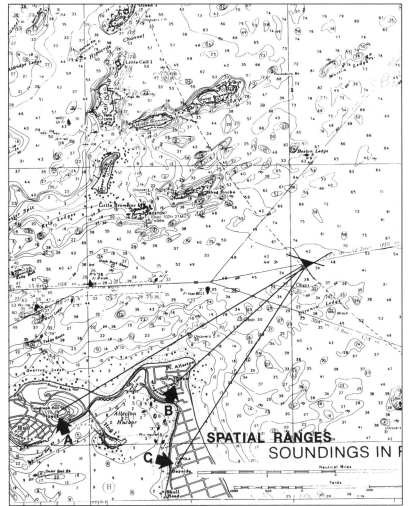

*If direct line visual ranges are not readily available, spatial ranges may be substituted. In this example, the tower at Point Allerton **B**), is just to the right of center between the tower at Telegraph Hill **A**) and the cupola **C**). When positioned over the search area, these objects will be in exactly the same relation to each other.*

FIGURE 4-5

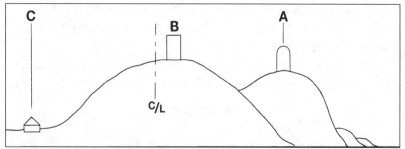

*This sketch illustrates the view from the **Kiowa** wreck site using the objects in **Figure 4-4** (on previous page). **A**) is the tower at Telegraph Hill, **B**) is the tower at Point Allerton and **C**) is the cupola. Illustration by Bill Carter, Jr.*

reliable and truly appreciated when rocking and rolling in less than perfect seas trying to figure out where you should be. (See **Figure 4-5**)

The second major method for reaching your desired location is to obtain compass or magnetic bearings. To accomplish this, simply draw a line from the wreck's position to any object on land. Using either a plotter or parallel rule and the chart's compass rose, a compass bearing can be calculated for the line you have just drawn. As with visual ranges, a second compass bearing should be recorded to achieve the two intersecting lines which will cross only at the desired location. (See **Figure 4-6**) One way of using magnetic bearings at sea would be to follow one of the bearings you have recorded with the boat's compass, while someone on board keeps watch for the second bearing using a hand-held compass. When the second bearing is correct, a buoy is tossed overboard marking the spot where the two bearings intersect.

The third major method for reaching that place in the sea where you hope soon to be, is to record sextant angles. By now you are probably thinking, "No way. Learn to use a sextant? You're crazy!" The truth of the matter is that using a sextant is really not difficult. With a bit of practice, it is easy to become proficient at using this rather simple instrument. Remember that this is the instrument that those who recorded shipwreck positions long ago often used. In keeping with the premise of using original data to locate wrecks, it would be worth using in many cases today.

Essentially, a sextant works by measuring two adjacent angles. You first need to select three objects on land that you will be able to see from the wreck site. These objects can very well be the same ones chosen for compass bearings or visual ranges. By drawing a line to each of the objects from the wreck site you will have created two angles that share a common side. Using a three-armed protractor, you can now calculate the degrees and minutes of each of the angles. You will, of course, have to learn how to read a three-armed protractor, but by placing the small hole in the center of the protractor over the wreck site and positioning the left arm on

FIGURE 4-6

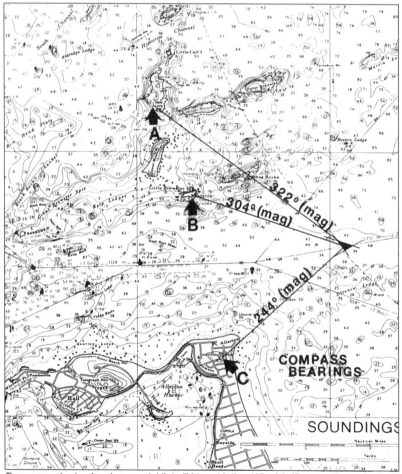

*Three compass bearings have been recorded that will intersect in the middle of the **Kiowa** search area. Bearing **A)** 322°, was taken from the twin chimneys on Calf Island. Bearing **B)** 304°, was taken from Boston Light and Bearing **C)** 244°, was taken from the tower at Point Allerton.*

Using a sextant from
the dive boat to line up
a position on land.

the left line, the center arm on the center line and the right arm on the
right line, this information can be easily recorded. (See **Figure 4-7**) At
sea the sextant will be used to line these objects up, moving your position until the angles are what they are supposed to be. When the
angles are correct, you are over the site. This method of reaching a
desired location at sea is very precise and can often be used when
other methods cannot. If you were searching for a wreck further offshore at a point where you could see land but not distinguish isolated
features, it might be possible to use sextant angles to fix a position
using large objects on land masses that you can recognize.

Using the three methods discussed, as a means of reaching the
target, may seem to be a lot of extra work. However, as anyone
who has spent time searching and searching and searching on a
calm, sunny day will tell you, it is better to spend extra time doing homework ashore than wasting time at sea. Another important point regarding these three methods is that anyone with just
about any type of boat can use them. In a time when most folks
seem to think that you cannot navigate without spending a tidy
sum of money on marine electronics, we would like to point out
that these methods are quite reliable and quite inexpensive. The
biggest expense would be purchasing a sextant, which can be
done on even the tightest budget with plenty of funds left over—
(assuming that you have a boat. If not, consider *that* the biggest
expense—or find a friend who already has one).

FIGURE 4-7

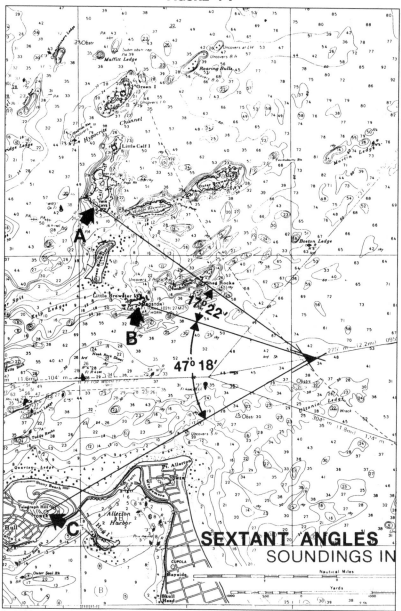

Sextant angles are recorded by measuring two adjacent angles. This example uses angles created from lines we have previously drawn for other methods. The top line has been drawn from the search area to the twin chimneys on Calf Island **(A)**. The center line was drawn from the search area to Boston Light **(B)**. The bottom line was drawn from the search area to the tower at Telegraph Hill **(C)**. Using a three-armed protractor, the angles between the three objects has been noted. When these angles are achieved at sea using a sextant, you will be directly over the desired site.

FIGURE 4-8

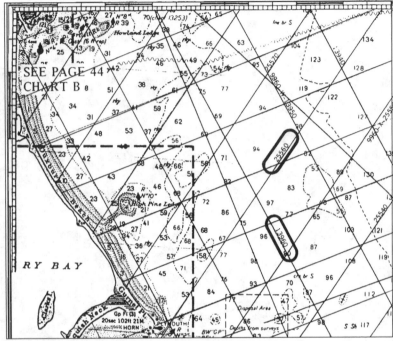

Loran numbers (circled) can be found on most modern nautical charts.

There is additional data that can also be recorded from a nautical chart which will help to ascertain the position you seek. Depth of water should naturally be noted as well as bottom contour. To most accurately survey this data, once at sea, some type of sonar is generally required. Numerous models are available as we will discuss in chapter five.

Another way of recording a position is the ever popular loran. You probably thought we would never get to this! Loran [lo(ng) ra(nge) n(avigation)] is a long-range navigational system which uses pulsed radio signals from two or more pairs of ground stations of known positions. A navigator uses the signals to establish his own position. Accuracy of the loran numbers depends on the sensitivity of the individual unit and the operator's ability to use the apparatus. If you have marked the position of where you think a wreck will be found and you have a loran on the boat, then by all means plot the loran numbers if they are given on the chart. (See **Figure 4-8**) Keep in mind, though, that numerous factors can effect the reliability and that the numbers you record should be used only as an additional aid to getting in the correct area. In the case of the *Kiowa*, loran numbers were not very helpful at all. Because of the wreck's close proximity to shore, and since loran is least reliable close to shore, it was the use of other methods that actually found the wreck. Loran is very good, however, for returning to a site that is already known. Once you have located a wreck, recording the loran numbers is an excellent way of making sure you can get back again.

Although it has been a principal navigational instrument for a number of years, loran is slowly becoming obsolete. Its replacement is Global Positioning Satellite navigation or GPS. GPS is a system that can position any object on earth using the principle of triangulation. Precise atomic clocks aboard GPS satellites are used to measure the time it takes an encoded radio signal to travel from the satellite to a GPS receiver. When signal travel times are calculated from four orbiting satellites whose positions are precisely known, the position of the receiver becomes known. Originally developed by the U.S. Department of Defense, the unprecedented accuracy of GPS is now available for commercial use.

HOW LORAN WORKS

Loran-C is a hyperbolic navigation system. This type of system is characterized by the use of groups of three or more fixed transmitter sites whose transmissions are time related in some way. The loran receiver is constructed to measure the time related variable. When the receiver is moved in such a way that the value of the measured variable remains constant; the path described by the receiver will be a hyperbola passing two transmitters monitored. Computed hyperbolas for equally spaced values of the variables are drawn on navigational charts as Lines of Position (LOP) for all transmitter pair combinations in a group.

The loran series of navigational systems transmits identifiable pulse groups from a group of transmitters known as a loran chain. A loran-C chain consists of a Master transmitter which provides the basic timing and two or more Secondary transmitters. Loran LOP's are determined by measuring difference in arrival times between the signal from the Master station and the signal from one of the Secondary stations. The LOP's for the Time Difference (TD) between the Master and all Secondaries are shown on a loran chart. The TD readings on the chart are in microseconds (0.000001 second).

The transmitter chain is identified by a four digit number specifying the Group Repetition Interval (GRI) of the chain in tens of microseconds. The GRI is a measure of how often the groups of loran pulses are transmitted. The GRI for any chain is found on the Loran-C chart for the desired area.

(courtesy of Raytheon, Inc.)

Finding your wreck will involve a considerable investment of time if it is to be done from scratch. It is not easy and requires a fair amount of patience, but if it were easy, everyone would be finding shipwrecks. It is however extremely rewarding in many ways. A diver today can easily dive wrecks without ever knowing anything about the vessel's history or without knowing anything about charts or navigation. Making the dive is only the tip of the iceberg in wreck diving. Reading a chart that an ill-fated captain may have read a century ago or searching for ranges that recorders of history notated in a now forgotten era are the larger portion of that iceberg, hidden from the view of all but the most curious. Putting together all the disjointed pieces, confidently sailing to a place at sea that many before you have sailed over and finding a shipwreck, are indeed the ingredients dreams are made of.

Chapter 5

The Physical Search

With research and chart work completed, the next step is discovery. Shipwrecks can be very elusive, though, and considering the amount of effort and time you have invested up to this point, it is imperative to follow prudent searching techniques to insure a successful outcome. Before ever leaving the dock, a well orchestrated game plan—a strategy of how you will conduct your search. There are numerous methods that can be employed to search for wrecks. The method chosen should be based primarily on what you expect to find. For example, if you are searching for a steel-hulled tugboat that sank in a storm in 1945 on a hard bottom in 125 feet of water, the wreck should be relatively intact. Based on the premise that the wreck is intact, not buried and not reduced to rubble from any prior salvage, then you have a number of viable alternatives available as methods of searching. If, however, the tug was made of wood and sank in 1860 in an area of high current and soft sand, only an engine and boiler may remain and even that might be buried. Such a scenario limits the number of methods that might be used.

The "Diver Search" is most useful on very old wrecks where little of the hull remains.

In addition to speculation on what will be left of the wreck, the search will also be influenced by the type of bottom. Some terrains do not lend themselves to certain methods of search. The following shipwreck search methods offer the diver a wide range of options to choose from depending on what is anticipated to be found, type of terrain and, last but not least, budget. Even the simplest of these techniques have been proven over time and will help a diver find wrecks.

Diver Search

Perhaps the most basic means of locating a shipwreck is to anchor over the spot where research indicates the wreck should be and go diving. A useful approach is for the diver to descend the anchor line, tie off a line reel to it, then move out in pre-established increments on a circular search. This technique is rather inefficient in comparison to some of the more sophisticated methods available, however it can produce results. If the wreck you seek is a very old wooden sailing ship, for example, which wrecked on a shallow rocky ledge, this might be a productive way of locating her. Since there wouldn't be much left of the vessel in this case, a thorough

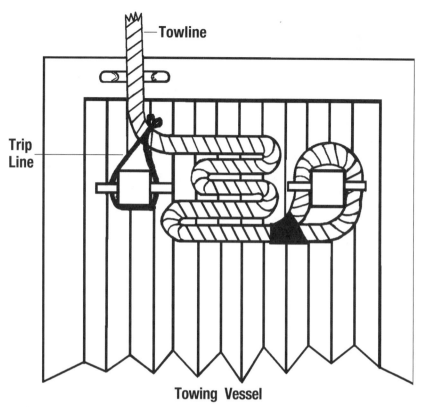

Towline

Trip Line

Towing Vessel

A trip line, thinner and weaker than the towline, should be tied to the tow line as an early warning of a snagged wreck.

diver search may yield small clues such as scattered fastenings or a lone deadeye indicating that you are at least in the correct area. You may not be able to effectively cover large sections of real estate using this procedure but hopefully at least the territory you do cover will be done so thoroughly.

Anchor Dragging

This technique of locating shipwrecks was quite popular in the early days of wreck diving in a time when marine electronics were not available. Today, it is rare to find divers employing this method, however, if you are working on a tight budget and have spent your savings on a new regulator instead of sonar gear, this technique will work. Quite simply, this method works by cleating off a tow line, with anchor attached, to the stern of the boat, paying out the

Of these three common anchor types, only the grapnel (right) and the folding stock type (center), are productive in hooking wrecks. While excellent for sand anchoring, the Danforth (left) is ineffective for this purpose.

line until it is on the bottom and then powering the boat ahead until the wreck is snagged. A length of heavy chain should be placed at the anchor end of the line to keep the anchor on the bottom as well as to reduce chafing. The length of line used in this procedure should be roughly four times the depth of the water. Once the towline is properly played out and cleated off to a strong bit, a smaller, thinner piece of line should be tied to the towline, after taking up slack, and also secured to a bit, creating a trip line. This way, when the wreck is hooked, the smaller line will part under the sudden strain allowing time to stop the boat before any damage is done to the boat or tow line. Note that it is possible for the anchor to "ride up" over the wreck. By having someone hold the tow line in their hand, the wreck may be felt even if the anchor did not snag by itself.

This procedure is best used when searching a bottom that is flat and free of large rocks. A sand or even a gravel bottom would be acceptable for anchor dragging. The choice of anchor type is also an important consideration. Best suited for this type of work is the grapnel type of anchor since it will not easily catch into the bottom but will effectively grab a wreck. Another choice would be a folding stock type anchor with the stock folded. Danforths or plow type anchor designs are not at all useful for this procedure due to the fact that by dragging them they become set into the bottom.

It is important to run the boat at a slow enough speed to keep the anchor on or very near the bottom. Moving too quickly will cause the anchor to "fly" up off the bottom where the only thing likely to be hooked is another boat on the surface! Once you have hooked something on the bottom it is necessary for a diver to go down and check it out. Your heart will pound and your thoughts will race anticipating what lies below. More often than not it will probably be a rock that the chart never indicated was there but, like frogs and princes, you'll have to dive a lot of rocks to find that one virgin wreck!

Sled Search

More efficient than the previous two methods, the sled search is also quite a bit of fun. It works by having the boat tow a device, which a diver holds on to, through the water. The sled can be designed a number of ways although the more hydrodynamic, the better. It should incorporate into its design an easy way of holding on and letting go. The sled can be made from a variety of materials with the focus on it being light-weight, durable and resistant to the marine environment. Painted or treated plywoods, plastic and plexiglass are just a few of the materials that have been used to make underwater sleds.

The advantages of this method over those already discussed are many. Compared with the diver search, sledding can cover a much greater area and do so nearly effortlessly for the diver. In comparison with anchor dragging, the obvious advantage is that a diver can see and has peripheral vision. By looking side to side a sledding diver can effectively cover a wider search area than could be accomplished by dragging an anchor. Should the diver spot

Photo by Bill Carter, Jr.

Bryan Carter holds a homemade underwater sled.

what looks like a shipwreck off to one side, he can "fly" the sled in that direction to get a closer look. If it is in fact a wreck, the diver can detach the sled from the tow line and glide to the wreck. Once on the wreck, the diver can send up a buoy or lift bag to mark the location. Sledding is an ideal way to locate wrecks that are less intact. Scattered wreckage can easily be missed with other techniques, but a diver on a sled can see small pieces that may hold a clue. Although quite productive, sledding is limited to physical considerations such as air consumption, depth and time of the dive. Naturally, this approach is quite ineffective, not to mention a safety concern, when working in water of limited visibility. The diver

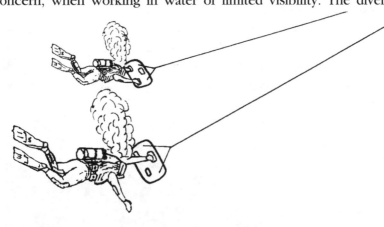

Illustration by Charles P. Zimmaro

Using underwater sleds, divers can visually cover large expanses when searching for wrecks.

using a sled must also be especially attuned to ascent rates, since when being towed it is possible to rise very quickly. Under any conditions, the boat operator and topside crew must keep extremely alert paying close attention to divers, potential obstructions and boat traffic. To re-emphasize an initial point of this chapter, a well orchestrated game plan must be in place before attempting any type of search, especially when divers are involved.

Trawl Door Search

Like anchor dragging, another method of locating wrecks that was quite popular during the early days of this sport is the trawl door technique. A fair amount of time may be needed to properly fabricate the parts needed for this approach but, in the absence of more sophisticated means of searching, the trawl door method can and has been used, yielding impressive results. In the way that fishing trawlers drag their nets to catch fish, the same concept can be used to drag a cable or line to "catch" shipwrecks. This technique employs the use of two "doors" with angled brackets which will keep the trawl doors in the correct position while under tow. Connected between the doors is a piece of line, cable or chain. The cable may be of any length, however the longer the cable the larger the doors must be. Attached to each of the doors is a towline leading to the towing vessel in the shape of a "Y".

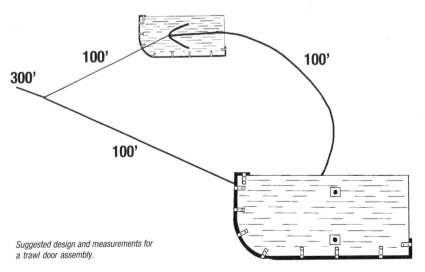

Suggested design and measurements for a trawl door assembly.

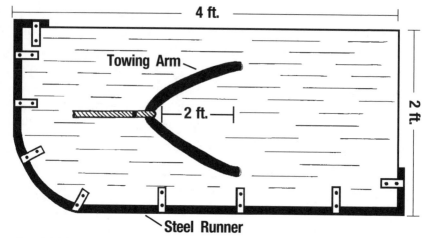

Suggested design and measurements for a trawl door.

The doors can be made from one inch exterior plywood with a quarter inch steel runner placed over the leading and bottom edge. The runner will add weight to the doors as well as provide protection. A one-half inch pipe, bent to the proper form, will serve as a towing bracket. The bracket or arm should be bent so that, while under strain, the leading edge of the door angles outward from the boat providing a constant strain on the drag line. Shackles should be used to connect all lines into the towing arm.

As with the anchor dragging method, a smaller line should be attached to the tow line and cleated off to act as a trip line when an obstruction is snagged.

A variation of this method is to use two boats trawling at the same speed with a drag line suspended between them. Trawl doors, cable, and tow line may be too much for one small boat to handle, however this alternative of using two boats and one drag line may be much more manageable.

Depth Finder

We have now reached the 20th century portion of our discussion—marine electronics. In a relatively short span of time marine electronics have come a long way, both in price and available features. For the purpose of this text we will avoid discussing the cost of various instruments since that is a variable that will continually change. It is safe to say that for a modest investment, a diver can purchase a suitable depth finder which can tremendously aid in the search for shipwrecks. Fathometers, recorders, fish finders and chromo-scopes are all types of active sonar. They may feature different ways of presenting the data but they all gather it in pretty much the same way. Simply stated, a transducer mounted underneath the boat emits a signal of sound that penetrates the water column until it hits an object. The signal then bounces back to the transducer. The time it takes for the signal to make its round trip is expressed in distance. Therefore, steaming along with the depth

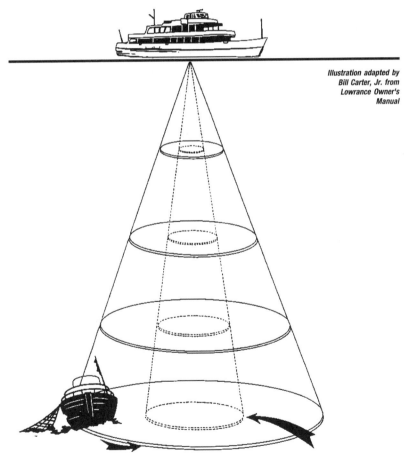

Illustration adapted by Bill Carter, Jr. from Lowrance Owner's Manual

Cone of signal emitted from depth finder transducer. Note the much wider area covered by the 20˚ transducer compared to the 8˚ transducer.

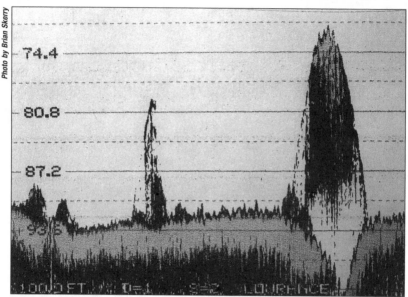

74.4

80.8

87.2

93.6

100.0 FT   0=1   S=3   LOWRANCE

Typical paper record from a depth finder. The high areas or "spikes" may indicate a shipwreck has been found.

finder on, provides constant signal that produces a "picture" of sorts of what the bottom looks like by calculating distance or depth. A boat traveling over a flat, featureless bottom in 100 feet of water reflects a constant depth until its sonar signal speed increases, indicating an upward slope of the sea floor on the screen. By displaying an image, either on paper or video screen, of the sea floor below, depth finders are an excellent tool for finding wrecks. Although these machines are fairly simple to operate, some practice is necessary to become proficient in recognizing shipwrecks. The signal emitted by the transducer is shaped like a cone with the widest portion being on the bottom.

The deeper the water being searched, the wider the area of the cone will be. Signal strength, however, is strongest in the center of this cone with intensity falling off at the edges. For this reason never drop the anchor on the first "hit" recorded. While searching with a depth finder you may only catch a piece of the wreck resulting in a smaller record on the machine. Adequate time should be taken to run thorough search patterns with the boat to assure a complete picture of the wreck below. To achieve a proper reading the boat must be traveling at a reasonably slow speed (no faster than headway speed). Using this technique to locate a large, intact wreck on a flat, sandy bottom is obviously much easier than searching for a broken up schooner amidst a rocky, boulder-strewn bottom but, with practice, even difficult terrain can be deciphered. Practice and plenty of experience will also come in handy when trying to distinguish between a large rock and a piece of wreckage.

Even the best interpreters of sonar records have erred, turning wreck divers into rock divers on more than one occasion. Regardless of which type of unit you decide on, using a depth finder will greatly improve your efficiency in the quest for locating and diving the forgotten fleets in the sea.

Side Scan Sonar

A significantly more advanced method of searching for wrecks is side scan sonar. Rather than projecting a conical beam straight down, as with a depth finder, side scan directs the signal (or sound wave) to either side resulting in an image of a much larger section of the ocean floor. The apparatus achieves this by dragging a cylindrical metal casing with stabilizing fins, called a tow fish, behind the boat. The tow fish has two transducers mounted on either side (port and starboard) and is connected to a recording device on the boat by a cable. While the tow fish is being towed on a straight course at a constant depth, the signal is emitted from and returned to the transducers at

Photo by Brian Skerry

Vince Capone and Rick Clinton ready a side scan towfish for deployment.

regulated intervals. The data obtained is transmitted via the cable to the paper or video recorder which essentially draws a "picture" of the sea floor below. As with any sonar, numerous variables can affect the incoming data including waves, currents, thermoclines or even changes in salinity.

There is a wide range of side scan systems available with features to suit just about any operation. Perhaps the most important consideration is the unit's frequency strength. Frequency will determine two key aspects of your search—area and resolution. Lower frequencies will cover larger areas but have poorer resolution. Higher frequencies do not penetrate great distances but do offer much higher resolution. A unit generating a frequency of 100 kHz will cover a distance of about 600 meters. A 500 kHz unit will cover a distance of only 150 meters but with superior resolution. Because of this trade-off, a lower frequency unit might be fine when searching for large, intact wrecks and would allow the searcher to cover huge expanses of underwater real estate quite easily. A search for an older, less intact shipwreck might require the use of a higher frequency unit capable of closely examining smaller portions of the sea floor. No matter which type of side scan unit a wreck hunter chooses, it will undoubtedly be an immense improvement over previous methods and a sure fire way to improve one's "batting average."

A final note regarding side scan. Unlike depth finders, side scan units are portable and can be easily taken from one boat to another. Before investing in your next dive boat, consider investing in side scan instead. I guarantee you will have no trouble finding plenty of boat owners willing to make room for you and your electronic friend.

Magnetometer

Another electronic marvel that has added a sizeable number to the "wrecks found" column is the magnetometer. Like side scan sonar, it is usually a portable unit consisting of a recording device, cable and tow fish. In simplified terms the magnetometer works by measuring anomalies in the magnetic field of the earth's crust. Any ferrous metals in a particular region will cause changes in the earth's magnetic lines and are detectable by a magnetometer.

Shipwrecks therefore, create considerable anomalies in the earth's magnetic field and are easily detected with the use of a magnetometer. With typical ranges of up to 1000 feet and the ability to detect wrecks above and below the sea floor, these devices can be a tremendous aid to locating wrecks. Naturally, in areas of high concentrations of iron deposits or where several other wrecks are known to be located, zeroing in on a probable new site can be difficult.

John Fish preparing to lower magnetometer towfish over the side.

Search Patterns

A key element of the well orchestrated search plan is to not only decide what type of search will be conduct (i.e., depth finder, sledding, etc.) but to determine how the actual search will be carried out. Once the desired target area is reached, a buoy should be thrown to mark the position. The most common buoy for this purpose is simply a plastic jug wrapped with one-eighth inch line and a weight on the end. The buoy will allow you to temporarily disregard shore ranges or monitoring electronics and allow you to concentrate on the search at hand.

Perhaps the two most popular search patterns are the circular pattern and the grid pattern. The circular search pattern is carried out by simply sailing the search vessel in concentric circles around

*Captain Eric Takakjian of the charter boat **Grey Eagle** with 80-foot marker buoy. In this case, the buoy assembly consists of a lobster pot marker, 1/8-inch line and a window sash weight.*

the buoy which was thrown to mark the initial position. The circular pattern can only be used when the choice of methods is using a depth finder. Any of the other methods that involve towing a diver or any apparatus behind the boat cannot effectively be done using this pattern. Anchors, trawl doors, and tow fish need to be towed in straight lines, eliminating this pattern as an option. (Divers would get much too dizzy!)

By far the more exact approach is to conduct a grid pattern search. This can be done by "squaring off" a section of the ocean or lake in the desired target area. For example, use the first buoy thrown as the center point in the grid and place four additional buoys at the corners of the area intended to be searched. If the boat is equipped with loran or GPS, the extra buoys can be eliminated. Instead, the parameters of the search area can be established with T.D.'s or latitude/longitude. If within sight of land, new ranges might be selected to facilitate piloting within the grid limits. For example, the search area might be confined within two fixed positions on shore that can be easily seen at a glance.

No matter how the grid is designed, it will help to take current direction into consideration first. If the current runs north to south, it will be easier to steer the boat if the grid is laid out north to south and east to west. Attempting to search by fighting a strong current

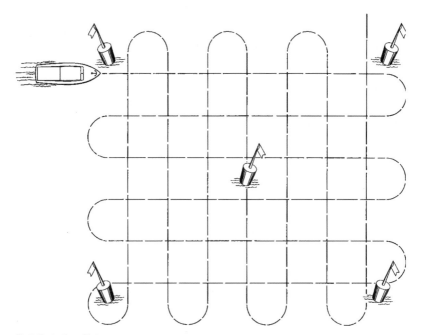

illustration by Aaron Hirsh

A basic grid pattern used for thoroughly examining a squared-off section of lake or ocean. Center buoy marks the initial, desired target location. Four additional buoys have been laid out as the parameters of the search area.

on an angular course can be difficult. It will be easier to pilot with the current's direction, directly opposite it or directly perpendicular to it. Current direction can be determined by watching the buoy that has been thrown or by consulting tide and current tables. An excellent source for this is the **Eldridge Tide and Pilot Book**.

Once the grid has been laid out the search can begin. Standard procedure is to cover the grid by repeatedly traveling up and back in one direction, then in the perpendicular direction. Like mowing the grass, each pass should overlap the previous one. Surprisingly, even large shipwrecks can be missed if every inch of the grid is not covered. Extra buoys should be available at all times because when that "hit" comes, the spot must be marked immediately.

Anchoring

If your research and chart work was sound and your searching procedure thorough, the reward will be a shipwreck. In order to dive the wreck, a small boat must be anchored in a way that will contribute to safe and efficient diving. If the diver or sled search method was used, the locating diver should have attached a buoy line to the wreck; the boat can initially be tied off to it. If the anchor dragging method was used, nothing further needs to be done. The boat is already anchored into the wreck. With the trawl door method the cable will be snagged into the wreck but you may want to swim down a separate anchor line that can be shackled to the wreckage then release the trawl rig and remove it from the water. If, however, the method of search used was any of the electronic means, the dive boat will hav e to be anchored over the wreck before the diving begins. When diving on shipwrecks it cannot be emphasized enough that safety is the most important concern. Having a line that leads directly to the wreck from the dive boat is an essential aspect of a safe dive plan. Divers must descend and ascend the anchor line to prevent surfacing away from the protection of the dive vessel. Anchoring near the wreck is not good enough. Even assuming that divers can find the wreck when they first descend, having to search for the anchor off the wreck at the end of a dive is not safe, especially with limited visibility. It is for this reason that standard operating procedure calls for anchoring into the wreck. Accomplishing this task first requires the selection of a proper anchor type. As we discussed in the section on anchor dragging, the anchor type best suited for hooking wrecks is the grapnel hook. The anchor must be large enough to hold the diving vessel securely in place even in rough weather and heavy enough to reach the bottom quickly when thrown over the side. Placing a length of chain (as much as ten feet) between the end of the anchor line and the anchor will add extra weight as well as reduce the risk of the anchor line chaffing against the sharp edges of the wreck. The weight of the chain in front of the anchor will also cause the hook to fall over to a better position for catching wreckage.

When attempting to anchor into a shipwreck, wind and current often come into play. Current direction can be determined by watching the buoy that was thrown to mark the wreck's position. Current is generally given precedent over wind since it will have a greater affect on your anchor line. The dive vessel should proceed into the direction of the current to a point ahead of where you want to anchor. The anchor should then be thrown and, once on the bottom, the boat's engine should be placed in neutral allowing the boat and anchor to drift back over the wreck, hopefully catching in the desired area. If the wind is as strong as the current and blowing from a different direction, hooking the wreck may require vectoring between wind and

Captain Eric Takakjian holding a shot line. In this case, the shot line consitsts of several lead weights attached to a chain which is then attached to an anchorline and a large Norwegian float. Using the shot line is an alternative to hooking the wreck.

current. If there is no current or wind, a bit of power from the boat in reverse may be necessary to solidly anchor into the wreck.

An alternative way of getting onto a wreck is to use what is often referred to as a shot line. Rather than using an anchor, a shot line is an anchor line with weight on one end and a float on the other. When the boat is positioned over the target area the weighted line is thrown over, much like the positioning buoy discussed earlier. The boat can then drop off a diver who will descend the shot line and physically tie off the end to the wreck allowing the boat to pick up the surface float, cleat off the line, cut the engines and wait for the diver to return with a report of what is below.

Getting Back

Unless the research was so precise as to have placed a boat right on top of the wreck, a few notes should be made before pulling up the anchor and heading for home. This is simply a matter of recording all the information that we discussed in the chapter on chart work, but this time you will be recording them from the known wreck site. Land ranges should be sketched out on a piece of paper, taking as many as possible. Magnetic and sextant angles also should be noted. Exact depth of water during the particular tide will prove helpful and, of course, if a loran or GPS is on board, detailed numbers must also be logged. Taking a few minutes to record this information will ensure finding the wreck on the next trip out.

While it may sound romantic and exciting, searching for shipwrecks is actually quite tedious. *Finding* shipwrecks is the part that is romantic and exciting! Unfortunately, *ye must seek before ye can find.* Seeking is best done on calm days, in pleasant weather. Days that are perfect for diving. It will take an incredible amount of restraint keeping your eyes glued to a depth finder while traveling in a grid pattern when you could easily be just a couple of miles away diving on a known shipwreck. It is for this reason, along with the vast amounts of detailed research and chart work needed to find new wrecks, that so many divers become content with diving the same old sites. There is certainly nothing at all wrong with diving existing sites over and over again. In fact, this repeatability and familiarity yields the best results in wreck diving. The true explorer, however, will never rest as long as there are mysteries to solve. But mysteries are not solved easily. This type of exploration demands patience and time. If done correctly, patience will lead to victory; and to the victor goes the spoils.

Chapter 6

Charter Boats

Thus far in *Complete Wreck Diving,* we have spent a fair-amount of time outlining a step by step methodology for locating shipwrecks. The vast majority of those who dive on wrecks however, do so, not by finding wrecks themselves, but by venturing out on a charter boat. The sinking of ships throughout the ages has spawned a modern day industry designed to afford divers access

Diving from a charter, like the **Gekos,** from Ocean City, Maryland, is by far one of the easiest ways to reach wrecks.

No crawling through the bilge to make repairs, no pulling up the anchor and no washing the boat at days end. Just relax and go diving.

to numerous wreck sites. Although in some parts of the world ship-wrecks make up only a small portion of the diving itinerary, in other locales they are the main attraction. Wreck diving charter boats have been servicing the northeastern United States, for instance, since the early 1960s; and it is doubtful that people would go to the trouble and expense of journeying to Truk Lagoon or Bikini Atoll if these places were "wreck-less."

Wreck diving via a charter boat is arguably one of the easiest ways to go wreck diving. Simply get on the boat with scuba gear, go diving and go home. No worries about navigating, finding the wreck, throwing the anchor, pulling the anchor, repairing mechanical problems, cleaning the boat, etc. Although diving from a charter boat frees you from many of these responsibilities, there are a number of considerations that should be resolved long before departure.

What to Look for Beforehand

Asking a lot of questions first is the safest way to avoid any misunderstandings or hard feelings later. First and foremost are the questions of destination and experience required to make the dive.

If adverse conditions prevent the boat from getting to the designated site, what are the alternatives, if any, and are you equally prepared for these dives? There have been plenty of instances when a charter boat's plan to take divers to a wreck in shallow water was changed, due to severe surge, to visiting a deeper site. Know *before* you go.

You will want to know the price of the charter and the duration of the trip. Will you have time to make two dives or only one? What is the policy on refunds? You may have driven 400 miles to dive the U-boat but the wind is blowing offshore, the boat can only make it to the artificial reef placed just beyond the inlet, and the captain intends to make his day's pay! Know *before* you go!

What To Bring

Space on board a dive boat is always at a premium. Even a large vessel can get crowded if gear is not properly managed. Tell the captain or crew what you intend to bring with you, to find out if there will be enough room. Some charter vessels have more room than others and space parameters vary with what part of the world you happen to be diving in. Bringing along that extra camera box or diver propulsion vehicle may not be a problem but it is best to ask first.

No matter how much or how little equipment you bring, it is your re-

photo by Brian Skerry

Dive gear strewn about the deck is an inconvenience to everyone on board. If your gear is not properly stowed, expect it to be lost or broken.

A fish tote makes an excellent gear container. Note line attached to tote being used to prevent it from sliding.

sponsibility to keep it out of the way. When you first get on the boat you should "stake out a claim"—an area in which to keep your gear. Before and after the dive your gear should be in that area, not strewn about the deck. Wreck diving can be an equipment intensive sport, however efforts must be made to consolidate gear when on the boat. Large gear bags are very popular but there are other even less expensive ways of stowing your equipment. Plastic boxes such as fish totes or containers that houseware companies produce are excellent ways of carrying, protecting and consolidating your gear. They will often fit neatly under a seat out of the way or even double as a seat if made strongly enough. A few vessels even provide gear storage for extended periods. Whenever any type of plastic box is used on a boat, it is a good practice to attach a length of line to it first. Boxes will easily slide across the deck if not secured. With a line attached there will always be a handy way of lashing them down.

Another topic of discussion before departure is how many cylinders to bring. Three singles, one single and a set of doubles, two sets of doubles, two singles—find out the typical dive profile for the charter you are going on, and do it ahead of time. Today, a fair number of larger charter boats are equipped with compressors, eliminating the need to bring more than one set of cylinders (or extra singles if the dive is shallow). If there is a compressor on board find out if air fills are included in the charter fee. Do not assume anything. Since we are on the subject of air (or gas) supply, which dictates time spent underwater, do not forget to inquire about the policy regarding decompression diving. Some boats do not allow decompression diving and you will be more than a little disappointed finding that out after you have spent the night before rigging double 120's and a 40 cu. ft. pony, planning for a marathon dive on that freighter in a hundred feet.

Know Before You Go

Another policy that can vary from boat to boat and from one location to another is that of taking artifacts. If your intent is to recover artifacts during your dive, make sure that it is permitted before stepping on board with an arsenal of tools in tow.

Most often, once the vessel is underway or once anchored on the site, the captain or crew will give a briefing regarding diving procedures and a description of the wreck to be dived. If something is not covered that you want to know—ask. Where should you enter the water and where should you exit? Is that oxygen hanging at twenty feet for everyone to use? Will someone be waiting to take my camera when I surface? Whatever your question, do not hesitate to ask it and remember that the answers may vary from charter boat to charter boat, all over the world.

Food

There is nothing like a day of wreck diving with time spent hanging on an anchor line and the invigorating smell of salt air to work up a voracious appetite. After one particularly long and chilly evening of wreck diving off the coast of Virginia, the authors exited the water, drudgingly climbing the ladder, only to be brought back to life with the smell of steaks being barbecued on the after deck. It doesn't get any better than eating a steak and mashed potatoes, ten minutes after a long, cold dive, under the stars on a gently rocking boat.

Although many charter boats will provide food such as sandwiches and cold drinks, do not wait for a bad case of the "scuba munchies" to find out that you should have brought your own. When packing food for a boat trip, it helps to keep things simple. Fruit, sliced vegetables or individually wrapped snacks travel quite well. Sandwiches should be well packaged to prevent water from coolers seeping in and ruining them. Re-sealable water containers are also handy since you will want to keep well hydrated for diving. You may also want to bring along a few straws for those times when seas get rough and keeping your mouth on the top of a soda can is difficult at best. When packing a cooler, try to get as much food as possible into as small a cooler as possible to conserve boat space. If diving with a buddy, consolidate food into one cooler to further conserve space. You should also check to see if the boat has a microwave oven on board. If so, you may decide to treat yourself to something a bit more exotic than just a sandwich.

Sleeping Arrangements

If a trip aboard a charter boat will involve being at sea overnight, you will want to inquire about sleeping arrangements. Should you bring a sleeping bag? Will you be asked to share a bunk and where is it located? If your bunk is located near the engine room or a running generator (or if you are sleeping next to a repugnant snorer) you will find sleeping much easier with a pair of earplugs. Some larger charter operators have private sleeping quarters, sometimes referred to as "staterooms." These accommodations may even include a private head and/or shower.

An extended stay on board will also mean extra planning regarding equipment but, this is again dependent on the boat size. If any of your gear, such as underwater lights or strobes, will require charging, you will have to know if the boat is equipped to handle your needs. If the boat does not have a generator to recharge batteries, extra ones will have to be packed. It is a good idea to bring extras of several things. As already discussed, space is at a premium so you cannot bring too many extras, however, 30 miles at sea is a long way to have come to miss a dive because your fin strap broke. A small, well stocked tool kit with extra straps, o-rings, etc., will be much appreciated when Murphy strikes, as he inevitably will.

Other Hints

Spending time on a boat, and therefore in the elements, can take its toll on your body; so it is a good idea to venture forth well prepared. Depending where you are in the world, you may be very hot or very cold. You might encounter driving rain or uncomfortable humidity. The tropical sun could burn you to a crisp or, if the wind is still, you might be harassed by relentless gnats and mosquitoes. Like a good Boy Scout, always be prepared. Rain gear, sunblock and bug repellent do not take up much room and can make a dive trip much more enjoyable. If traveling offshore for longer than a day trip, consider packing extra clothes in a way to protect them from the ever present humidity encountered on boats. Large plastic bags with zip lock closures work very well for this purpose. Before stepping onto a boat, many divers replace their everyday footwear with rubber boots which are ideal for walking on decks awash with sea water. Eye protection is extremely important, particularly at sea, so a couple of pair of sunglasses should always be stowed along with the essential dive gear.

When diving from a charter boat keep in mind that the captain and crew have a responsibility to get you to the wreck and bring you back to the dock—that is it. Although many crew members or mates will go out of their way to help you, you should not expect it. If the mate has been especially helpful you may want to consider tipping as a token of appreciation. There are no set rules regarding this subject. Most mates work on dive boats as a way of diving without having to pay, as well as gaining experience in handling boats. On some boats, however, the mates work for tips and it is customary, in fact, to tip.

In addition to your questions, the boat's rules and how best to prepare for a charter trip, there are other considerations regarding charter boats as well. The U.S. Coast Guard has established rigid safety regulations for all passenger-carrying vessels requiring that the boat's certificate and the captain's license be prominently displayed. When diving from a vessel that is under U.S. jurisdiction, divers are cautioned to ensure that their dive charter boat displays a U.S. Coast Guard certificate and that the vessel is not loaded beyond the number of passengers it is certified to carry. Most other countries will have similar regulations to which boat owners and captains must adhere. The boat should also be stocked with an adequate First-Aid kit and oxygen to handle emergencies.

As the dive industry continues to grow, we will most likely see an increase in the number of wreck diving charter boats. For the diving consumer, this is a good thing. It will provide greater access to the wrecks we want to dive. As any consumer knows however, buyer beware. When we investigate closely any product or service, we realize that some are better than others. Better, can simply be a matter of personal taste, or, in the case of diving, it can equate to much more. Running a safe and knowledgeable wreck diving charter boat requires a lot of work and a great deal of experience. There are many factors that can influence a successful day of wreck diving and many of those are influenced by the captain and crew of the boat you are on. Although the crew's primary responsibility is to get you to and from the wreck site, a knowledgeable crew provides more. While economics are always important, it is more important to have a level of comfort with the captain and crew you have selected to go diving with. Today, with a boat and electronics, almost anyone can take you to a wreck. However, not just anyone can provide information crucial to enjoying the dive. Going with someone that knows the layout of the wreck, water conditions, potential hazards, keeps an alert eye on surface conditions and knows what to do when problems occur, is invaluable for safe wreck diving. We sometimes take for granted a captain that can put us precisely on the section of a wreck we wanted to dive. We may also take for granted the mate who dragged the anchor to an area we asked to be in. Wreck diving is a highly specialized sport that demands a great deal of dedication from anyone that chooses it for recreation. Any wreck diving captain and crew worth their salt is equally as dedicated. They *also* dive wrecks and are aware of the concerns wreck divers have. If a nondiving friend offers to take you out to a wreck to go diving you may willingly accept the offer, but do so recognizing that you are pretty much on your own. You should not expect too much, since the friend knows nothing about diving. When paying a charter boat to take you out, it is nice to know that you are in the hands of professionals. In most cases, you should not have to be overly concerned about an inept captain or crew, but it does not hurt to check around. Perhaps the best method of obtaining information about a charter boat is to ask other divers. Although most divers will have their preference, they will not give a bad report unless it was duly earned. If you cannot find anyone familiar with the boat you are interested in, do not hesitate to ask a few more questions of the captain. A captain who dives and is well acquainted with the wreck you are interested in will gladly tell you whatever you want to know. Spending just a few minutes discussing such topics should give you the answers you seek.

A final point regarding charter boats. Although we may all like to think that we are capable of diving any wreck a particular charter boat may be headed to, one should not let their ego stand in the way of safe diving practices. It is human nature to become offended if the captain questions our experience, but such questions

Photo by Brian Skerry

Larger charter boats can get divers to some interesting offshore sites. The **Seeker** runs out of New Jersey.

are for everyone's benefit. Keep in mind that the captain may never have seen you dive and is not attacking your character, but simply trying to run a safe operation. A charter boat is a business and therefore is not in the habit of turning away customers. If you are questioned about your dive history, consider that a good sign. Any boat that would take anyone, anywhere, is a boat that you should really think twice about getting on. If you hope to dive with a charter operation that does not know you and you feel you are qualified to make the dive, consider providing references. Names of other captains that you have dived with that will vouch for your experience. Even with such references, the final say belongs to the captain and you must respect that decision. A bit of diplomacy and understanding goes a long way.

Charter boat diving can provide some of the greatest enjoyment you will find in wreck diving. The time you spend underwater is only a fraction of the time leading up to and following the dive. The camaraderie found in the relaxing atmosphere of a well run charter boat is hard to beat. Diving from a vessel that meets regulations, asking questions and treating the boat and crew with respect is a successful formula for charter boat diving that will guarantee hassle free wreck diving every time.

Charter boat diving can provide some of the greatest enjoyment you will find in wreck diving. The **Horizon** runs out of San Diego, California.

Chapter 7

Gearing Up
Wreck Diving Equipment and Pre-Dive Preparation

Choosing the correct tools for a specific job has long been regarded as a crucial element for the successful outcome in any task. Before one can choose these tools, however, it is necessary to firmly understand the job at hand. This is especially true when it comes to wreck diving. To properly equip a diver to explore shipwrecks we must thoroughly understand shipwrecks as dive sites.

Like fish in the often quoted proverb, there are plenty of wrecks in the sea and no two are exactly alike. Though it would be convenient to provide the definitive wreck diving equipment check list or the step by step unabridged wreck diving technique guide, it is not that simple, due to the uniqueness of sunken ships. Shipwrecks cannot easily be grouped. They do not fall into well defined categories complete with nice, neat rules for diving them. As we discussed previously, there are countless wreck types found in a variety of geographical settings, all deteriorating at different rates resulting in innumerable potential dive sites. Such an assortment of shipwreck types leads to countless diving scenarios.

A key element in the gear selection process, is the type of wreck diving you are planning to do. This is readily apparent when we focus on extremes, i.e. a diver diving a tropical wreck

Patrick Rooney prepares for a cold water wreck dive.

in 40 feet of water will undoubtedly wear considerably less gear than a tri-mix diver in the North Atlantic diving a 200-foot site. The necessity of specific gear is more subtle however, when we move away from the extremes, and focus on the mid range of wreck diving. Since we cannot state that "when diving wrecks in 30 feet of water you will need only certain gear;" or that "when diving sites between 100 and 150 feet of water you must add these certain items;" the solution is to evaluate each wreck individually and prepare for the dive by equipping yourself to handle the worst possible scenarios that could arise.

The more gear a diver wears, the more critical gear management becomes. Eric Takakjian has strategically placed additional equipment, such as a stage bottle and Argon suit inflation bottle, in an easily accessible fashion for this deep water dive.

Though it is impossible to precisely evaluate a wreck that you have never dived, it is possible to ascertain factors, such as depth or potential penetration, that will influence your decision. You can, of course, get carried away with this approach, by carrying gear that you will never need and that may actually impede your performance, which is why prudent evaluation of each dive is necessary.

Self-Sufficiency

With this in mind, the primary force dictating a wreck diver's choice of equipment should be self-sufficiency. Self-sufficiency in wreck diving is not unlike self-sufficiency in many other aspects of life. To be a self-sufficient driver, for instance, you must first learn how to drive, be sure to have contingency plans and equipment for emergencies (like a spare tire in the trunk) and then gradually gain the experience that comes from driving on a lot of different roads. The major difference between the two is that if you run out of gas while diving, you can't simply pull to the side, turn on your flashers and wait for help. As a diver, you must prepare yourself to be completely self-sufficient. A diver gearing up for wreck diving must consider potential problems and equip himself or herself to deal with them accordingly. The potential problems a wreck diver may encounter generally fall into two categories: equipment malfunctions and shipwreck hazards. It may well be that none of your diving equipment will ever malfunction and of course, not all wrecks are hazardous. But, if you are prepared for the worst, then you should be able to handle any situation that arises.

Equipment Management

In addition to selecting the gear best suited to the wreck environment and maintaining a high degree of self-sufficiency, the well-rigged wreck diver must also pay close attention to equipment management. Placing all of the gear you bring with you in a manner that makes it readily available is crucial. When a crisis occurs underwater, there is no time to fumble for gear. Equipment must be arranged so that it can be reached immediately when needed. Placing one's gear in the same position every time, is a good way of preventing wasted time when you need to find something quickly.

The further a diver progresses with wreck diving, the more equipment intensive the sport can become, resulting in the need for serious forethought of how every new piece of gear should be carried. Equipment management goes even further, however. When diving shipwrecks, you will need to be as streamlined as possible. Hoses, straps and gauges, not to mention all of the additional paraphernalia taken along, must be kept close to the body to prevent getting caught in the wreck. Standing on the boat, a diver may *appear* to be streamlined but once in a horizontal swimming position, gauges, bags and clipped tools will fall out like landing gear on an aircraft. If a

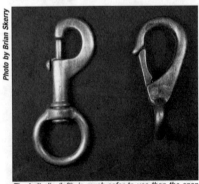

The bolt clip (left), is much safer to use than the snap hook (right).

hose is too long and may present a potential snag, get rid of it. Custom high or low pressure hoses can be ordered. It is a never ending process of fine tuning and managing your equipment in an effort to improve your safety margin. Throughout the following discussion of equipment and methods of rigging equipment, we will often suggest the use of clips or tie wraps. How a diver decides to attach pieces of gear is extremely important and while you will have to find the method that best suits you, there are items that we strongly recommend you stay away from. One very dangerous type of clip is the snap hook or boat clip. When used to attach tools or bags to a brass ring or D-ring, the item clipped can easily become unclipped, but even more importantly, when worn on a diver's body, they can snag lines, nets and cables severely entangling the diver. Much more preferable, is the bolt or gate clip which can only be opened by the diver. Attention should also be given to tie wrap selection. Nylon tie wraps are stronger than plastic, and wraps that consist of any metal should be avoided since corrosion will likely occur.

Diving Equipment

To best understand a wreck diver's arsenal of equipment, simply imagine regular diving gear with a severe dose of paranoia thrown in. It is with this attitude that we approach the discussion of wreck diving equipment. The equipment on which we will focus includes only those pieces that relate directly to wreck diving, or standard items that need to be somehow modified for the shipwreck environment. We will not, for example, discuss snorkels. Though they are a useful item and you will most likely carry one

On a hot, sunny day, Roland Pelland finds putting on a heavy dry suit is less than pleasurable.

Tom Mulloy makes a fashion statement wearing coveralls to protect his drysuit underneath.

Jeff Pagano has added kneepads made from rubber inner tubes to protect this vulnerable area of a wreck diver's suit.

with you, your choice of snorkel will not in any way affect your exploration of a wreck.

Exposure Suits

Although much of a wreck diver's equipment is designed to deal with adverse conditions, some of the most basic gear should be selected simply because its design is conducive to the wreck environment. Since wrecks are very abrasive environments, the thermal protection a diver chooses should also be quite resistant to punctures or tears. Even in the warmest of waters it is a good practice to wear some type of suit to guard against the jagged metal and sharp edges found on most wrecks. A rugged wetsuit will usually offer necessary protection against these abrasive concerns, as well as giving the primary benefit of thermal protection.

The choice of suit thickness will obviously depend on local conditions. In colder waters a 1/4" wetsuit will insulate a diver quite well, adequately providing defense on both counts. Should the diver be planning prolonged exposures in cold water or be

EFFICIENCY & RELIABILITY OF WETSUITS vs. DRY SUITS

Water Temperature	WETSUITS			DRY SUITS		
	1st Dive	2nd Dive	3rd Dive	1st Dive	2nd Dive	3rd Dive
70°F	100%	100%	100%	100%	100%	100%
60°F	100%	90%	80%	100%	100%	100%
50°F	80%	70%	50%	100%	100%	100%
40°F	50%	25%	**	100%	85%	75%
32°F	**	**	**	100%	75%	55%

** Not recommended unless involved in a life saving rescue.
* Chart based upon 30 minute dives at a depth of 50 feet, with a one hour surface interval between dives, during a 3 dive day.

diving to greater depths where compression would reduce the insulating capacity of a wetsuit, then a dry suit should be considered (see above table "Efficiency & Reliability of Wetsuits vs. Dry Suits"). In recent times, dry suits have become increasingly popular with a wide variety of styles to choose from. Many divers will invest in a dry suit, using it in all climates, warm or cold, by varying the layers of garments worn underneath. The choice of dry suit is strictly a matter of personal preference with advocates of all types lining up behind their top choice. If it keeps you warm and dry and allows you to comfortably explore shipwrecks, you have made a wise investment. Since some dry suits, particularly those constructed of vulcanized rubber, are less abrasion-resistant than suits made of other materials such as neoprene, a pair of coveralls can be worn over the suit for added protection. Available at just about any work clothes store, the coveralls will need to be "customized" to allow access to inflation and exhaust valves, but will keep the dry suit free from tears and looking like new. The downside to coveralls is the additional drag they produce while moving through the water.

Regardless of whichever type of thermal protection you choose, the Achilles' heel for wreck divers is invariably their knees. Bearing the brunt of the abrasive onslaught of shipwrecks, the knees are the most abused portion of a diver's anatomy. To combat this malady, kneepads can be added to prolong the life of the suit. A simple yet rugged kneepad cut from a rubber inner tube that can be slipped on before each dive is all that is needed to ensure the extra protection.

Buoyancy Devices

The next consideration should be focused on buoyancy devices. While it is generally accepted that buoyancy devices should always be worn when diving in a wetsuit, some would argue that with certain dry suits a buoyancy device is unnecessary. While this *may* be true with some suits on some dives, a diver in deep water will definitely appreciate having one. The deeper a diver descends, the heavier he or she will become. Without a buoyancy device, this diver will be forced to continually inflate the dry suit to an uncomfortable level. It is much better to put just enough air (or other gas) in the suit to be comfortable, using the buoyancy device to offset the weight at depth. Dry suits have also been known to tear and

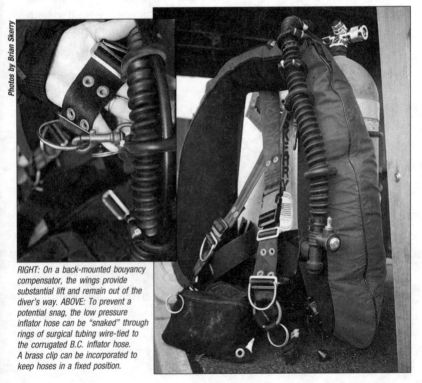

Photos by Brian Skerry

RIGHT: On a back-mounted bouyancy compensator, the wings provide substantial lift and remain out of the diver's way. ABOVE: To prevent a potential snag, the low pressure inflator hose can be "snaked" through rings of surgical tubing wire-tied to the corrugated B.C. inflator hose. A brass clip can be incorporated to keep hoses in a fixed position.

flood, effectively disabling the buoyancy created from an inflated suit. Even with a 1/4" neoprene dry suit, which has a fair amount of buoyancy without being inflated, a large tear could severely affect the diver's ability to make a controlled ascent.

Another reason that wreck divers have historically opted not to wear a buoyancy compensator is because their design impeded access to dry suit valves or D-rings on the chest area. Necessity being the mother she so often is, along came the return of the back-mounted B.C. Fitting between the back plate and tanks, the back-mounted B.C. stays out of the way of other gear and close enough to the body so as not to present a problem when swimming around wrecks. Though this design of buoyancy device has seen a resurgence in popularity among wreck and cave divers in recent times, the concept has actually been around for quite some time. In an effort to further streamline this device, wire tied rings of surgical tubing can be placed on the corrugated inflator hose through which the low pressure inflator hose from the regulator's first stage can be "snaked," preventing the hose from making an arc which could easily get hung up on surrounding wreckage. On one of the rings of surgical tubing, a brass gate clip can be added providing a means of attaching the B.C's inflator hose to a fixed point where it can be easily reached (such as to a D-ring). Some brands have the low pressure hose inside of the corrugated inflator hose.

Providing upwards of 50 pounds of lift, the back-mounted B.C.'s are well suited for the diver venturing to depths that require the carrying of stage bottles which add considerable extra weight. As a practice of redundancy, many divers will stack two sets of back-mounted buoyancy devices together in the event a malfunction renders one ineffective.

Breathing Systems

Since we have touched on the all important "R" word—redundancy—our next area of focus should be on gas supply. As mentioned earlier, when exploring shipwrecks, it is a good practice to expect the worst. In doing so, like a well-trained Boy Scout, the wreck diver will always be prepared. Breathing is something we should first and foremost be prepared to do. It is imperative to design a system that will give more than enough gas for a given dive, and one with redundancy in the event of a malfunction.

Redundancy in a breathing system must be a completely separate system; not simply an octopus. All the air in the world will do you no good if your regulator's first stage malfunctions, which is exactly what once happened to Brian Skerry. While making a dive on the United States submarine *Bass* he was making the swim along the sand from the stern section to the bow section when his primary regulator literally stopped working. At 160 feet his first thought was "This can't be happening." His second thought was "There's a lot of water over my head." His next thought as I reached for it was "Thank God I have a pony bottle." Though it was at the beginning of his dive and he still had a full set of double 80's on his back, it was his pony that got him up the anchor line.

Remember also, that shallow wrecks are not necessarily safer to dive than deeper wrecks. There are wrecks in shallow water where portions of the vessel actually break the surface but, if penetrated, can be places of severe disorientation and hazards with strong surge pounding though deteriorating hulls. Deep or shallow, it is quite easy to get oneself into situations that require extra time. Making sure that you have *more* than enough gas will never be regretted. Short of stepping back on the deck of the dive boat with the ship's bell, there are few feelings as good as surfacing with 1500 pounds still left in your tanks. Though the wreck diver has numerous options available in regards to tank configurations, the following are some of the more common systems found in use today.

Single Tank

The most basic breathing system that can be used to explore shipwrecks is the single tank configuration. This system should only be used when planning dives on shallow wrecks for short duration. If there is even a remote chance that a decompression situation might occur or a penetration of the wreck might be carried out, this system should be disregarded. Many divers have excellent air consumption rates, but it is not only a limited air supply that makes single tanks less than desirable. It is primarily due to the lack of redundancy that single tank configurations offer. With only one tank and one regulator, there is little room for error.

The single tank system can be made slightly more versatile by adding a bit of redundancy. This can be achieved by the addition of a pony bottle or the use of a "slingshot" Y valve allowing the addition of a completely separate regulator. Even with these modifications, the single tank system is severely limited. As with any system you decide on, you must consider the inherent risks of the dive and ask yourself if the system chosen will allow you to respond.

Photo by Brian Skerry

Redundancy can be incorporated into a single tank with the addition of a pony bottle.

Independent Doubles

When venturing into deeper water, or as a means of simply adding greater safeguards to a breathing system, a double tank configuration is the logical next step. The easiest way to accomplish this is to merely band together two single tanks attaching a regulator to each one.

Using this configuration the diver must switch from the regulator first used to the second regulator at some point during the dive. A common practice is to use 1/3 to 1/2 of the air supply in the first tank before switching to the second. Using this method, a substantial gas reserve is always maintained in the event of a malfunction.

For the diver wearing a dry suit and a buoyancy device, it is recommended to attach each low pressure inflator hose to a different regulator. This way, in the event of a valve or regulator malfunction, at least one method of buoyancy can be maintained.

The addition of a second regulator means finding an acceptable way of rigging it, in keeping with the practice of good gear management. There are numerous methods available, with a common practice being to wear one regulator under your chin, held there by a loose fitting and removable piece of surgical tubing, with the other regulator clipped to a D-ring on a short lanyard. The second stages should also be differentiated, so there is no confusion as to which one you are using. This is accomplished in a number of ways, from using two very different second stages to marking them with tape to installing noticeable different mouthpieces. No matter how you choose to rig the regulators, the key is to make sure that they can be reached immediately when needed and will not get lost amongst other gear. The two pressure gauges necessary with this system can be taped, velcroed®, or held together with

A pony botttle is easily added to a set of manifold doubles creating redundancy in the system.

surgical tubing, to create a compact instrument package. If you use a color-coding system of marking your second stages; the same coding can be used to distinguish each pressure gauge.

Manifold Doubles

Another version of the double tank configuration is the addition of a manifold, creating a system capable of accessing the gas in both tanks simultaneously. With the basic double manifold design, a single regulator is used eliminating the need to switch regulators during the dive. The obvious downside to this is the lack of

Patricia Morton climbs on board wearing a set of doubles with an isolation manifold.

redundancy. Should the manifold or regulator malfunction, there are no options. An example of just how dangerous this lack of redundancy can be is illustrated in a story told by veteran diver and charter boat captain Larry Keene of Ocean City, Maryland. "While diving the wreck of the German submarine *U-853* off Block Island, Rhode Island (in 130 fsw) several years ago, I had a first hand lesson in

Richie Kohler makes redundant regulator instantaneously available by attaching it with surgical tubing held loosely around his neck.

the importance of a backup system. I was exploring inside the forward torpedo room when in the confined space, I rubbed against some sharp, jagged metal along a bulkhead which literally sliced my regulator hose in two! All the air in my double tanks completely drained out in seconds causing a maelstrom of bubbles. I forced myself not to panic, exited the loading hatch and thankfully saw my buddy about 30 feet away near another hatch. I had two choices; swim to him or head for the surface. I made the decision to swim to him and buddy breathe. I made it to him. He immediately understood the situation and we were able to buddy breathe to the surface. I'm lucky I did not have to decompress. From that moment on I never went diving without a redundant system."

This system can be enhanced to include redundancy with the addition of a pony bottle. There are those divers, particularly those engaged in deep diving, who refute the advantage of carrying a pony bottle with the argument being, so little gas will be of no use in an emergency. Once again it comes down to evaluating each dive individually. Granted, a 15-cubic-foot pony will be of little use on a dive to 300 feet, but on a 70-foot dive it may well save your life. If the system you are using is a basic manifold on double tanks, then a pony is a wise addition.

A very simple method of attaching a pony bottle to the doubles involves nothing more than a length of stainless or galvanized rod and two hose clamps. By inserting the rod between the tanks inside the tank bands, catching the two hose clamps, the pony can be snugged up securely leaving no loose pieces that could become entangled.

A variation on the manifold doubles is to employ the use of a manifold with an isolation valve. Basically, this design incorporates the advantages of the two previous systems, by allowing two regulators to be mounted for redundancy, yet accessing the entire gas supply from either regulator. With the isolation valve open, the diver does not have to switch regulators during the dive, but does have a completely separate system as a back up. In the event of a catastrophic gas loss, such as with a free-flowing regulator or ruptured burst disc, the isolation valve can be closed, maintaining the integrity of the non-malfunctioning unit and providing a controlled method of return for the diver.

Although this design is rather attractive, practice will be needed to effectively close the isolation valve—especially in an emergency. Unless you are extremely limber (or double jointed), it may be necessary to loosen the waist strap of the backplate so that the tanks can be pulled into a position where the valve can be handled. The waist strap should not be undone in this procedure, only loosened to allow upward movement of the tanks, (a good reason for leaving the waist strap a bit long). Practice emergency procedures such as these in a pool first, then progress to shallow open water before relying on these techniques during a deep dive.

Because Murphy himself is an avid wreck diver, many divers choose to add further redundancy to this configuration with a pony bottle. It should be re-emphasized that simply having a redundant system is no guarantee of survival. Whether it is a second regulator mounted to a manifold or a pony bottle configuration, the second stage of the regulator *must* be instantaneously available. Having a redundant regulator hanging by your side will do little good when your primary just breathed its last breath and you are fumbling in the silt and rust of a sunken U-boat's interior. Learn how to use whichever system you choose.

Regulators

No matter which configuration of tanks you opt for, they will only be as good as the regulators attached to them. When allotting funds for equipment, this is one area not to skimp on. In wreck diving, you are likely to encounter conditions that will put a regulator to the test. Depth, current, silt and cold are just some of the ingredients a wreck diver's regulators must endure. The regulator must be capable of delivering all the gas a diver demands of it under any condition. At rest, most regulators will perform acceptably, however volume of gas delivered under heavy breathing loads is the crucial test of performance. The same criteria should be used to select one's backup regulator as well. Should the primary malfunction, you will *need* a reliable redundant regulator that is able to step up and take over.

We would also like to emphasize at this point, the benefits of using a DIN fitting system. DIN is a German industry standard in which the first stage of the regulator is screwed into the tank valve. The system features a captured o-ring seal. Designed for pressures higher than 3000 pounds, the DIN fitting is ideal in the wreck diving environment where the accidental bumping of a regulator and valve could unseat a standard o-ring/yoke assembly causing a rapid gas loss.

Knives

There is a certain bit of irony that is felt when you have researched a wreck for years, searched and searched for it at sea, finally find yourself swimming its lonely decks, knowing you are the first to ever be there, then coming upon hundreds of feet of monofilament and scores of codfish jigs. It is true, shipwrecks are not only the domain of wreck divers, but are equally sought after

---

COMMON LOCATIONS FOR WEARING KNIVES

- Front of Thigh
- Side of Thigh
- Inside or Outside of Calf
- Forearm
- Bouyancy Compensator Hose
- Back of Gauge Console

Remember, redundancy is important. At least two knives should be worn and placed in different locations. Should you become entangled, you may not be able to reach one of the knives.

Think

- Where can it be easily reached?
- Where will it not increase the likelihood of becoming entangled?
- If you cannot reach one knife due to entanglement, where should the second knife be worn?

Fishing nets and divers don't mix. Carrying at least two sharp knives is the best way to prevent a mishap.

A fishing knife converted into a diving knife. A sheath made of weight belt webbing has been sewn to a piece of neoprene and glued to the diver's suit.

by fishermen as well. Sport fishermen seek the proliferation of species found on these accidental reefs and while dragger vessels would prefer to avoid the wreck itself, often find themselves hung solidly into one as a hazard of their occupation. Add to the nets and monofilament, tether and ascent lines abandoned by other divers and you have a perfect environment for entanglement. For this reason, a key piece of equipment for the wreck diver is a knife.

A visit to any dive shop will reveal a plethora of choices of knives, many with unique features. The most important feature for the wreck diver is that it can cut you out of entanglement. Having a large rugged knife that can double as a pry bar may be useful, but the primary function should be to cut line. Some of the sharpest knives around, designed specifically for cutting line, are those made for commercial fishermen. Available at most fishing supply stores, these knives can be aptly transformed for diving. If you don't want to use the sheath supplied, a suitable one can be made by sewing weight belt webbing and adding a snap closure. It can then be fastened to the back of a console or even sewn to a piece of neoprene and glued to your suit for easy access. Though these knives may rust after several dives, they are generally inexpensive enough to replace when needed.

An alternative to a knife, for some wreck divers, is to take along a pair of surgical shears. If you feel you possess the dexterity necessary to operate them, shears will work just fine, with cutting power capable of slicing a penny. As a rule, at least two knives should be carried at all times. Since getting tangled on a wreck can be a serious problem, and considering how easy it is to drop a knife, you may even want to have three. Remember to arrange the knives strategically so that they are easily reached when needed.

Lights

Although not always necessary on dives when ambient light is sufficient, a dive light is a very useful tool for seeing under fallen timbers or beneath collapsed bulkheads. More often than not a light will help the diver find things, such as artifacts, that would otherwise be missed. It will also come in handy for signaling a buddy, should you need to get their attention. If penetration is part of the dive plan, a light is mandatory. Redundancy being the key word, at least two and preferably three dependable, powerful dive lights must be carried when going inside. Imagine the sensation of swimming through a decaying labyrinth in total darkness and you will always remember to carry reliable backups. As with most gear, personal preference will dictate an individual's choice. This choice must include a light that is bright enough to illuminate well, the stygian darkness of a sunken ship's interior and provide adequate burn time.

Burn time is a result of power source. Dive lights are powered either by dry cells or rechargeable batteries. If used often, rechargeable lights are more cost effective. They generally provide intense light, perfect for wreck diving. The downside of rechargeables however, is that the burn time curve is sharp, meaning that when

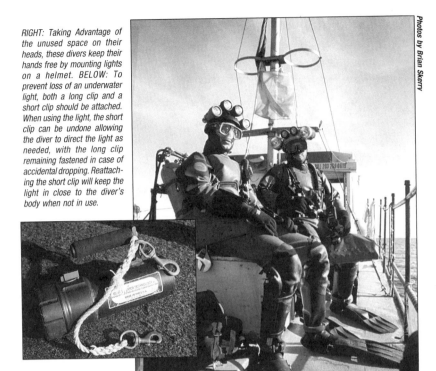

RIGHT: Taking Advantage of the unused space on their heads, these divers keep their hands free by mounting lights on a helmet. BELOW: To prevent loss of an underwater light, both a long clip and a short clip should be attached. When using the light, the short clip can be undone allowing the diver to direct the light as needed, with the long clip remaining fastened in case of accidental dropping. Reattaching the short clip will keep the light in close to the diver's body when not in use.

they start to die, they go fast. Obviously, this is not good when you are deep inside a wreck. Dry cells on the other hand, while often not as bright, do give fair warning of their impending demise with a steadily dimming beam. It is a good practice to choose a rechargeable dive light as a primary and a dry cell light as a backup offering a more reliable form of redundancy.

Since wreck divers often find themselves with their hands full, many opt to mount lights on a helmet taking advantage of the otherwise unused space on their head. Most lights can be affixed to a hockey or skateboarding helmet, or units initially designed for cave divers, specifically for this purpose, can be purchased. To prevent dropping a hand held dive light, a line can be attached with two clips secured at varying distances. By clipping both to a D-ring, the diver can keep the light close to the body and out of the way, yet unclip only the short clip when using the light, keeping the line always attached should the light be dropped.

Lines To Remember

When it is finally time to come up at the end of a dive, it is a comforting feeling to behold that precious anchor line right where

Jeff Pagano goes over the side with a sisal ascent line strapped to his back.

A diver unreels an ascent line after tying the loose end to the wreck. A more preferred method is to attach the loose end to a lift bag and sending the bag to the surface. The line attached to the reel is then cut and tied to the wreck.

you left it, guiding you back from whence you came. History has shown, however, that the best laid plans can fall to waste (otherwise we would have no shipwrecks!). It is not difficult to become disoriented on an unfamiliar wreck or the anchor line might chafe on wreckage, parting the line. Though every effort must be made to locate the anchor line, there are times when the diver must ascend without it. Aware of these realities, the fully-rigged wreck diver should be equipped to deal with the problem of having to ascend without the anchor line.

The contingency plan favored by many experienced wreck divers calls for carrying an ascent or "up" line that will serve as their own anchor line of sorts, in the event of a problem. Constructed in various ways, the most common up line consists of 300 feet or more of 1/4" biodegradable line, like sisal, wound onto a dowel (such as a broom handle) with circular disks at each end to keep the line from falling off. A few inches of the dowel should be left on each end so that can be held with both hands. The up line is most commonly attached between double tanks by means of surgical tubing or slices of inner tube, and is only removed when needed.

By attaching the end of the line to a lift bag, inflating the bag and allowing the line to peel off towards the surface; the diver then cuts the line, tying it to the wreck, effectively creating his own anchor line on which to as-

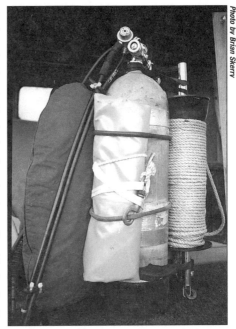

Photo by Brian Skerry

Lift bags can be mounted on the side of tanks, out of the way, held in place with surgical tubing.

cend. With the lift bag marking your position, the surface crew on the dive boat knows where you are and can keep a lookout for surface traffic that might interfere. The lift bag can be rigged to the ascent line in advance or clipped to a D-ring, or secured against the tanks with strips of inner tubes or surgical tubing.

Lift bags come in a variety of sizes designated by pounds of lift. Even a small bag with 50 pounds of lift is adequate for this purpose. However, a larger bag will fare better in a current. As we will see when we get to our discussion of artifacts, they have multiple uses. While on the subject of lift bags, we should discuss the proper method of inflating them. Filling a lift bag with the second stage of a regulator is a potential hazard, it could easily freeze in a free-flow position. Instead, a simple device, called interestingly enough, a lift bag inflator, can be plugged onto any low pressure inflator hose allowing the diver to rapidly and safely "shoot" a bag.

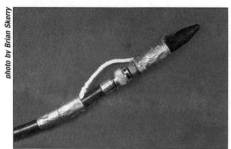

A lift bag inflator attached to a low pressure inflator hose. A piece of strin taped to both the hose and the inflator will prevent accidental loss.

Although a less desirable method, in severe currents, wreck divers in a "no anchor line" predicament may elect to send a lift bag up attached to a line reel, once they have begun their ascent, and drift with the current. This type of line reel is commonly constructed of stainless steel with a large diameter spool capable of holding several hundred feet of 1/8" line. It should not be used in the same manner as an ascent line due to the small diameter of the line. In a current, it would be extremely difficult to hold on to for any length of time if tied to a wreck. Much smaller than an ascent line, the line reel can be attached to a D-ring for easy access.

Although the line reel is most often associated with penetration, it can also serve as an excellent reconnaissance tool. In situations where visibility is poor and the wreck unfamiliar, the line reel can be clipped to the anchor line, allowing the diver to explore the wreck without fear of getting lost.

A considerably smaller piece of line that will come in handy on many wreck dives is the "Jonline". Named for its inventor, veteran diver Jon Hulburt, the "Jonline" is used while decompressing on days when the sea is rough, the current strong, or when too many

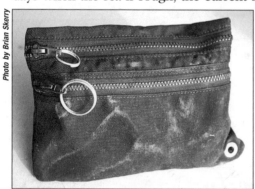

divers are clustering at the same stop. Generally no more than ten feet long, the line is either clipped off to or looped around the anchor line allowing the diver to reduce the shock of pounding waves. A "Jonline" can be easily stowed in a

Zippered pouchs are useful in carrying small items, can be modified for easy access with dive mitts by adding split rings to the zippers.

Steve Bielenda uses a "Jonline" to make a decompression hang more tolerable. PHOTO INSET: The wreck reel has many applications.

pocket of your suit, B.C., or in a pouch on the waist strap of your tank. When using a pouch, which is equally useful for carrying other small items, it helps to modify the pull tab of the zipper. Sliding on a split ring or any larger handle of sorts will make finding and opening the zippered pouch considerably easier.

Weight Belts

Losing one's weight belt, while wearing a dry suit inside a wreck, can really mess up your day. In fact, there are few times, if ever, in penetration wreck diving that a diver would want to shed his or her belt. One way of assuring that the weight belt stays in place is to use two buckles instead of just one. The addition of a second buckle helps to eliminate the chance of an accidental loss due to a diver rubbing against a piece of wreckage which can open the quick release. Buckles made of metal are generally preferred to plastic ones due to the gripping power metal has on the nylon weight belt material. Metal buckles also seem to stand up to a bit more abuse and can be easily repaired if damaged.

Signaling Devices

In wreck diving, unlike some other diving specialties, self-sufficiency does not only apply to the time spent underwater. Even with ascent lines, line reels, and lift bags, it is possible to find yourself at the surface and no dive boat in view. If the anchor line parted, the boat may have drifted before the crew became aware of the problem. Fog may have formed, obscuring the view or you may be at the mercy of a current, unable to swim against it.

If you have tied off an ascent line, then remain with the lift bag and secured line to the wreck, since the boat's crew can always find the wreck again. Sometimes however, even when it seems as though nothing can go wrong—it does.

Several years ago a diver returning to the dive boat after a dive on the *Andrea Doria*, was checking his video camera on the swim back to the ladder. When he looked up, he realized that the current had carried him past the boat, and was too strong to swim against. He could see a mate filling tanks on the stern, but his shouts for assistance could not be heard over the noise of the air compressor. It was about 30 minutes before his dive buddy, who was still decompressing when the diver left the anchor line, returned to the boat and reported him missing. By then the errant diver had drifted out of sight and a fog had set in inhibiting a search effort with the dive boat's small chase vessel. The dive boat's captain prudently dropped styrofoam cups into the water every few minutes until the fog cleared hours later, just before dark.

The search party eventually found the diver who had ditched his weight belt, double tanks, pony bottle, regulators, and gauges. Prior to discarding his tanks however, he removed a piece of duct tape and taped his dive light to his arm to help rescuers find him at night. Drifting in the shipping lanes enveloped in fog, 50 miles south of Nantucket, is a precarious position for a diver to be in to say the least, but bad things do happen—especially at sea! To make oneself easier to locate in the event of such an occurrence, a signaling device should be carried. Had this diver carried a signaling device, the crewman may have heard it and directed an immediate rescue.

The traditional standby has always been a whistle which can work fine, but there are additional alternatives. Other commercially available products include the Dive-Alert which attaches to a low pressure hose to create a high pitch sound when used or the Safety Sausage that can be inflated making the diver more visible on the surface. A small strobe can be attached to a B.C. hose or secured to a shoulder strap and can be activated at night.

Technical Toys

As wreck diving continues to grow, there will undoubtedly be grand innovations in equipment, making the quest safer, easier and more productive. Currently there are numerous pieces of gear including everything from dive computers, that give much more accurate decompression profiles of multilevel diving, to diver propulsion vehicles which allow divers to effortlessly tour wrecks and can even be used to blow sand away as a means of locating artifacts.

Underwater metal detectors can also be advantageous, particularly when combing a wreck site for buried artifacts. Metal detec-

A tremendous aid in multi-level wreck diving is the dive computer. These electronic devices provide constant calculations of no-decompression limits, time underwater, depth and even cylinder pressure in some models.

tors vary greatly in capabilities, and options should be considered before making an investment. Some units are affected by salt water and are best used only in fresh water. Other models can be tuned to reject "trash" such as pop tops. More sophisticated units can detect very small valuable items buried beneath the sand. Who knows, maybe on a day when you get blown out from an offshore site and reluctantly dive an old wooden inshore wreck with a metal detector in hand, you just might make the find of a lifetime.

Before concluding our discussion of wreck diving equipment, we return to this chapter's opening thought. While it is crucial to choose the correct tools for the job, it is more important to know how to use them. The most important piece of gear a diver will ever own is his or her brain. Good judgment cannot be bought, and purchasing the finest equipment in the world will not in itself make you a good wreck diver. The wreck diver must be comfortable and competent with every piece of gear carried. Comfortability, comes from diving with the same gear often. Competency, is attained by *using* specific pieces of equipment frequently enough so that their use becomes second nature. From time to time, practice removing the ascent line from your back and sending up a lift bag, when the anchor line *is* in sight. Use your knife to cut monofilament during a dive when you are *not* entangled. Use a Jonline on a day when there is hardly any current and you're the only one hanging.

Practicing these skills under controlled conditions when you *do not* have to use them is the best way to prepare for the day when you do. Any wreck diver worth his salt, has progressed to this point by diving often and experiencing many conditions. "Seasoning" comes from exposure to all that shipwrecks and the sea have to teach us. This is not learned in any prescribed time frame nor is it realized from making any certain number of dives.

To refer once again to the analogy of driving a car, it would be ludicrous to enter the Indy 500, having just received your driver's license, even if you owned a race car. It is just as unwise to attempt to dive wrecks that require experience which you have not yet attained, even if you have all the equipment needed to make the dive. There is an old proverb which says "A good archer is not known by his arrows, but by his aim." Proceeding methodically and progressing gradually, gaining the experience each wreck has to offer, is the best way to improve one's aim.

Billy Deans uses an Aquazepp diver propulsion vehicle while diving the wreck of the Civil War ironclad U.S.S. **Monitor**. Note the video camera mounted on top.

Lift bags are used by wreck divers to send ascent lines to the surface and retrieve artifacts. The diver in the photo above is inflating the bag with his regulator. A preferred method is to use a lift bag inflator, such as the one shown on page 164.

Chapter 8

Diving the Wreck

Adrenaline coursed through the diver's body as he methodically dressed in his gear, while thoughts of sunken riches below saturated his mind. Jumping off the boat, he soon settled down on the shipwreck and began to explore. Cautiously venturing inside, his eyes adjusted to the darkness allowing him to better navigate the submerged labyrinth. Squeezing past a collapsed bulkhead, he entered the cargo hold as the rhythmic beating of his heart picked up its tempo. At last he gazed upon the stuff of dreams. He had indeed found treasure.

Photo by Brian Skerry

Whether shallow or deep, certain procedures must be followed to ensure safe wreck diving.

A lot has changed in the pursuit of wreck diving since the mid-5th century B.C. when a diver named Scyllias recovered treasure from sunken Persian galleys. But one thing has not. An essential, innate human catalyst is curiosity and few pursuits can re-ignite this dormant inferno like that of exploring sunken ships. Unlike other aspects of diving, exploring shipwrecks requires a degree of dedication from beginning to end. While the diver can simply cruise around the wreck with no set plan, it is usually better to follow certain procedures or routines as a way of increasing safety and productivity, no matter what your goals.

Once the wreck has been hooked, it is time to suit up and go diving. As was discussed in Chapter 5, divers should always descend and ascend the anchor line, unless another prearranged method is called for. To assist divers in swimming to the anchor line, a gerry or granny line can be employed. The gerry (shortened from geriatrics) line, is simply a line running from the anchor line to an after cleat on the boat. The end tied or clipped to the anchor line is often weighted (a heavy shackle is commonly used) so that the diver jumping in off the stern of the boat has only to follow the gerry line to where it connects to the anchor line, perhaps 15 or 20 feet down, to begin descending to the wreck.

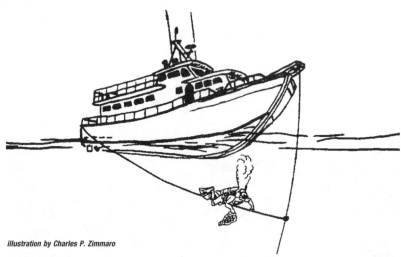

illustration by Charles P. Zimmaro

Attached to an after cleat on the boat and to the anchor line, using a "gerry line" is the most efficient way of beginning a descent.

Upon reaching the wreck, the first diver down must "tie in." Tying in, is nothing more than making sure that the anchor line will be there when it is time to come up. This can be done using several methods, one of the easiest being taking along a length of line and physically tying the anchor to the wreck. If a shot line was used instead of a grapnel hook, the chain can be unclipped from the weight

Photos by Brian Skerry

Tying the anchor to the wreck will prevent it from coming free and ensure a safe ascent at the end of the dive.

Frank Nardi checks the anchor on the wreck of the steamship **Oregon,** making sure it is secure.

and reclipped or shackled to the wreck. Care must be taken to see that a solid piece of wreckage has been selected to tie to. Attention should be focused on making sure that chafing of the anchor line will not occur. A chain shackled around a piece of wreckage usually works best, instead of a rope to prevent chafing. Consideration of tide or current changes are key since either might swing the line into a different position during the dive. Even though the first divers down will make the tie in, every diver reaching the bottom should check to see that the line is secure.

Because getting back to the anchor line at the end of the dive is so important, it may be wise to attach flashing strobe lights to it,

Making mental notes of identifiable wreckage, such as this anchor and winch on the wreck of the **Proteus** off North Carolina, will help guide you back to the anchor line.

Mike Drainville swims along the keel of a newly discovered wooden wreck as a method of maintaining orientation.

creating a homing beacon which can usually be seen from quite a distance. If the line has been tied in, you will want to untie it before the last diver climbs back on board. Simply by untying the hook however, will not guarantee that it can be pulled up. To make sure of that, the hook should be carried to the sand away from the wreck or placed on the wreck in such a way that it can be easily retrieved. Remember that if it falls back into the wreck and gets hooked again, you will either be making another dive or doing the "anchor jig" from the deck of your boat, until it is free.

As you begin to explore the wreck, particularly if you are unfamiliar with the site, you should be closely surveying all that you see. By noting things that are seen, a path back to the anchor line can be memorized. Use natural navigation methods and try to remember the placement of boilers, engines, capstans or anchors and where they are in relation to each other. If visibility is poor, you may not want to stray too far from the anchor line, becoming intimate with a rather small area of the wreck. The alternative is to clip off a line reel providing a direct path back. When you do venture forth it is helpful to do so by following natural lines of the ship that are easy to recognize. For instance, if you are exploring an old wooden schooner, it may be best to swim along the keel since it is the center line of the vessel. From there you can branch out. If the wreck is a more modern vessel, traveling along the gunwales may be the best path to follow. Learning each nuance of the wreck will make future dives less rigid. Disorientation is not uncommon on unfamiliar

Filmmaker, Nick Caloyianis, penetrates an open hatch on a German U-boat to capture interior sequences.

wrecks, especially those not intact. Knowledge of the ship's construction and following procedures like those outlined above will greatly diminish the chances of getting lost and increase your chances of enjoying the wreck and seeing wondrous things.

Hazards

In Chapter 7, when discussing wreck diving equipment, we emphasized that much of the gear that a wreck diver carries is in preparation for dealing with potential hazards that might be encountered. We offered suggestions for handling problems with entanglement, abrasion, poor visibility, no anchor line, etc. There are, however, additional environmental hazards that the wreck diver must consider. The hazards of this category are best dealt with by improved diving technique rather, than with specialized gear.

Currents

Found in all depths of water, in good visibility and bad, in warm water and cold, and in oceans throughout the world, current is per-

Once a wreck has been entered—the stakes increase!

A sideways sink inside **Andrea Doria**. The interiors of shipwrecks can be disorienting.

haps the most common hazard found while diving wrecks. If the current is tidal, the wreck should be dived at slack tide at a time when the water speed is negligible. If, on the other hand, it is ocean currents you are up against, there is not much you can do except get in the water and see if it is diveable.

Veteran wreck diver Gary Gentile for years was fond of kidding with charter boat captains by stating, "If you can hook the wreck, we can dive it." On one trip to the *Empress of Ireland* in the St. Lawrence river, however, where the current can truly scream, Gary amended the statement, to "If you can hook the wreck, we can get in the water."

Although using a gerry line will make getting to the anchor line quite a bit easier, in a strong current just getting to the wreck can be a chore. Rather than expending energy kicking against it, pull yourself down the line steadily, hand over hand. When the authors dived the U.S.S. *Monitor,* in 1990, a mooring system was in place which divers were to be dropped off at to begin their descent (by law we could not anchor the wreck or tie off to the mooring placed 100 feet away from the wreck). Due to a severe current, we were dropped up current and rapidly drifted back to the one float still marking the mooring's position. A momentary distraction and we would have not been able to grasp the float as we shot past. The strong current continued all the way to the bottom, 230 feet below the surface. Also, we had to keep looking directly ahead, or our face masks would have been pulled from our faces because of the current. Working hard at that depth increases the chance of nitrogen narcosis and carbon dioxide build up, but conserving energy will help prevent this. Using primarily our hands and arms to pull us with a constant steady rhythm, we reached the bottom and viewed the legendary warship. Fortunately, the current is not always that severe on this historic shipwreck.

Once on the wreck, pulling yourself along, reducing the need to kick, is a much easier way of getting around and conserving energy. Whenever possible, dive on the lee side of the wreck, away from the force of the current. Remember also to start the dive by swimming against the current, so that at the end of the dive it should be an easy drift back towards the anchor line. If the wreck is broken up and not contiguous, scattered sections can be reached by vectoring against the current, staying low to the bottom.

Surge

Surge is most noticeable on shallow wrecks, another factor to consider while discussing potential hazards. Waves breaking over and around inshore wrecks can create a surge that will alternately push and pull. This action can cause a sudden loss of control and throw a diver into jagged metal or other harmful objects. If you suspect a strong surge before diving a shallow wreck, it may be wise to add a bit of extra weight to help you hold your ground on the bottom. Surge can also be present on deeper wrecks.

Depth

The word deep is a relative term and while depth itself is not a hazard, it does require a heightened awareness of potential problems that can occur. Depth is a diving challenge that must be met

Intact wrecks like the **Ethel C,** off the coast of Virginia, are generally found in deeper water. Depth, then adds further complexities to a penetration dive.

gradually. A diver must be extremely comfortable in a given depth range before venturing into deeper water and even then should only progress in small increments. The deeper one ventures, the less room there is for error. Therefore, a diver must be confident that he/she can respond to any problem that might occur on any dive that is made. The deeper a diver descends, the more rapidly gas supplies are depleted and decompression obligations increase. Equipment management becomes especially crucial since there is no time to be wasted when a piece of gear is needed. In 40 feet of water, having to cut oneself out of monofilament or having to reach back to close an isolator manifold because of a free-flowing regulator is a real inconvenience and a potentially serious problem. In 200 feet of water, either of these scenarios becomes severe. The time allowed to solve these problems is greatly reduced at the deeper depth. A diver should have encountered the range of potential wreck diving hazards at shallower, more comfortable depths, before hoping to solve them when encountered at greater depths.

Depending on the depth of water and the individual diver, nitrogen narcosis can also become a severe hazard when diving deep wrecks. There is no shame in encountering narcosis. The diver must recognize it for what it is and plan dives accordingly. In many cases, nitrogen narcosis can be quite noticeable in a diver venturing to first time depths for which he/she is simply not yet prepared or accustomed. But, given enough dives at gradually increasing depths, that same diver may have no noticeable effects. However, nitrogen narcosis is unpredictable at best.

As was mentioned previously, lack of time to solve problems is a key factor in deep diving. Under the influences of nitrogen narcosis, a diver's response time is slowed even further, emphasizing the importance of being able to react instinctively. Narcosis levels can be reduced by switching breathing gases and cutting back the amount of nitrogen present; however, this is an area for only the most experienced divers and should not be used by inexperienced divers as a means of achieving depths for which they are not yet prepared.

Decompression is a necessary fact of deep wreck diving, and must be planned for accordingly. When conducting decompression dives on wrecks, adequate time must be allowed for returning to and locating the anchor line. Dive time and gas supply must be carefully monitored to allow for a safe ascent. Although a dive may be planned for a certain duration, it must in reality be dictated by gas supply. Decompression schedules must be well rehearsed and stops should be written down and carried where they can easily be referenced, such as on a slate or laminated paper fastened to a gauge console. Though dive computers can make things a lot simpler, they should not be relied on entirely. Any piece of equipment can malfunction. Proficiency with decompression tables is a must and should be consulted along with the use of computers in any profile. A great deal could be written at this juncture regarding decompression theory and practice; however, as is mentioned in the introduction to *Complete Wreck Diving*, the intent of this text is to address issues that apply only to diving shipwrecks. While decompression will be confronted by most wreck divers at one time or another, it is not unique to wreck diving and is abundantly covered in numerous other sources. For this reason, we have kept from lengthy discussion of the biology and physiology of decompression. What is rather unique to wreck diving, however, is decompressing in the open ocean with one's hands full of equipment. There is nothing particularly difficult about ascending an anchor line and stopping for a prescribed amount of time at a designated depth. The challenge comes from doing so while hanging in a two-knot current and bouncing up and down in a four-foot sea while trying to keep one hand on the anchor line and the other on a camera system or bag of tools. When conditions like these prevail, a healthy dose of stamina is perhaps the best thing to bring along.

Stamina and a Jonline, that is. Remember also that you will want to remain slightly negative (buoyancy that is, not attitude!) when hanging. You can always add air to your buoyancy device if you want to remain neutral, but under no circumstance do you want to be buoyant when reaching your decompression stop.

Anchor line etiquette is equally important. Be considerate of others decompressing. Keep an eye on that crowbar you have dangling from your wrist and try not to tie up all the space on the line between ten and fifteen feet as you hang vertically. Proper buoyancy, use of a Jonline and a touch of consideration and you and your "hanging mates" should be able to ride out even the most foul weather amidst the overcrowded and dreaded "cluster hang."

Shipwreck Penetration

In the solitude of the rusting, tranquil leviathan, you glide effortlessly across the sullen decks, seeking remnants of a bygone age. Inevitably, you come to an open hatchway, beckoning you to enter and cross into the next dimension. Lying in a prone position,

Photo by Brian Skerry

The wrong way to enter a submarine hatch.

still on the deck, your dive light stabs the awaiting darkness, as your eyes trace along with the beam, hoping to glimpse a familiar object, amidst a world of disarray. Your heart picks up the pace of its rhythmic pounding, because it is now aware of the decision your brain has made. Purging the air from your suit, you drop feet first through the portal, your tanks scraping the sides of the hatch, as you fall inside, coming to rest in a billowing cloud of silt on a debris-laden floor. Through the silty cloud, you can see above you the chartreuse green light in the shape of the hatch you have passed beyond. Moving only a few feet ahead, inspecting every inch of uncharted territory, you frequently glance back for the reassurance of the glowing green light. When you reach a point when the view of your exit becomes obscured by the trail of disturbed sediment, you carefully turn around, fighting the urge to race back, and slowly move towards the comforting aura. Exiting, you feel exhilarated, having entered the abyss and returned. You ascend the anchor line, recharged and already contemplating the next foray into the unknown.

A bit dramatic perhaps, but a wreck diver's first penetration dive, is nothing if not dramatic. While it is true that much can be seen and found and enjoyed on the exterior of shipwrecks, sooner or later, human curiosity will prevail and you will venture inside.

It is a natural progression in the evolution of a wreck diver to seek out the answers to the question of what lies beyond the exterior of a wreck's hull. Whether in search of artifacts, (the engine room telegraph for instance, will only be found in the engine room of an intact wreck), or simply because, like the mountain—it is there—divers will eventually go inside.

It becomes quite apparent however, that once you enter the interior of a wreck, the stakes increase dramatically. No longer can you simply come to the surface should a problem arise. Add to it that the interior of a decaying shipwreck is a very disorienting place and you begin to realize the complexities associated with penetration. One of the best quotes describing the view inside a shipwreck comes from commercial diver Ted Hess while working on Peter Gimbel's 1981 *Andrea Doria* project when he said "You know, it looks like somebody scooped up a big ol' house, dropped it from about a hundred feet, then came along with a bulldozer and shoved the whole damn thing in a cave."

Diving in a disorienting, overhead environment is understandably reason enough to proceed cautiously, but there are additional concerns that must be considered as well.

One of the first concerns is poor visibility. Even in relatively clear water, fallen debris lying below a swimming diver can be easily disturbed, causing the fine sediments, rust and silt, that have been collected for years, to be disturbed. If enough silt is kicked-up, it can cause what is termed as "siltouts", which can quickly extinguish any visibility that once existed. Even if you are extremely careful, exhaust bubbles can dislodge rust particles and overhead

John Lachenmeyer demonstrates the proper way to enter a sunken submarine.

silt, creating a rainfall of rapidly deteriorating visibility conditions. Divers must use kicking techniques that won't disturb silt layers. Pulling yourself among wreckage and not kicking or minimizing fin strokes often prevents dangerous siltouts.

Next on the list of concerns is depth of water. As was mentioned previously, depth in itself does not have to be considered a hazard; however when penetrating a shipwreck, it certainly adds to the complexities of the dive. Since intact wrecks are most often found in deeper water, the diver must prepare for the concerns associated with deep diving. These concerns include gas supply, decompression schedules and nitrogen narcosis.

While it is not the intent of this text to discuss in any great detail the particularities of deep diving, we do wish to emphasize that the interior of a shipwreck is not the place to gain one's initial experience. A diver must be comfortable with a given depth before attempting a penetration. Just about anything that can happen outside a wreck can happen on the inside, and oftentimes, hazards inside multiply geometrically. For instance, the diver could become entangled by fallen wires inside the corridor of the wreck. As the diver moves to get free, silt is kicked up, causing disorientation and forcing a longer bottom time while searching for the exit. Assuming the diver finds the exit, the additional time spent on the bottom may have depleted his or her gas supply and result in a longer or unplanned decompression. The concerns of shipwreck penetration can, however, be addressed in a safe manner by following certain procedures and techniques.

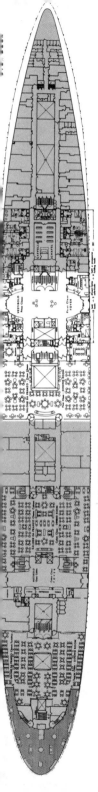

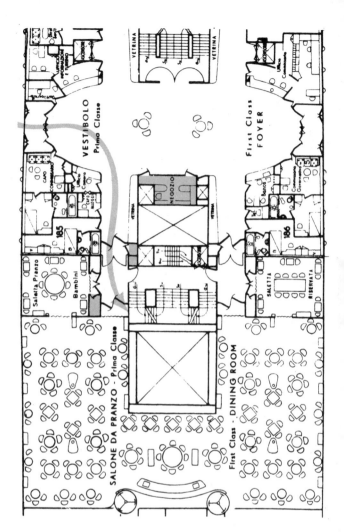

The arrow indicates the path divers follow through the hull and into the corridor, at 205 feet, to recover china and crystal from the *Andrea Doria*. A china cabinet, shown in grey above the arrow's point, collapsed and the contents fell onto the bulkhead below. A crystal cabinet, also shown in grey, is below and to the right of the china cabinet. The gift shop, shown in grey, is below the opening to the corridor.

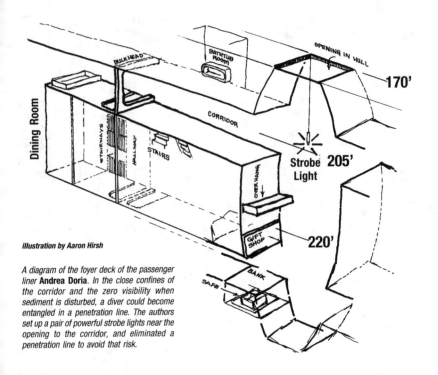

illustration by Aaron Hirsh

A diagram of the foyer deck of the passenger liner **Andrea Doria**. In the close confines of the corridor and the zero visibility when sediment is disturbed, a diver could become entangled in a penetration line. The authors set up a pair of powerful strobe lights near the opening to the corridor, and eliminated a penetration line to avoid that risk.

Penetration Lines

When considering penetration, many divers automatically think of using lines to guide them in and out of the wreck. Penetration lines can be a useful tool; however, they can equally become a severe hazard. Swimming through a rusting, collapsed maze in limited visibility, pulling behind you a thin nylon line, is not any guarantee of getting back out. Penetration lines are notorious for wrapping around divers if not continuously managed. They may also slip into areas that the diver did not come through, making exiting the wreck extremely confusing. Lines can also break, chafe, or be cut and should never be trusted completely.

If a penetration line is to be employed, it is best to use a line reel such as the type discussed in Chapter 7, wound with non-floating, braided line. The line should be tied at a point just outside the entrance/exit and at a point just inside the entrance/exit. Securing the line in this manner, at two points, is done as a precaution against a severed line.

When tying off the line, the diver must be sure to tie to a secure piece of wreckage that is free from sharp edges which might cut the line. As the diver ventures forth inside the wreck, periodic tie offs or wraps should be made to prevent the line from falling into "traps". The line should be kept taut, but not tight, since a tight line is easily severed by sharp wreckage. Ideally, the penetration line should be run along a constant bulkhead (i.e. the portside bulkhead), to prevent entanglement.

When returning, the line should be reeled in slowly and never should the diver pull himself along it to get back. A penetration line should never be cut and tied off at the furthest point, just because the diver did not want to take the time to reel the line in. Anyone planning to use this method of penetrating a wreck must also make sure to notify all other divers on the boat. There is enough to be concerned about without having another diver cut your line because it was in their way.

Progressive Penetration

The alternative to using a line to explore inside shipwrecks, is not to use one. The mere thought, however, of swimming through such a chaotic world without help, is enough to start one's heart beating faster and breathing rate to increase. But perhaps, this is as it should be. To abandon fear and place faith in any tool is unwise. Better to allow apprehension to flourish than to bury it with a false sense of security. Penetration of shipwrecks can safely be carried out without the use of a line by practicing a gradual or progressive technique of exploration. Using this technique, the diver enters the wreck, carefully examining and memorizing very small sections before moving on. By familiarizing oneself with each small section of a wreck over a period of many dives, the diver is much more able to rely on him/herself to find the way out under adverse conditions. Granted, it will take considerably longer to explore the wreck using this method, but shipwreck penetration should not be viewed as a race. The steady accumulation of first hand knowledge of a wreck in this manner is also a remedy for the monotony that is sometimes experienced when frequently diving the same site over and over again. Conducting an ongoing progressive penetration is stimulus enough to want to return to a wreck that would otherwise hold little interest. Remember also, that wrecks continue to change as they decay. If you have been away from a wreck for a while, do not rely on old recollections from which to navigate.

There is nothing preventing a diver from employing a combination of the two techniques discussed. Using a line only as a back-up, while gradually learning limited sections of the wreck is certainly a viable option.

Regardless of which method you prefer, there are several techniques and procedures that, when followed, will increase the safety and enjoyment of wreck penetration. The very first thing divers should be in the habit of doing before penetrating a wreck, is learning something about the place they will be venturing into. Once again we return to research. Although it may not be practical to always have researched a ship before journeying inside, doing so may give you an edge. While it is true that the interior of a sunken ship rarely looks very much like a builder's blueprint, studying the plans will often indicate features that can act as landmarks on your trek through this labyrinth of lost time.

Buoyancy Control

Buoyancy control is a technique that should be regarded as an art. With adequate visibility being so critical for safety, and silt being so easy to disturb, buoyancy control must be practiced and mastered before venturing inside. By maintaining neutral buoyancy, a

---

BOUYANCY CONTROL

Always important in wreck diving, bouyancy control becomes critical when penetrating a shipwreck. Tips include:

- Achieve a neutral attitude
- Move slowly
- Pull yourself rather than kicking
- Maintain slow, steady breathing
- If air must be added or expelled from suit or compensator, it should be done in brief measures. Add or dump small amounts of air, check bouyancy, do more if necessary.
- Picking up objects such as artifacts or the laying down of objects such as tools can affect bouyancy.

AIR MANAGEMENT

Many factors encountered within wreck diving can affect a diver's gas consumption. Depth, currents and work load are just a few. The wreck diver must allow sufficient gas supply at the end of the dive to locate the anchor line, ascend and fulfill any decompression obligation. The longer the hang, the more gas that will be needed for that portion of the dive.

While dives are typically planned for a designated amount of time, in many cases gas supply will actually dictate the duration of the dive. For instance, a 20 minute dive to 150 fsw is planned; however, after 15 minutes, the diver has only 1200 psi left in his tanks. Considering the time it will take to get back to the anchor line and complete decompression, the dive is terminated at 15 minutes instead of staying the planned 20 minutes. Conversely, if a dive is planned for a prescribed time limit, the diver should not stay longer just because plenty of gas remains. Dives should be planned for a certain amount of time or a certain remaining level of gas—whichever comes first.

diver can move through sections of sunken ships effortlessly, keeping disturbed silt to a minimum.

Speaking of moving through wrecks, we must emphasize that all movements should be made slowly. Reaching quickly into the muck for a dish or hammering rapidly on a porthole will soon have you looking like "Pigpen" as you move within a cloud of dust to find the exit. Fins should be used sparingly and should not be dragged behind as you move forward. "Finger walking" is the best method of propelling oneself through the wreck. A deliberate forward motion achieved by pulling rather than kicking is your best assurance of maintaining suitable visibility on the return trip.

Keep in mind, also, that many wreck interiors are places of narrow, confined spaces that only one diver at a time should enter. Most often, with two or more divers in such spaces, visibility becomes completely obscured and safety compromised. In such cases, a buddy team should prearrange for one diver to enter, while the other waits at the entrance/exit, shining a dive light as a homing beacon. A final word in regards to entering hatches on sunken ships: although it may seem quite obvious, hatches are best penetrated feet first. At least one of the diver's hands should remain outside as the slide inside is made. All equipment should be kept close to the body and some air vented from the suit or BCD. Entering a hatch head first is unsafe. If for any reason you should become stuck, there is little recourse (not to mention the severe embarrassment of dying in this position).

Geographical Differences of Wreck Diving

The year is 1942. Two freighters, sisterships, are sailing the Atlantic Ocean carrying cargo. One has left New York, bound for Portland, Maine, the other is plying southern waters off the Dry Tortugas. As fate would have it, both are torpedoed by German U-boats, and come to rest in exactly 150 feet of water. Fifty-odd years later, divers have located the wrecks and plan to dive them.

Although the ships are quite the same, the dives are very different. When we discussed the elements that will effect a shipwreck's decay in Chapter 2, we focused on geography as a key contributor to a wreck's condition. When we discussed hazards of wreck diving earlier in this chapter and in Chapter 7, we emphasized such things as cold, depth and currents as realities of wreck diving for which we must prepare. What we hope to stress in this section is that wreck divers need to recognize the vast differences inherent in shipwrecks of various regions. A healthy respect must be given to diving in any area you are not familiar with.

Divers used to diving in warm, clear waters, regardless of how long they been diving, must consider themselves novices when entering cold, dark and poor visibility water. Diving in cold water can increase stress as well as make you more susceptible to decompression sickness. While it is generally assumed that if a diver is competent in cold, dark water, he can dive anywhere in the world, we must guard against overconfidence. Many regions may appear easy to dive, but a closer inspection could reveal difficult conditions not immediately evident. A warm, clear, tropical site for instance, could contain a strong ocean current or a dangerous down-welling and the cold, dark water diver may not have had previous current diving experience to this degree. Local divers will usually have perfected procedures that work best for their region. When diving wrecks in an unfamiliar area, consult local divers regarding conditions and procedures.

Marine Life

Perhaps one of the greatest added benefits of diving wrecks is the thrill of seeing the abundance of interesting marine life that make the wrecks their home. When a ship sinks in the ocean, it becomes an artificial reef providing a home to many marine crea-

Even ardent artifact hunters can't help getting excited when visited by a passing shark.

tures. In the absence of natural reefs in many regions, it is interesting that man, albeit unintentionally, has provided the basis for fascinating ecosystems—shipwrecks. They provide large areas of hard surface for colonizing marine organisms, and after a few years each wreck is an entire ecosystem. They are not only oases in a desert of sand, but they also increase biologic productivity. It is stunning to see for the first time the incredible beauty and diversity of marine life that has taken up residence in or around a sunken ship.

On some wrecks, the growth of marine organisms is so dense that it completely obscures the structures of the vessel. Depending where in the world you are diving, you might see a turtle on a tanker in Truk or swim by a sculpin in Scapa Flow. Even the most ardent artifact hunter can be found exuding enthusiasm after an encounter with a manta ray or passing hammerhead shark. Certain inhabitants of shipwrecks are the reason many divers seek out shipwrecks in the first place. We refer, of course, to the lobster, which can be found in most ocean waters of the world. Found nestled under fallen beams or beneath rusted plates, these delectable denizens occupy shipwrecks of nearly every region. Whether it is the North American, spiny, or slipper lobster, divers will be seeking

Beautiful marine life, such as this school of spade fish on a North Carolina shipwreck, aesthetically enhances any wreck dive.

them out on shipwrecks. If you intend to catch lobsters while wreck diving, be sure to obey state laws regarding licensing and size limits.

When attempting to catch lobsters or anything else for that matter, a diver should never just blindly reach inside a hole. There is always the chance that a species of hazardous marine life has made that hole their home and will not appreciate a hand thrust through the front door! Although you will unlikely ever encounter man-eating moray eels, a bit of caution is prudent. Stonefish, lionfish, goosefish and countless other potentially hazardous species of marine life will be found on shipwrecks, and although few if any have ever been known to be aggressive, even accidental antagonization can result in injury. The best approach is not to touch any animal you see, unless you are after lobster, and beware of reaching inside dark and foreboding crevices.

By proceeding logically and methodically, diving shipwrecks will get more exciting with each dive. The more you see, the more you will understand. The more problems you have to solve, the more experience you will garner. As you dive more and more wrecks, you will become confident with navigating around even scattered wreckage and appreciate ship construction. As you continue to dive wrecks, you will also unconsciously gain a subtle appreciation for rough seas, smooth seas, strong wind, a calm wind, currents and depth, geography and history, your own mind and body, and of course, ships in the sea. With a bit of common sense and an adventurous soul, you too, like Scyllias, may soon be gazing upon the stuff of dreams.

photo by Brian Skerry

An atlantic wolffish finds a home on the wreck of a wooden schooner in ninety feet of water off the New England coast.

Two projectiles for six-inch guns and clips of rifle ammunition inside one of the U.S. armored cruiser **San Diego**'s many magazines. The steel I-beam rests on the tip of one of the projectiles. Ordnance such as this is considered to be hazardous when recovered by divers.

Chapter 9

Shipwreck Identification

If the shipwreck you are diving is the result of your research, chart work, and searching, congratulations! The hard work has paid off. Even though you have located a shipwreck, it may not be the one you were looking for. Proof will need to be obtained to confirm your discovery. Identifying a wreck need not only be the

Photo by Brian Skerry

Finding the ship's name still painted on the stern makes the task of identifying an unknown wreck quite easy.

A cannon recovered from the British ship-of-the-line **Culloden** *in about 20 feet of water, near Montauk, Long Island, New York, was marked with a monogram. A figure 2 entwined in a "G" is the Royal Cypher of King George II (1727-1760). The cannon was cast some years before the* **Culloden** *was launched in 1776. The "22" to the right of the crown was probably a manufacturer's code.*

domain of the wreck finder. There are many wrecks that are dived regularly, yet remain unidentified. There are also numerous wrecks that are misidentified—and no one has taken the time to set the record straight.

When attempting to identify a shipwreck, it may require working backwards with your research. Obviously, the task is made simple by swimming past the name painted on the stern or finding the quarterboard lying in the sand. Locating the bell is often a way of solving the mystery, but not always. Still, artifacts found on unidentified shipwrecks will often indicate the period in which a ship sank and provide clues to its nationality. Prime examples are coins and cannon. Dated coins give an index to the period of the wreck, but not always the nationality of the ship.

Certain coins had a wide circulation in international trade, especially Spanish coins. The gold doubloon and the silver pieces of eight were standard coins of international commerce in the 17th,

18th, and early 19th centuries. Pirates and privateers preyed upon Spanish galleons, further distributing the species. Also, sailors often kept coins as souvenirs of the ports they visited, a practice which continues even today. Coins from several countries

The numbers "56-2-0" on the **Culloden** cannon indicate the weight in hundredweights, quarters and pounds.

The National Maritime Museum, London, England, believes the letter "G" on the **Culloden** cannon's trunnion is the initial of the manufacturer, but, could not trace which one. A similar letter is on the trunnion of one of the cannons recovered from the Barrier Reef, Australia, where they had been jettisoned from Captain James Cook's ship, **Endeavour**.

may be recovered from one wreck site. Cannon usually bear the date they were cast. The date not only indicated the age of the cannon to the armorers in the ordnance depots, but also the internal condition of the cannon.

Scandinavian and British cannon of the late 17th, 18th, and early 19th centuries often have the date

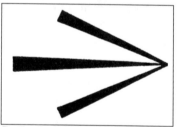

The "broad arrow" was and still is the mark of British Government ownership and will be found on various artifacts such as cannon and cannon balls. The mark may signify that an unidentified shipwreck is a British warship.

cast in one of the trunnions, (trunnions are the side "protrusions" of a cannon that when fitted into a carriage, allow the muzzle to tilt up or down). However, the date was not always in four numerals. In many cases only the last two numerals were expressed. Thus, "97" could be 1697, 1797, or 1897. The molding forms used in different periods is important for determining the century. A

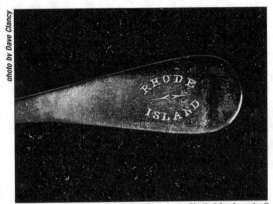

*Tableware, such as this fork from the side-wheeler **Rhode Island,** sunk off Bonnet Shores, Rhode Island was often imprinted with the ship's name.*

"crowned rose," for example, would indicate 1697, as the crowned rose was not used during the reigns of the Hanoverian kings. British cannon of the latter part of the 18th century also possessed serial numbers that may be confused with dates. However, the serial numbers were usually stamped in rather than embossed, as were most date marks. If the date was stamped in the end of the trunnion, the initials or full name of the cannon's maker is also present. A cannon's serial number can be used to identify the wreck.

The British Admiralty recorded the serial numbers of cannon a ship was armed with in both the warship's records and the ordnance department's records. Also, changes in ordnance during the warship's service would be recorded.

French cannon of the 18th century frequently bear the date in full in the base ring. The "Fleur-de-Lis" was used as the armorial emblem of the kings of France. French cannonballs from the French and Indian wars, recovered from Lake Champlain and Lake George in upstate New York, are stamped with the heraldic device, while British cannonballs possess the "Broad Arrow."

The number and size of cannon will usually date the wreck and furnish evidence as to the type of warship. The ordnance of different classes of warships during the 18th and 19th centuries were closely defined by admiralty regulations for British and French warships. American regulations, however, were not as rigid. The U.S.S. *Ohio,* a ship-of-the-line, now sunk in about 20 feet of water in Greenport Harbor (Long Island, New York), was classed as a 74. However, the warship carried anywhere from 84 to 104 guns, depending on the decision of her various captains. The Bureau of Ordnance Gun Register lists the *Ohio's* armament in 1845 as 90 guns.

Anchors went through a gradual evolution from the late 15th century to the early 19th century. Examples found on wrecks seldom show distinctive characteristics and are difficult to date.

The types of wood used in the

The gudgeons of some warships have the ship's name stamped in them. A brass gudgeon recovered from the British ship-of-the-line **Culloden**, with the ship's name misspelled when it was cast at the foundry. A broken pintle pin protrudes through the gudgeon socket. The function of gudgeons and pintles is illustrated on page 33.

construction of hulls often will furnish clues in identifying a vessel. Ships built in North America were frequently constructed of pine, while cedar may indicate the West Indies or Mexico as the place of construction. British and Spanish shipbuilders favored oak. Fastenings from the hull often can be used to date a shipwreck to a period within 50 years of its manufacture (see fastenings on page 41)

Tableware is sometimes imprinted with the ship's name or the steamship company's name. The Cunard Line steamship *Oregon,* which sank in 1886, was identified in this manner. Beginning in 1958, Long Island scuba divers heard reports of large codfish being caught on a wreck referred to as the *Oregon.* The location corresponded to what was known of the Cunard liner's sinking, but names applied to offshore wrecks are often wrong. As an example, "Tea Wreck" off Jones Beach, Long Island is actually the *Acara.* She happened to be carrying crates of tea when she sank; from time to time they would pop to the surface, thus "Tea Wreck."

In 1960, a group of 20 divers in ten diving teams launched an effort to identify the *Oregon.* They hoped to find identification such as the silverware bearing the ship's name that they had recovered as positive identification of another wreck, the *Black Warrior.* That was probably expecting too much, but measurement of the boilers, or some distinctive machinery might serve the purpose.

Divers from two boats searched for the wreck in midsummer without the benefit of today's sophisticated loran (Long Range Aid to Navigation) units. Several marker buoys were dropped to set up a search pattern. The depth recorder traced out a wreck and buoys were set in preparation for diving. A shark's fin temporarily halted operations, until a baited rig landed the 8 1/2-foot, 140-pound blue shark.

Two of the divers, Charles Dunn and Graham Sneidiker wrote, in an article for *Skin Diver:* "Our first dive to the remains of the *Oregon* was one of the most rewarding experiences we have enjoyed in our diving career….Directly below us was a jumble of machinery and boilers representing what had once been an engine room….The decks had collapsed downward; everything was in a complete shambles….We spotted a porthole lying on the deck and tried to pick it up but it was much too heavy to handle. More portholes were seen. They must have dropped from wooden deckhouses which had long since vanished through decay…"

They were disappointed despite their porthole finds. They had nothing to prove the wreck's identity. They hoped that their 15 feet ten-inch measurement of one of the boilers would help if nothing more definite was found. They alerted other dive teams to search areas other than the engine room. Lift bags of the other teams soon began to pop to the surface. The first had a porthole attached; others contained plates, cups and chamber pots bearing the Cunard Steamship Company emblem. Other plates bore the Guion Line insignia. The *Oregon* had belonged to the Guion Line prior to being sold to Cunard. Positive proof of the wreck's identity had been made.

Bottles recovered from shipwrecks may also help to determine the approximate time period a ship sank. The ability to identify bottles made by hand, either free-blown or mold-blown, or manufactured by automatic bottle production machines is an aid in dating them. Uneven glass thickness and bubbles within the glass often indicates an old bottle. Determining the approximate date of bottles usually depends on knowledge of manufacturing methods and types of bottles, based on their contents and the periods during which specific types were used. The following clues may help you determine the age of a bottle and possibly the approximate date of the ship's demise. However, bottles on a wreck site may have been discarded there by fishermen, and may be misleading.

Hand-blown Bottles: Can be either free-blown or mold-blown. Bubbles are common because the glassblower collected the molten glass from the top of the vat with his blowpipe, and bubbles are always present at the top of any boiling mass.

Free-blown Bottles: Produced until about 1860. The glassblower used puffs of air and various turnings and twirlings to produce a unique type of bottle. This type is never perfect in symmetry, and no two are identical. Naturally, there are no mold marks.

Pontil Bottles: Free-blown bottles from 1618 to 1866. When the body of a bottle was blown, the glassblower had his assistant dip the end of a pontil rod into molten glass. This molten glass was then fused to the bottom of the bottle, which was still hot. The glassblower then freed his blowpipe and made final touches to the neck and lip of the still red hot bottle. When finished, a sharp tap separated the bottle from the pontil rod. The resulting rough scar (pontil mark) is a circle of sharp, jagged glass that adhered to the bottom of the bottle.

Some pontil marks were ground smooth with iron oxide or powdered iron. Such oxidized deposits, called iron pontils, are often found on the bases of bottles produced in the 1850s.

Mold-blown Bottles: Open and closed molds were developed after invention of the blowpipe, about 100 B.C. However, it was the development of hinged brass molds in the 17th century and hinged iron molds in the 18th century that allowed gradual replacement of free-blown bottles in Europe. In America, molds were not commonly used before the 19th century.

To produce a mold-blown bottle, the glassblower lowered his blowpipe, with a red hot blob of glass on the end, into the open mold, then blew steadily until the glass assumed the shape of the mold.

When a bottle is made in a mold, seam marks remain. The raised lines or ridges are left on the exterior surface when the hot glass is forced out the interstices between parts of the mold. The marks identify the type of mold used in the bottle's manufacture. Knowing the time periods from which the various molds (two-piece, three-piece, paste, etc.) were used provides a basis for the approximate dating of bottles. One made in a three-piece mold would have three seams. Three-piece molds were in use from 1806 to 1889. Late 19th century bottles with no seams were usually European in origin and were spun-molded (turned in a greased mold during production) to prevent seam formation. However, close inspection of the bottles reveals horizontal striations on the glass surface.

Sheared Lip: The glassblower's assistant cut the blown bottle free from the blowpipe with a pair of shears. There is no ring, band, or collar on this type of bottle. The visual appearance of the lip is aptly described as "sheared lip." The sheared lip indicates a bottle that was probably blown between 1800 and 1830.

Laid on Ring Lip: During the 1840s glassblowers attached a ring of glass to the top of the sheared lip. The "laid on ring" is usually obvious.

Raised Letters: Bottles embossed with raised letters were produced from 1790 to date.

Black Glass: Due to impurities in the glass mix, some early (approximately 1700-1880) blown bottles appear black or dark olive green in color.

Capping Devices: The "closed mold" era improved lips to the point that capping devices were developed in the 1870s. The "crown cap" was invented by William Painter in 1895. Crown caps are still one of the most frequently used forms of drink type bottle closures. A screw top bottle was probably made by an automatic bottle production machine.

Michael J. Owens invented the automatic bottle making machine in 1903. Bottles produced by automatic machines usually have a mold line running from the base through the lip. If mold marks are not present, the bottle is probably free-blown.

There is an abundance of reference material to help determine the approximate date a bottle was manufactured. One source is *The Illustrated Guide to Collecting Bottles* by Cecil Munsey. Trademarks, brand names, and other marks and symbols of identifica-

Photo by Brian Skerry

This beautiful clock from the freighter **Trojan,** *recovered by Bob Cartier, bore the vessel's original name,* **Orion.**

tion found on bottles are datum points in determining the age of a bottle. An excellent source for the identification of such marks is *Bottle Makers and Their Marks* by Julian Harrison Toulouse. The book includes bottle identification marks by bottle makers from the mid-1st Century A.D., to 1970.

Other pieces of the ship may also contribute to her identity. Boiler gauges or a clock might actually have the vessel's name embossed on the face or perhaps the manufacturer may have records helpful in identification. Bridge equipment, such as a telegraph or a binnacle, may equally have markings. Capstans are often fitted with brass covers fully identifying the ship by name. Sound research, a careful eye and a bit of luck might even reveal the location of a builders plaque, which will unequivocally answer the question once and for all.

In the end, the identity of nationality, period, and size of a ship may be established from the artifacts recovered. This evidence can be compared with records of known shipwrecks for the particular area in which the wreck is located. Artifacts will present evidence, but the whole complex of clues to the ship's identity should be considered before conclusions are drawn.

Jon Hulburt surfaces with treasures from the wreck of the **Andrea Doria**.

Chapter 10

Artifacts

One of the greatest aspects of wreck diving is the thrill of discovery. Discovering a wreck is perhaps the ultimate thrill, but finding a prized artifact is a close second. Returning home with a nautical souvenir that you found and recovered is a feeling unlike any other. An artifact by definition is an object made by man, so just about anything brought up from a wreck qualifies. The word actually comes from the Latin *arte factum*, meaning something made with skill.

Always remember, one man's trash is another man's treasure. Each wreck has potentially different artifacts waiting to be discovered. Some divers favor china or dinnerware while others are only interested in brass. Some find only personal effects meaningful and others are driven by only by one-of-a-kind finds, like a ship's bell. Whatever your taste, there is an ocean full of opportunity waiting.

How to Get Them

You do not have to find a virgin wreck to find artifacts. Very few, if any wrecks, have been picked clean of recoverable objects. All that is necessary is careful observation. Green areas of patina

Dinnerware, such as these dishes on the wreck of the steamer **Metis** off the coast of Connecticut, is an artifact prized by many divers.

Tom Packer and Steve Gatto with the find of a lifetime— the helm and stand recovered from the freighter **Ethel C**.

on a wreck indicate non-ferrous metals: copper, brass and bronze. Sea-weeds, barnacles, mus-sels, sea anemones, and other marine organisms often cover and obscure artifacts. Many marine or-ganisms need a solid sub-strate for attachment. On shallow wrecks, artifacts completely buried by sand may be found by checking under tufts of seaweed.

A basic search tech-nique for artifacts, espe-cially on older wrecks, is to find an undisturbed area of sand immediately to the side of the wreck. In deeper water, either side will do; in shallow water, the side closest to land may be more produc-tive. If there is a surge, anchor to the wreck with one hand and fan the sand with the other. If there is a current, fan in the direction of the flowing water. The sand will be carried away with the current with-out reducing visibility in the immediate area. Continuous fanning will produce a hole and may expose artifacts. Patience is the key. You may have to remove a couple of feet of sand to find something. If a portion of an object appears, do not rush to pull it out. Carefully continue to fan the sand away until the artifact is completely exposed. In trying to pull objects free of the sand, delicate items such as cup handles and ornamental structures may be broken. In addition, the artifact may be oxidized to an underlying piece of wreckage.

Inside a wreck, such as the German submarine *U-853*, which lies in 130 feet of water off Block Island, Rhode Island, there may be a layer of loose sediment several feet deep. Fanning would quickly destroy visibility. Carefully probing with your hand will disturb less sediment, but even that will reduce visibility to zero after a period of time. At that point, not only is recovery of artifacts done by feel alone, so is exiting the wreck. Working in zero visibility requires care when placing objects in a net bag. Divers often surface and eagerly look into their net bag for the artifact they thought they had recovered, only to find the bag empty because they had missed the bag's opening and left their find inside the wreck.

Henry Keatts recovered artifacts from the *Andrea Doria*'s first-class china area that were simply resting on top of the sediment. The previous dive team had missed bagging them while working in zero visibility.

Another technique for artifact recovery is to look under pieces of wreckage. Many divers only look straight down into openings but wrecks flatten out as they break up; artifacts may be on ledges of wreckage. Remember, look to the sides in case there are layers of wreckage.

Research is often the key to finding artifacts. Knowing where to find the galley and dining saloon will produce more crystal and china than swimming aimlessly around or through a wreck. Knowing that a porthole is attached on the *inside* of the ship will also save time.

In addition to those already mentioned, there are other techniques that can be used to increase one's odds of surfacing with a prize. The first of these is learning to use the "wreck diver's eye." The wreck diver's eye is nothing more than the ability to see things on the wreck. Nature almost never produces perfectly straight, sharp or angled objects, as humans do using tools, so it is important to look for shapes that are a little too perfect. Even when covered with marine growth, the shapes can usually be discerned by a careful eye. Sometimes, in fact, marine growth can actually lead you to an artifact. Certain marine organisms will actually absorb metallic salts from an object to which they are attached. On the

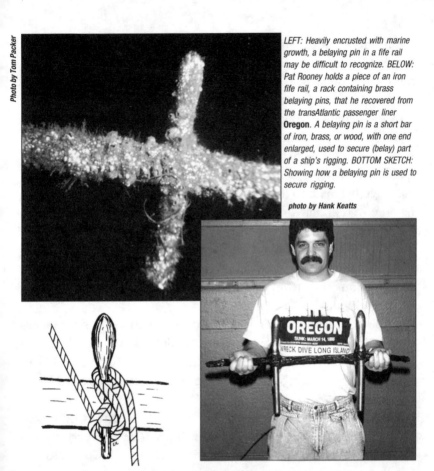

LEFT: Heavily encrusted with marine growth, a belaying pin in a fife rail may be difficult to recognize. BELOW: Pat Rooney holds a piece of an iron fife rail, a rack containing brass belaying pins, that he recovered from the transAtlantic passenger liner **Oregon**. A belaying pin is a short bar of iron, brass, or wood, with one end enlarged, used to secure (belay) part of a ship's rigging. BOTTOM SKETCH: Showing how a belaying pin is used to secure rigging.

photo by Hank Keatts

wreck of the steamship *Oregon* sunk off Long Island, New York, for instance, some anemones found on top of the massive engine were green in color, while surrounding anemones were not. Removal of the anemones yielded brass valves beneath. The animals had absorbed the salts from the brass, giving them a green color. The next step in this process, which is actually an extension of the first, is use of your imagination. Since many artifacts are partially buried, when something catches your eye, you have to try to imagine what the rest of it might look like or what it might have been used for. This is when knowledge of vessel types and ship construction is especially useful. Using this technique, even wrong guesses will produce some nice finds and no one ever has to know that what you found was not what you were looking for. Once you believe that you have found something worthwhile, you should determine what it is made of. Artifacts made of glass, pottery or even wood are easy enough to identify, but determining the type of metal an artifact is made of involves a third step—"feel." When struck with a hammer, iron objects have a soft, almost mushy feel, very different from the solid, hard feel that brass or bronze offer. Unless you have something really special, most iron or steel artifacts that have been underwater for a long period of time are not worth the effort of bringing to the surface. Brass, copper or bronze are more noble, more easily conserved and usually yield more interesting artifacts. Tapping potential artifacts with a hammer before removing them may reduce wasted effort on unwanted pieces. By going slowly, being alert and using these steps, your artifact to dive ratio should increase.

Tools

Unless you are fortunate enough to find artifacts "just lying there," some time will need to be spent in removing them. To accomplish this, tools will be needed. Since each artifact is unique in its manufacture, how it is attached, and how it is encrusted, each piece must be evaluated as to its removal. Specific tools may be

Photo by Bill Carter, Jr.

Basic wreck tools include a mason's chipping hammer, chisel, and tool bag.

To prevent loss of tools used underwater, they should be fitted with brass clips or lanyards.

required to complete the job and we cannot list every tool that might be used by wreck divers. If you are looking for artifacts, a good tool to bring along is a mason's chipping hammer. Not too large or heavy, the hammer can be used to test the "feel" of potential artifacts as well as to remove many smaller items. A crowbar is also quite useful and can be carried on the back of your tanks, like an ascent line, only to be taken off when needed. Smaller tools such as screwdrivers, wrenches or hacksaws can be carried in a bag without fear of losing them. Many divers opt for the mesh "bug" bag, which is also large enough to place many artifacts into afterwards. Inside the bag, you may want to keep a screw top jar which can be used to hold small pieces that would otherwise slip through the mesh openings. The only drawback to these bags is that the mesh material catches very easily on wreckage. If using one, make sure to keep it from dragging on the wreck. The alternative is to use a smaller wreck tool bag, designed specifically for carrying tools on wrecks. Generally made from a heavy nylon or codura material with brass grommets at the bottom, these little bags are quite rugged and are easily carried, although not large enough to hold much in the way of artifacts. Any tool that you plan to use for wreck diving should be fitted with a brass clip and/or lanyard to further prevent loss.

Once the artifact has been removed, you will need to decide how to get it back to the boat. If it is too large or heavy to be carried, another means will be needed. Perhaps the most common method of bringing heavy artifacts to the light of day is the use of a lift bag. A line tied to the lift bag should be securely tied to the artifact and the bag inflated. Be especially careful not to over inflate the lift bag. Put just enough air in the bag to get it started, helping it along with your hands. Although the flexible walls of the lift bag will accommodate the increase in pressure as the bag rises, too much air will cause the bag to clear the surface and dump with potential loss of the artifact. One way to prevent this loss, even if the bag should dump, is to tie the end of your ascent line to the artifact as well, be-

Photo by Brian Skerry

A large bronze window from the wreck of the passenger liner **Proteus,** *off Cape Hatteras, North Carolina, was brought to the surface with the use of a lift bag.*

fore sending the bag skyward. When it reaches the surface, cut the line and tie it to the wreck. This way if the artifact should fall back to the bottom, it can be retrieved by finding your line and following it to the artifact.

Another method of bringing up artifacts is to use a marker and retrieval buoy. This system can be made from a 1/4" polypropylene line with a bolt snap on one end and a small float on the other. Properly coiled, a diver can carry several of these buoys to a wreck site. To use, the bolt snap is attached to the artifact, the buoy released and forgotten until the diver completes his or her dive. Upon returning to the boat, the diver can retrieve the artifact by hauling up the line. This

Photo by Bill Carter, Jr.

A marker and retrieval buoy can be used to mark smaller artifacts which can later be pulled up to the dive boat.

Photo by Marcia Skerry

Brian Skerry displays the binnacle stand after recovery. INSET: This 18th century, bronze, dolphin-based binnacle stand from the wreck of a schooner barge. **Inset photo of binnacle underwater by Brian Skerry**

system is best used on shallower wrecks since it would be impractical to coil hundreds of feet of line and carry it on a D-ring. On shallower wrecks, and with artifacts weighing less than 100 pounds, this system will work extremely well.

The most important point with regard to artifact recovery is conservation. The techniques of restoration and conservation require expertise and commitments of time, patience, and money. If you are not certain that you want the artifact, or if you lack the expertise, time, or money to conserve it, do not disturb the historical object. Mistakes in handling or improper attempts at conservation may lead to irreversible damage. Before an archaeologist would remove an artifact, he or she would map the wreck and document it with photos.

Conservation of Artifacts

Many divers feel that sunken ships and their artifacts should be left as they were found for others to dive and enjoy as long as they last. Others believe that a wreck's artifacts should be recovered before they are lost to the ravages of the sea. This debate has raged for many years and will no doubt continue for many to come.

Unfortunately, thousands of artifacts from shipwrecks that are of interest to historians and archaeologists have been allowed to disintegrate by sport divers. Often it was not intentional, but rather it was owing to a lack of information which could have prevented the loss. Any diver who is uncertain of the correct procedure for conserving an artifact should *keep it wet and seek professional assistance.*

Recovered artifacts deteriorate in varying degrees; the purpose of this section is to acquaint the diver with various methods of conserving those historical objects for posterity. Artifacts that have been buried deep under sediment will usually be recovered in excellent condition. However, exposed artifacts that have deteriorated to such a degree that they cannot be restored should be left in place. All that should be taken is photographs.

Field Preparation

Of utmost importance, the artifact should be protected immediately after surfacing. When objects are removed from the water,

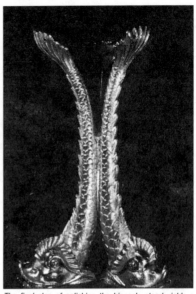

Dolphin-based binnacle stand during acid treatment in child's wading pool.

The final step of polishing the binnacle stand yields a mirror-like image.

they are exposed to a new environment and may deteriorate quickly. Too often, a recovered object is left on the deck of a boat in direct sunlight and exposed to air. It should be kept wet, preferably in a plastic bucket of water, or a water-filled cooler. The surrounding water will prevent exposure to air and protect against mechanical damage. Beach towels and paper towels may be used as packing.

Objects encrusted with coral should be kept in salt water. After the encrustation is removed, they may be stored in freshwater. Small artifacts may be transported in water-filled Ziploc® plastic bags. Large objects such as cannon may be wrapped in wet cloth or paper towels, or Saran Wrap®.

Conservation

Archaeologists refer to the artifact preservation process as "conservation." It is the term we will use throughout this volume. The first step is to clean off the material that detracts from the artifact's appearance (mud, etc.). The calcareous secretions of barnacles and tube worms can be left as a reminder that the artifact came from the sea. However, they can be easily removed from metal by an overnight soak in a weak solution of muriatic acid or a strong detergent and laundry-bleach solution. *All of the chemicals and chemical baths listed in this section should be kept out of reach of children and disposed of responsibly.* Also, it is wise to wear a respirator and safety goggles when handling solvents or acids. Do not smoke in the presence of flammable or volatile solutions.

A wooden serving mallet can be dehydrated with use of denatured alcohol.

*Part of a wooden trunnel and the remains of a plank from the U.S.S. **Ohio** that was conserved with turpentine and boiled linseed oil. The artifact had been in salt water for 100 years.*

Artifacts that have been submerged in salt water must be soaked in successive baths of freshwater, to remove the salts, for at least three months, the longer the better. The length of time depends upon the size of the object, the type of wood and the length of

*Copper coins recovered from the 1809 wreck of the East Indiaman **Admiral Gardner**. The coin on the right was submerged in a bath of distilled white vinegar (a dilute solution of acetic acid) for 24 hours. Then it was cleaned with a tooth brush and polished with a thick paste made from baking soda and water.*

time it was underwater. Change the water at least once a week, preferably every day. Chlorine is often present in tap water, so distilled water is better if it is available. Small objects may be placed in the holding tank of a toilet where the water is replaced with each flushing. However, that technique should not be followed if a cleaning agent for the toilet's bowl is kept within the holding tank. Also, determine that the artifact does not interfere with the toilet's working mechanism. A child's wading pool or an old bath

Artifact Recovery & Treatment Record

Shipwreck _____

Location _____ Artifact # ____

Date of Recovery _____ (Dive Log entry)_____

Description of Artifact: _____

_____

Condition of Artifact:_____

Field Prepartion of Artifact: _____

Dates of Treatment Record: _____

Treatment Summary: _____

tub, outside the home, may be used for large items. A string attached to the tub's plug allows the water to be emptied periodically without having to submerge your hand into the foul water. Large objects may require fabrication of holding tanks lined with polyester resin or PVC pool liners. Another method for large objects such as wooden ship's timbers or cannon is to place them in a freshwater pond or stream. The running water of a stream will carry away the salts as they are leached from the artifact. With that method, the object may be left submerged for a shorter period of time.

All aspects of conservation treatments should be recorded for future reference, especially if the artifact's restoration is not satisfactory. An "Artifact Recovery Sheet and Treatment Record"can be devised, typed and then photocopied to record information. Photographs of the artifact should be taken before and after treatment. Ideally photographs should also be taken of the object on the wreck before its recovery.

Wood

After soaking wood in fresh water, it must be dehydrated before conservation. Dehydration is accomplished by immersing the wood in three successive baths of denatured ethyl or wood alcohol, each bath at least one week. The first bath should be 40% alcohol and 60% water, the second 60% alcohol, and the third 100% alcohol. After dehydration, one of several procedures may be followed for conservation.

One method is to place the wood in two successive baths of xylene. The first bath requires one week. Xylene is a flammable isomeric hydrocarbon; do not use the solution near a flame, and keep the solution containing the artifact in a tightly sealed container. When the wood is in the second bath of xylene, paraffin (a flammable, waxy, solid hydrocarbon mixture) chips should be added until a saturated solution of paraffin is obtained. You will recognize saturation when paraffin becomes recrystallized around the edges of the solution. Leave the wood in the saturated solution for approximately four weeks. When the wood is removed, allow the xylene to evaporate from it. Remember, xylene is flammable. After evaporation, there will be a coat of small crystals of paraffin left on the surface. A gentle brushing will remove them. The advantage of this technique is that the artifact should retain its original shape because paraffin has replaced the water within the wood.

A faster method of conservation after dehydration is to slowly dry the object, and then place it in a one-to-one solution of turpentine (a volatile solution) and boiled linseed oil for approximately two weeks. The solution leaves the wood with a more natural look. However, sometimes flat pieces of wood will warp as they dry. The procedure will leave a distinctive odor in the wood which will dissipate after a period of time.

Nonferrous Metals
Gold and Silver

Oxidation occurs with varying rates in different metals. Gold is one of the most corrosion-resistant metals and usually requires no treatment. However, there may be calcareous encrustations, and some alloys of gold tarnish, due to close underwater association with other metals. The calcareous material may be removed, leaving the gold with a bright finish by soaking it in a 10% solution of nitric acid (10 parts acid to 90 parts water). Always add acid to water never water to acid.

A silver artifact submerged in salt water may be completely converted to silver sulfide and no attempt at restoration should be made.

Silver artifacts with a black surface corrosion may have a core of sound metal; they should be cleaned in an electrolytic bath. Superficial black corrosion may be removed by submergence in a 15% ammonium hydroxide solution. Both gold and silver should be run through successive freshwater baths. Silver objects may be polished with a mild abrasive paste of baking soda and water, or a commercial polish. The surface grease and abrasive may be cleaned with alcohol. Several coats of an acrylic plastic (Krylon® Crystal Clear) may be applied by spray or brush to retain the luster.

Copper, Brass and Bronze

Gold and silver are seldom found on shipwrecks but other non-ferrous metals such as copper, brass, and bronze abound in fastenings, sheathing, fittings, and instruments. Copper and its alloys resist the corrosive effect of seawater.

Remove calcareous growth or oxidized conglomerate from the metal by tapping it gently with a rubber hammer or a piece of wood such as a 2 x 4. If a metal hammer is used, be careful not to damage the surface of the metal. Use safety goggles to protect your eyes from flying pieces of encrustation. If the growth is difficult to remove, place the object in a bath of muriatic acid (one part acid to six parts water) for 24 hours. Muriatic acid is a 20% solution of hydrochloric acid that may be purchased at hardware stores or swimming pool supply stores. When diluting acids always add acid to water never water to acid. Strong acid solutions may splash or explode if water is added to them.

Small bubbles forming on the surface of the artifact indicates the acid is dissolving the calcium carbonates. If the bubbles stop forming and the encrustation remains, discard the old acid solution and prepare a fresh one. If the artifact is left in the acid too long, ferric oxides will form, causing a permanent discoloration of the metal. Strong acid solutions may cause pitting on the surface of the artifact. The acid bath should be in a glass or plastic container covered by a lid in a well ventilated room, or preferably outside. A plastic trash can may be used for large objects. Rubber gloves should be worn to protect the skin from irritation when handling artifacts that have been in the acid bath. When the encrustation feels like paste, remove the artifact from the acid bath and rinse it in fresh water, then scrub it with a wire brush. Use safety goggles while brushing the object. Place the artifact in a freshwater bath for at least 24 hours to remove the acid from the metal. Following the last bath, a fine wire brush or an electric drill may be used to restore the original color. A cloth buffing wheel with jeweler's rouge (a polishing compound) should then be used to buff the surface. Future polishing can be eliminated by sealing the metal with a clear polyurethane varnish or acrylic plastic spray or paint. The sealing process requires several coats, especially if a spray is used.

The acid bath will remove the green patina from these artifacts. Patina (verdigris) is the result of oxidation, but does not harm the underlying metal. Some divers prefer to leave the patina, finding it more attractive than a highly polished natural finish.

Objects too large for acid baths may be sandblasted to remove their encrustations. Fine sand should be used; coarse sand will pit the surface metal.

Wooden ships were often sheathed with copper plating so the leaching copper salts would kill the shipworms before they could do damage. By 1850, shipbuilders were using brass spikes as well as tree nails (wooden pegs) to attach planking to the ribs of warships and better-made merchant vessels. As sunken ships lie on the bottom, the copper in the brass continues to leach out saving the immediately adjoining wood from shipworms and other wood boring organisms. The wood becomes mineralized and hard in texture. Often the impregnated wood is all that remains of a ship's plank or timber. Combinations of wood and metal pose special conservation problems. Since each type of material may require different treatment, you may want to separate the materials. If that is not possible, or you prefer not to do so, you must compromise on the treatment you use.

Scattered ammunition cannisters in one of the U.S.S **San Diego**'s many magazines. Each cannister contains a bag of gunpowder for the armored cruiser's six-inch guns.

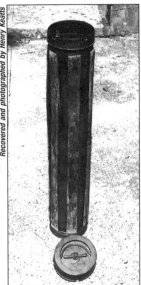

An ammunition cannister from the **San Diego**. The artifact is composed of a copper container with oak slats and a bronze lid. After successive freshwater baths the wood slats were covered with masking tape and the copper container was sandblasted and sprayed with three coats of clear acrylic plastic. The lid was cleaned with muriatic acid before being coated with clear acrylic plastic.

Pewter and Lead

Pewter and lead undergo little deterioration in salt water. Brushing and successive freshwater baths to remove salts is usually sufficient treatment for those materials. The original luster of pewter may be restored by polishing with a paste of baking soda and water or a commercial pewter polish. Clear polyurethane varnish or acrylic sprays may be applied to retain the luster. Lead oxide coatings on lead artifacts may be removed by submergence in a 10% solution of acetic acid prior to soaking them in freshwater baths.

Ferrous Metals

Ferrous metals include iron, wrought iron, and steel. Artifacts recovered from freshwater require minimal treatment compared to those found in salt water. Objects from freshwater may only have

*A cannon recovered from the British warship **Culloden** is on display in the East Hampton Town (Long Island) Marine Museum. Conservation of the cannon was only partially successful. Exterior sections separated and repairs were made with auto body putty (note the lighter colored area on the right).*

a thin surface layer of oxidation while those recovered from the ocean may have oxidation ranging from superficial flaking to deep pits and shards.

Iron artifacts from salt water provide some of the most difficult problems for conservation, which is generally less successful. Iron objects submerged in salt water usually convert to iron oxide. In some instances, nothing will remain of the original artifact other than a hollow form of iron oxide or coral-encrusted conglomerate. The object may be used as a mold to produce a replica of the original artifact, or X-ray photography may be used to reveal the original form and record it, but it will disintegrate quickly if exposed to air.

Freshwater artifacts with little oxidation may be cleaned with a wire brush or steel wool. Air dry and remove any light rust, then apply several coats of polyurethane, acrylic plastics, or lacquers. Some prefer to coat the artifact with several layers of a flat black rust-preventing paint, such as Rustoleum®, rather than polyurethane as a final step. The flat paint leaves a dull, non-wet appearance. If beads of rust appear on the surface of the paint, carefully brush them off and apply polyurethane.

Objects recovered from salt water will usually have a thick layer of oxidation or encrustation. In addition, the metal is impregnated with salt and water that will cause it to swell, crack, and flake away. To prevent that happening, the salt and water must be removed from the artifact, and the metal must be protected from moisture in the air.

The first step in conservation is to remove encrustations. Large objects should be tapped gently with a piece of wood (a 2 x 4) or, if necessary, with a hammer. Never strike a glancing blow because it often damages the iron. Strike directly at the artifact. Small objects may be submerged in a bath of 10% nitric acid to remove thin layers of calcareous encrustations. Freshwater baths should follow, as described for ferrous metals above. Then, treatment in an electrolytic bath, or with a 50% ethylene glycol (antifreeze) solution will often stabilize the metal.

Electrolytic Bath

If an iron object has a substantial solid core beneath the encrustation, it may be treated in an electrolytic bath, where the iron is, to some extent, reconstituted with ions from a sacrificial metal. Use a plastic or glass container filled with enough 5% baking soda solution (95 parts water, preferably distilled water, and five parts baking soda) to completely cover the artifact. The solution is the electrolyte. A steel rod or plate, preferably stainless steel, may be used as an anode (positive pole). Place the steel rod so that part of it extends above the surface of the solution. Attach the positive wire of a power supply to it, keeping the point of connection out of the solution. The artifact is made the cathode (negative pole) by wrapping it with steel wire, preferably stainless steel. If the artifact is encrusted, remove part of the encrustation to assure contact between the wire and the metal within. Attach the negative wire of the power supply to the end of the artifact wire that extends above the solution. A direct current may be applied by using a six and/or 12 volt battery charger. Three amps is sufficient for even large objects such as a cannon. Low amperage is important for small artifacts to avoid damage to the metal. One-half amp is sufficient for delicate items.

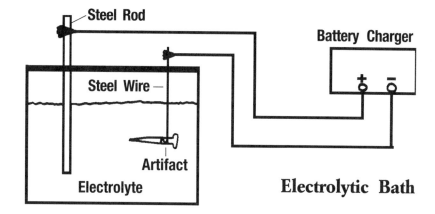

Electrolytic Bath

Bubbles appearing at both poles indicate that the reaction is taking place. If bubbles do not appear, check the connections. The solution will become discolored and should be occasionally changed and the anode (steel rod or plate) washed. In a few days the artifact will slowly begin to take its original shape.

Do not leave the artifact in the solution when the power supply is turned off. If you do, the object will plate. Experimentation with old pieces of iron is recommended to avoid irreparable damage to irreplaceable artifacts.

Solutions other than baking soda, may be used as an electrolyte, 5% lye or 5% sodium nitrate for example. The paper by Don Hamilton, listed at the end of this section, contains designs of various electrolytic systems. After electrolysis, iron objects must be boiled to remove the electrolyte.

Ethylene Glycol

After treatment in freshwater, an iron object may then be soaked in ethylene glycol to replace the water. This agent inhibits rust and is compatible with the protective coating of fiberglass resin that is applied after drying. The resin should be catalyzed lightly to allow the mixture to soak in before hardening. The resin leaves a glossy, wet appearance.

If an artifact is small, ethylene glycol or fiberglass resin may not be needed. After removing the object from freshwater, it is allowed to dry slowly, then painted with several coats of Rustoleum® flat black paint.

Glass and Ceramics

Glass and ceramic items from shipwrecks may range from crated cargo to dining room china. Those artifacts are usually quite stable and require little treatment other than cleaning with dilute muriatic acid followed by freshwater baths. Do not use acid on unglazed artifacts.

The primary problem with objects recovered from salt water is the soluble salts that probably have been absorbed. Upon drying, the salts migrate to the surface and crystallize, often exerting enough pressure to disrupt the surface and glazes. The artifacts should be submerged in successive freshwater baths. If the surface begins to flake after drying, spray the object with clear polyurethane varnish or acrylic plastic.

If ink or paint decorative patterns and insignias are on top of the glaze, an

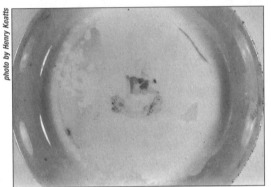

photo by Henry Keatts

*A piece of dinnerware recovered from the White Star Line's **Republic**, which sank in 1909. The steamship line's insignia was imprinted after glazing and some of the paint has dissolved.*

Recovered and photographed by Henry Keatts

*The dish on the left is from Cunard Line's the **Oregon**, which sank in 1886. The other dish is a piece of First-Class china from the **Andrea Doria**, which sank in 1956. In both cases the imprints were made prior to glazing.*

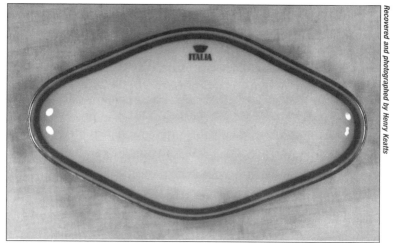

*A First-Class condiment dish from the **Andrea Doria** has very delicate gold leaf trim around the outer edge that is easiily damaged during the cleaning process.*

acid bath may remove it. Gold leaf trim is always on top of the glaze and is very delicate; it should not be scrubbed or placed in acid baths. Oxide or carbonate stains may be removed by carefully using cotton swabs dipped into vinegar or bleach. Do not let the solution run onto gold leaf or paint trim, and wash the object well with freshwater.

Bottles predating 1750, after cleaning and before drying, must be placed in a bath of wood or denatured ethyl alcohol to remove the water. Then they should be air-dried for a short period, before several layers of clear spray polyurethane are applied.

Sediment inside a bottle may be loosened by probing carefully with a tool such as a wooden dowel. More resistant deposits may require a metal probe such as an icepick or wire coat hanger. Wash the loosened material out of the bottle with water. A bottle brush and a glass detergent may be used to clean the interior. Bottles with the original contents intact are often unique and very difficult to preserve without losing their contents.

Earthenware artifacts are often damaged by salt crystals and should be submerged in successive freshwater baths to leach out the salts. Surface encrustations should be removed by scraping or brushing. Acid treatment may damage unglazed objects. Soaking the artifacts in a detergent may help loosen encrusted dirt.

Unglazed clay artifacts such as smoking pipes should not be cleaned of calcareous deposits. After submergence in freshwater baths allow the object to air-dry. The artifact will shrink slightly and the encrustations will fall off. Stains may then be removed with a mild detergent and a soft toothbrush.

Leather

After freshwater baths, leather must be dehydrated in successive alcohol baths, then treated in xylene and paraffin (see wood earlier in this chapter).

Paper

Surprisingly, paper deeply buried in sediment may survive for a long period on a wreck. Log books and charts in remarkably good condition have been recovered from sunken German U-boats after almost 50 years under water. However, paper will usually disintegrate upon drying if the proper conservation treatment is not followed. If the paper artifact is not too fragile, it should be placed in successive freshwater baths. After the baths, paper can be stored frozen in Ziploc® bags in a frost-free freezer. If the artifact is fragile, place it directly into the freezer. Next the paper may be soaked in 1% methyl cellulose (Methocel) for five days. Then remove the artifact and spread it between two sheets of Mylar® (thin strong polyester film).

Disclaimer

This section is intended only as an introduction to the conservation of artifacts. Additional information may be obtained from numerous archaeological journals and conservation books. Further reading and experience with some of the introductory methods may lead a diver to modify the procedures that have been described.

Further Reading

Clarke, Richard, and Susan M. Blackshaw (editors). **Conservation of Iron, Maritime Monographs and Reports 53**. National Maritime Museum, Greenwich, England, 1982.

Davison, Sandra. **The Conservation of Glass**. Butterworths, London, England, 1987.

Florida Division of Historical Resources. **Cleaning and Stabilizing Metal Artifacts by Means of Electrolysis and Protective Coatings.** Tallahassee, Florida.

Hamilton, Don L. **Conservation of Metal Objects from Underwater Sites: A Study in Methods. Texas Memorial Museum Miscellaneous Papers 4**. Austin, Texas, 1976.

Lane, Hannah. **"Some Comparisons of Lead Conservation Methods, Including Consolidative Reduction." Conservation and Restoration of Metals, Proceedings of the Edinburgh Symposium,** Edinburgh, Scotland.

Lawson, Eric. **"In Between: The Care of Artifacts from the Seabed to the Conservation Laboratory and Some Reasons Why It is Necessary."** Beneath the Waters of Time: The **Proceedings of the Ninth Conference on Underwater Archaeology, Texas Antiquities Committee Publication No. 6**, pp. 69-91. Austin, Texas, 1978.

Macleod, Ian. **"Conservation of Corroded Copper Alloys: A Comparison of New and Traditional Methods for Removing Chloride Ions." Studies in Conservation 32**, pp. 25-40, 1987.

Merk, Linda. **"A Study of Reagents Used in the Stripping of Bronzes." Studies in Conservation 23**, pp. 15-22, 1978.

Muhlethaler, Bruno. **"Conservation of Waterlogged Wood and Wet Leather."** ICOM Travaux et Publications XI, Editions Eyrolles, Paris, France.

Oddy, W. Andrew. (editor) **"Problems in the Conservation of Waterlogged Wood" Maritime Monographs and Reports 16.** National Maritime Museum, Greenwich, England, 1975.

Olive, John, and Colin Pearson. **"The Conservation of Ceramics from Marine Archaeological Sources" Conservation in Archaeology and the Applied Arts, Proceedings of the 1975 Stockholm Congress**, pp. 63-8, **International Institute for Conservation of Historic and Artistic Works**, London, England, 1975.

Pearson, Colin. **Conservation of Marine Archaeological Objects**. Butterworths, 1987.

Robinson, Wendy. **First Aid for Marine Finds, Handbook in Maritime Archaeology No. 2,** National Maritime Museum, Greenwich, England, 1981,

Singley, Katherine. **The Conservation of Archaeological Artifacts From Freshwater Environments.** Lake Michigan Maritime Museum, South Haven, Michigan, 1988.

Bachmann, Konstanze. (editor), **Conservation Concerns**. Washington, DC, Smithsonian Institution Press, © 1992.

Koop, Stephen. **"The Use of Acryloid B-72 in the Treatment of Archaeological Ceramics: Minimal Intervention"** Mat. Res. Soc. Symp. Proc. Vol 185:591-596, 1991.

Leigh, David. **First Aid for Finds.** Rescue and Department of Archaeology, University of Southampton Great Britain, 1978.

Oddy, Andrew. **The Art of the Conservator.** Pennsylvania, Smithsonian Institution Press, 1992.

Pearson, Colin. **Conservation of Marine Archaeological Objects.** London, Butterworths, 1987.

Sease, Catherine. **A Conservation Manual for the Field Archaeologist.** Regents of the University of California, 1987.

Displaying Artifacts

Once the artifact has been conserved, you will want to proudly display it. Certainly, you can simply place the artifact in plain sight to be admired, but there are more creative ways to display your find. The following photographs are examples of how some divers have chosen to do just that.

Artifact Controversy

The recovering of items from sunken ships is hardly anything new. Since the very first time a ship sank, people have been trying to bring back from the deep what was lost. The controversy surrounding shipwrecks and artifact recovery stems from two primary areas. The first is the question of ownership and salvage rights. The second area of controversy revolves around the historical significance of a wreck and the fear that valuable information may be lost in the salvage process.

This lamp made from a deadeye shows one of the creative ways artifacts can be displayed.

In spite of these very valid concerns, time has shown us that wreck diving has fostered significant archaeological and historical research. Wreck divers have also collected rare artifacts from vessels that have rested at the bottom of the sea for decades, even centuries. The recovery, identification, dating and conservation of these historical objects have attracted both amateur and professional archaeologists. A great deal has been gained by wreck divers who have dedicated enormous amounts of time and money in pursuit of our sunken past.

Proponents of forbidding divers from taking anything from shipwrecks argue that divers are destroying these submerged cultural resources. In reality, wrecks that lie in the ocean are naturally being destroyed at a steady rate. The sea is cruel to all that does not belong in it.

A common-place artifact, such as this porthole, can be transformed into a functional piece of nautical decor.

Even the sturdiest steel hulls cannot withstand the combined forces of wind, waves, current and corrosion. If a wreck diver recovers a porthole, conserves it and displays it, more people will benefit than if it were left to dissolve in the sea. The wreck diver should never, however, destroy one part of a wreck in order to recover

A brass porthole rim from the Long Island steamer **Maine** has been transformed into a piece of art by Tom Mulloy with the addition of stained glass. The scene shows the steamer on the rocks at Execution Light where she sank.

another. Additionally, conservation is the moral responsibility of a diver who removes a relic from a sunken ship. As we have discussed, the techniques of restoration and conservation of underwater artifacts are complicated, time-consuming and costly. If you are not committed to dedicating the time necessary to do things right, then do not even begin. Individual sport divers, however, have repeatedly displayed their capability to preserve historical artifacts. Marine artifact exhibits presented at museums, historical societies and dive symposiums by dive clubs have been instrumental in educating the public in the maritime history of this nation.

In defense of those who are concerned about destroying valuable historical information, it must be emphasized that much of mankind's history lies at the bottom of the sea. While most shipwrecks will not contribute much in the way of new information, there are those that will. The accessibility of historic shipwrecks has made them vulnerable to destruction by inexperienced or uninformed sport divers. Once a site is destroyed, the knowledge that might have been gained is lost forever. A diver who discovers a shipwreck of historical significance, within state waters, should inform the appropriate state agency. The diver could request permission to work with state appointed archaeologists. There are well defined techniques by which a site may be systematically explored and by which artifacts from it may be recovered, conserved, and identified. Divers recognizing the importance of sharing such a find are truly bridging the gap between wreck preservationists and artifact collectors. As is true in most debates, nothing is black and white. Not every wreck should be protected; however, there are those that should, even if only long enough to be properly studied. Until now, we have focused our discussion on wrecks that lie in the sea. However, as we have seen throughout this book, there are countless wrecks that rest in freshwater environments. Although wrecks in fresh water will decay, the process takes significantly longer. The argument of rescuing an artifact from the elements loses much of its validity in the context of freshwater wrecks. Divers today can descend the anchor line to view 19th century sailing ships sitting upright on a lake bottom perfectly intact. Taking artifacts from a wreck like this would deprive scores of other divers from the thrill of seeing such a wondrous site. Even non-divers may soon get to experience such thrills as the science of underwater telepresence is perfected. The debate of right and wrong becomes even more clouded as such issues are considered. There are many viewpoints and the debate will likely continue for some time. Rather than debate what should be, let's take a look at what is.

Admiralty Law

Before a wreck diver begins diving a wreck and recovering artifacts, a bit of knowledge regarding the law is helpful. Provided here in layman's terms, is a general overview of admiralty law as it applies to shipwrecks. Most nations have enacted their own laws pertaining to this subject. Our discussion here will be focused on the laws of the United States of America. When diving wrecks in other countries, consult that nation's laws.

Law of Finds vs. Law of Salvage

For centuries, this area of admiralty or maritime law was defined by the complementary theories of Law of Finds and Law of Salvage. Basically, the Law of Finds can be interpreted as "finders keepers, losers weepers." If on the other hand, the wreck was not legally abandoned—that is, it still had a lawful owner—then anything salvaged should be turned over to the admiralty court for an adjudication of a liberal salvage award to be paid from the proceeds of a judicial sale of salvaged property. As with any laws, however, there is the matter of interpretation. Quite often, when a vessel sinks, the owner is paid by an insurance company. The insurance company then becomes the owner of that sunken vessel. The factors that dictate a vessel's abandonment include such things as lapse of time, non-use by owner, and location of the shipwreck. If for instance, the owner of a shipwreck, such as an insurance company, knows the location of the wreck, yet does nothing with it for years, the wreck may be considered abandoned. If, however the location is unknown or the technology to salvage the wreck does not exist, time limit may not be a factor. In the well-documented case of the treasure laden steamship S.S. *Central America*, even though the wreck had been lost since 1857, the insurance company argued that they still owned the wreck since the technology to locate and salvage her in 8,500 feet of water did not exist until present time. Their argument was found to be legitimate; they were entitled to a percentage of the value of the insured shipments of gold recovered by the salvagers (in this case the salvagers received 90% of the value of the salvaged gold).

A contrasting example involves the wreck of the famed luxury liner *Andrea Doria,* which sank less than 40 years ago. Although the exact location was known and the technology to dive and salvage her existed, the insurance owners did nothing to protect their title to the shipwreck in the face of repeated salvage operations. In 1993 veteran wreck diver John Moyer, interested in recovering several artifacts from the wreck, sought a legal injunction to prevent others from interfering with his efforts. He did so based on the premise that the *Andrea Doria* was in fact abandoned and that the law allowed "finders keepers." The injunction was granted and John was given the right to salvage the wreck and keep whatever he recovered.

If a wreck is considered abandoned and title is granted to the finder under the theory of the Law of Finds, the finder must meet certain obligations as well. Title to abandoned property is acquired by a finder who demonstrates "occupancy," which is defined as taking possession of property and exercising dominion or control over it. "Occupancy" has also been defined as occurring where the finder has both intent to acquire specific property and has realized that intent through control of property. In other words, finding an abandoned wreck is not enough to claim ownership. You must be working the site on some type of regular basis to maintain title. Great Britain, for example, follows the year and a day rule, stating that a found wreck returns to abandoned status if left untouched for a year and a day. So, if you find a wreck and can clearly prove that it has been abandoned and that it could have been found and salvaged by others, then perhaps you are the new owner. That is providing that it lies outside state waters!

Abandoned Shipwreck Act

Enacted in 1988, the Abandoned Shipwreck Act says that states have the responsibility for management of a broad range of living and nonliving resources in state waters which includes shipwrecks. Any wreck embedded in state property, which includes all inland waters such as bays, lakes, rivers, and oceans extending to the states seaward boundary, which is three nautical miles, belongs to that state. Regarding the seaward boundary, there are two exceptions, Texas and Florida. Texas which for quite some time remained independent as the Lone Star Republic and Florida which was a Spanish possession, each have seaward boundaries of three marine leagues or nine nautical miles. Individual states then have jurisdiction over wrecks and the removal of artifacts. The right to file a salvage claim on state owned shipwrecks in admiralty court was abolished by the Abandoned Shipwreck Act. A diver must therefore consult state laws before attempting to recover artifacts from state owned abandoned wrecks.

Abandoned Shipwrecks

§ 2101. Findings

The Congress finds that—

(a) States have the responsibility for management of a broad range of living and nonliving resources in State waters and submerged lads; and

(b) included in the range of resources are certain abandoned shipwrecks, which have been deserted and to which the owner has relinquished ownership rights with no retention.

(April 28, 1988, P. L. 100-298, § 2, 102 Stat. 432.)

HISTORY; ANCILLARY LAWS AND DIRECTIVES

Short title:

Act April 28, 1988, P.L. 100-298, § 1, provides: "This Act may be cited as the 'Abandoned Shipwreck Act of 1987'. "

§ 2102. Definitions

For purpose of the is Act [43 USCS §§ 2101 et seq.]

(a) the term "embedded" means firmly affixed in the submerged lands or in coralline formations such that the use of tools of excavation is required in order to move the bottom sediments to gain access to the shipwreck, its cargo, and part thereof;

(b) the term "National Register" means the National Register of Historic Places maintained by the Secretary of the Interior under section 101 of the National Historic Preservation Act (16 U.S.C. 470a)

(c) the terms "public lands", "Indian lands", and "Indian tribe" have the same meaning given the terms in the Archaeological Resource Protection Act of 1979 (16 U.S.C. 470aa-47011);

(d) the term "shipwreck" means a vessel or wreck, its cargo, and other contents;

(e) the term "State" means a State of the United States, the District of Columbia, Puerto Rico, Guam, the Virgin Islands, American Samoa, and the Northern Mariana Islands; and

(f) the term "submerged lands" means the lands—

(1) that are "lands beneath navigable waters," as defined in section 2 of the Submerged Lands Act (43 U.S.C. 1301)

(2) of Puerto Rico, as described in section 8 of the Act of March 2, 1917, as amended (48 U.S.C. 749);

(3) of Guam, the Virgin Islands and American Samoa, as described in section 1 of Public Law 93-435 (48 U.S. C. 1705); and

(4) of the Commonwealth of the Northern Mariana Islands, as described in section 801 of Public Law 94-241 (48 U.S.C. 1681)

(April 28, 1988, P. L. 100-298, § 3, 102 Stat. 432.)

§2103. Rights of access

(a) **Access Rights.** In order to—

(1) clarify that State waters and shipwrecks offer recreational and educational opportunities to sport divers and others interested groups, as well as irreplaceable State resources for tourism, biological sanctuaries, and historical research; and

(2) provide that reasonable access by the public to such abandoned shipwrecks be permitted by the State holding title to such shipwrecks pursuant to section 6 of this Act [43 USCS § 2105],

it is the declared policy of the Congress that States carry out their responsibilities under this Act [43 USCS §§ 2101 et seq.] to develop appropriate and consistent policies so as to—

(A) protect natural resources and habitat areas;

(B) guarantee recreational exploration of shipwreck sites; and

(C) allow for appropriate public and private sector recovery of shipwrecks consistent with the protection of historical values and environmental integrity of the shipwrecks and the sites.

(b) **Parks and protected areas.** In managing the resources subject to the provisions of this Act, States are encouraged to create underwater parks and areas to provide additional protection for such resources. Funds available to States from grants from the Historic Preservation Fund shall be available, in accordance with the provisions of title I of the National Historic Preservation Act [16 USCS §§ 470a et seq.], for the study, interpretation, protection, and preservation of historic shipwrecks and properties.

(April 28, 1988, P. L. 100-298, § 4, 102 Stat. 433.)

Abandoned Shipwrecks *continued*

§ 2104. Preparation of guidelines

(a) In order to encourage the development of underwater parks and the administrative cooperation necessary for the comprehensive management of underwater resources related to historic shipwrecks, the Secretary of the Interior, acting through the Director of the National Park Service, shall within nine months after the date of enactment of this Act [enacted April 28, 1988] prepare and publish guidelines in the Federal Register which shall seek to:

    (1) maximize the enhancement of cultural resources;

    (2) foster a partnership among sport divers, fisherman, archeologists, salvors, and other interests to manage shipwreck resources of the States and the United States;

    (3) facilitate access and utilization by recreational interests;

    (4) recognize the interests of individuals and groups engaged in shipwreck discovery and salvage.

(b) Such guidelines shall be developed after consultation with appropriate public and private sector interests (including the Secretary of Commerce, the Advisory council on Historic salvors, archeologists, historic preservationists, and fisherman).

(c) Such guidelines shall be available to assist States and appropriate Federal agencies in developing legislation and regulations to carry out their responsibilities under this Act [43 USCS §§ 2101 et seq.]

(April 28, 1988, P. L. 100-298, § 5, 102 Stat. 433.)

§ 2105. Rights of ownership

(a) **United States title.** The United States asserts title to any abandoned shipwreck that is—

    (1) embedded in submerged lands of a State;

    (2) embedded in coralline formations protected by a State on submerged lands of a State; or

    (3) on submerged lands of a State and is included in or determined eligible for inclusion in the National Register,

(b) **Public notice of location.** The public shall be given adequate notice of the location of any shipwreck to which title is asserted under this section. The Secretary of the Interior, after consultation with the appropriate State Historic Preservation Officer, shall make a written determination that an abandoned shipwreck meets the criteria for eligibility for inclusion in the National Register of Historic Places under clause (a)(3),

(c) **Transfer of title to States.** The title of the United States to any abandoned shipwreck asserted under subsection (a) of this section is transferred to the State in or on whose submerged lands the shipwreck is located.

(d) **Exception.** Any abandoned shipwreck in or on the public lands of the United States is the property of the United States Government. Any abandoned shipwreck in or on any Indian lands is the property of the Indian tribe owning such lands.

(e) **Reservation of rights.** This section does not affect any right reserved by the United States or by any State (including any right reserved with respect to Indian lands) under—

    (1) section 3, 5, or 6 of the Submerged Lands Act (43 U.S.C. 1311, 1313, and 1314); or

    (2) section 19 or 20 of the Act of March 3, 1899 (33 U.S.C. 414 and 415).

(April 28, 1988, P. L. 100-298, § 6, 102 Stat. 433.)

INTERPRETATIVE NOTES AND DECISIONS

Review of district court's decision is premature until district court determines whether Abandoned Ship Act is constitutional so as to allow its application in case where shipwreck is embedded in lakebed owned by state. Zych v Unidentified, Wrecked & Abandoned Vessel, etc, (1991, CA7 Ill) 941 F2d 525.

State has colorable claim to ownership of shipwrecks discovered privately on bed of Lake Michigan resulting in dismissal of federal court action to decide ownership due to state's Eleventh Amendment immunity, because (1) 43 USCS § 1311 makes clear that states have title to all lands and natural resources beneath navigable waters within their boundaries an d(2) 43 USCS § 2105 grants title of vessels embedded on state submerged lands to state and it is not unconstitutional interference with grants of admiralty jurisdiction to federal courts, Zych v Unidentified, Wrecked & Abandoned Vessel, Believed to be SB "Lady Elgin" (1990, ND Ill) 746 F Supp 1334, summary judgement gr (ND Ill) 1990 US Dist LEXIS 16760.

§ 2106. Relationship to other laws

(a) **Law of salvage and the law of finds.** The law of salvage and the law of finds shall not apply to abandoned shipwrecks to which section 6 of this Act [43 USCS § 2105] applies.

(b) **Laws of the Untied States.** This Act shall not change the laws of the United States relating to shipwrecks, other than those to which this Act applies.

(c) **Effective date.** This Act shall not affect any legal proceeding brought prior to the date of enactment of this Act [enacted April 28, 1988]

(April 28, 1988, P. L. 100-298, § 7, 102 Stat. 434.)

HISTORY, ANCILLARY LAWS AND DIRECTIVES

References in text: "This Act" referred to in this section, is Act April 28, 1988, P. L. 100-298, 102 Stat. 432, which appears as USCS §§ 2101 et seq.

National Parks and Marine Sanctuaries

An exception to the Abandoned Shipwreck Act is those wrecks which lie within a National Park or Marine Sanctuary. National Parks are under the jurisdiction of the United States Department of the Interior, and Marine Sanctuaries fall under the jurisdiction of NOAA, (National Oceanic and Atmospheric Association), which is a branch of the Department of Commerce. Shipwrecks located within either of these are regulated not by the state, but by the individual branch of the federal government. Examples of National Parks where shipwrecks are found include Florida's Key Biscayne National Park and Michigan's Isle Royal National Park. A prime example of a Marine Sanctuary is the shipwreck U.S.S. *Monitor* located off Cape Hatteras, North Carolina. However, as time goes by more and more sanctuaries are being designated and it is likely that shipwrecks will be found within them as opposed to a single site like the *Monitor*. Before diving any wreck which is located in either a National Park or Marine Sanctuary, consult the proper agency for up-to-date regulations.

Warships

Another exception to the previously stated rules regards that of sunken warships. Regardless of when they were lost or where they lie, warships sunk in action are deemed to have never been abandoned by the sovereign owner. The validity of this assertion, however, has been called into question in several recent cases.

Dr. William S. Dudley, Senior Historian of the Naval Historical Center, Washington, D.C. states the Navy's position on sunken U.S. Navy warships and aircraft: "The U.S. Navy's policy towards wrecked and sunken ships has been guided by admiralty law. The United States does not lose its title to any vessel as a result of wrecking or sinking, regardless of the passage of time. Unless the United States legally abandons title in the manner directed by an act of Congress, the shipwrecks and their contents, including human remains, are U.S. property and are considered watery graves. Any persons attempting to salvage American Government vessels do so at their own risk and subject to the prior rights of the U.S. Government. This legal doctrine was set forth in the Hatteras, Inc. v. the U.S.S. *Hatteras* case by the U.S. District Court for the Southern District of Texas in 1980. The judge stated that the common law doctrine of abandonment had no application in the case. Only Congress has the power to divest public property under the property clause of the Constitution.

"The new and improved underwater breathing equipment allows benign individuals wonderful opportunities for underwater research but this also allows less nobly motivated souls the chance to disturb, deface, desecrate, or destroy naval shipwrecks while hunting for souvenirs or treasure.

"The staff of the Naval Historical Center is attempting to create within the Navy Department an awareness of the potential for abuses of historic underwater sites for commissioned aircraft, as well as ships, and to establish a new mission for the Center. Unfortunately, this comes at a time when we have been warned of greater austerity in future defense budgets. Thus our ability to hire additional personnel to undertake this new mission is in doubt. For a while, at least, we will have to be content to monitor naval wreck sites, to collect information systematically, to cooperate with authorities who have more access to the sites than we do, and finally to alert those in positions to affect government policy in Congress that the Navy has a new-found but abiding interest in historical maritime archaeology."

U.S. NAVY OBJECTIVES

The Navy's objectives in underwater archaeology are to:

- Monitor U.S. Navy underwater wreck sites.
- Help protect the Navy's legal interests.
- Prevent destruction of historic Navy shipwrecks.
- Discourage looting of Naval artifacts.
- Provide sanctity of watery graves of American seamen.
- Encourage Naval archaeology/historical studies.
- Encourage non-intrusive surveys of wreck sites.
- Encourage preservation and display of artifacts retrieved.
- Encourage historical understanding of related Naval events.

One of the gray areas encountered within this category of shipwrecks is with warships that were scuttled. The scuttling of a ship would appear to be an act of abandonment; however, Naval officials might argue otherwise. While it is the opinion of admiralty legal experts that a scuttled warship is in fact abandoned, further cases may need to be decided before the matter is truly clear-cut.

What has been made clear throughout this chapter is that recovering artifacts is no small task. While opportunities abound for exciting finds, attached to them is a price tag of responsibility. A wreck diver interested in recovering artifacts must be well versed on applicable laws, take the time to remove artifacts correctly without damaging other sections of the wreck, conserve the artifact and display it in a manner befitting a nautical antique.

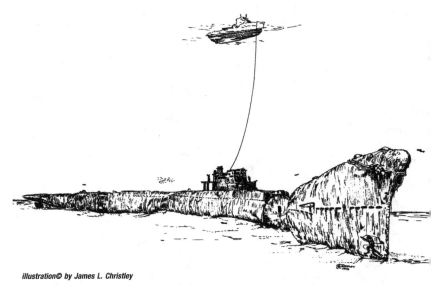

illustration© by James L. Christley

*The U.S. submarine **Bass** was sunk as a target off Block Island, Rhode Island, in 1945. The wreck, in 160 feet of water, is a popular dive site.*

Brian Skerry prepares to photograph the German submarine **U-85**'s 88-mm deck gun. The U-boat is in 90 feet of water off North Carolina.

Chapter 11

Sunken Ships
and Salty Shutters
Making Images of Shipwrecks

In the middle of a busy city, while walking down a sidewalk, a bus passes by and the smell of the diesel fumes, for an instant, reminds you of standing on the after deck of a charter boat on a morning's trip to a favorite wreck site. The sound of a country church's bell tower transports you to a time when, once anchored

Shipwreck images convey the drama and excitement of wreck diving.

at sea, a bell buoy rang in the distance to the rhythm of the rolling waves. In the course of living our lives, we file away experiences as memories, memories that can lie dormant for years, only to be awakened by a sound, a scent or a taste. Perhaps the most powerful of the senses is sight. Even though our lives are played out in continuous motion, we store memories as individual scenes. Looking at a photograph, one can vividly recall a time that otherwise might have remained in the subconscious. Images need not be from one's own life, however, to stir emotion. We may view a seaside painting of John Stobart and be taken away to 19th century Baltimore or study a photograph of a ship being tossed about in icy seas during a winter storm and feel glad that we are safe and warm.

Within the world of wreck diving lies the potential for countless emotion stirring images. An artifact can be admired, but an image actually takes you there. Shipwreck images can convey drama, solitude or danger. They can illustrate adventure or discovery. Photographs create a mood. A brightly lit, clear water tugboat photo gives a very different feeling than one of a dim, green water, somber submarine. Like all image making, underwater photography is one's own interpretation of a moment in time. It is the sum of one's knowledge of shipwrecks and how a particular scene is viewed. The way the amberjacks circle a towering mast, or a diver's efforts to squeeze through a hatch, are frozen for eternity when the shutter is opened and closed.

Aside from these more ethereal views of shipwreck photography, a camera can also be a useful tool in shipwreck identification and familiarization. Reviewing photographs of an unfamiliar wreck site can aid in navigating the site on a future dive. For artists interested in sketching a wreck site, even technically poor photos can be useful for evaluating the present condition of various sections. For the technically ambitious, a photo mosaic can be completed, giving an overall view of a wreck site by piecing together multiple images taken in succession from a constant angle and depth.

Although a diver need not be extremely experienced before attempting wreck photography, he or she must at least be quite comfortable with the surrounding environment. If one is just starting out in pursuit of shipwrecks, it is a good idea to become accustomed to the gear and the wreck environment before taking a camera in tow.

Still Photography

Still photography is one of those pursuits that can be as simple or as complex as you would like it to be. If your goal is to produce images that can be shown to family and friends who will not be overly critical of quality, then photography can be rather simple. If, on the other hand, your goal is to publish your work or make public presentations, the heavy metal band AC/DC put it best when they said, *"It's a long way to the top if you want to rock and roll."*

In either case, photography is best learned in a controlled environment. A shipwreck is not a controlled environment. The aspiring photographer should learn the basics about film, lenses, light meters and various camera functions before slipping beneath the waves. As with all of wreck diving, know your equipment. For the purposes of our discussion, we will limit our focus to 35mm photography.

In underwater still photography, there are two options available: amphibious cameras and housed cameras. A housing is a capsule of sorts in which a surface camera is

Photo by Brian Skerry

A diver squeezing through the hatch of a submarine is an adventure captured for eternity by the wreck diving photographer.

mounted. On the front of the housing in front of the camera's lens is affixed a port. A dome port would be used for wide-angle lenses, a flat port for longer lenses. If you already own a camera, a housing may be the answer to begin taking underwater pictures. Housings are available in quite an extensive range, from less expensive plexiglass to the higher end, precision cast, anodized aluminum models. One of the great advantages of using a housing is the ability to house a single lens reflex camera. A single lens reflex camera simply means that you see through the lens. With this type of camera, you can better compose the photograph. Another advantage is the wide variety of interchangeable lenses that are available.

Photo by Brian Skerry

Two options for underwater photography include a housing like the one manufactured by Aquatica (left) or an amphibious camera like the Nikonos III (right).

Unfortunately, wreck diving is a harsh environment on camera gear. While any housing can allow you to produce quality images, not every housing will stand up equally to abuse. At 150 feet, in a decompression situation, there is not much you can do when your housing begins to fill with water. This brings up another point—depth rating. Not all housings are created equal in this regard. When purchasing your first housing, a depth rating of 160 feet may seem fine, but in a couple of years when you were hoping to shoot the propeller of the *Andrea Doria* in 220 feet, dare you take a chance? You will obviously need to evaluate your objectives in relationship to your budget before buying. Aside from the risk of flooding and ruining an expensive surface camera, perhaps the only other downside of using a housing is size. Since many wreck divers jump into the water wearing the equivalent of a hardware store on their backs, carrying any "extra" gear can be a real drag - literally. Although great strides have been made in reducing the size of many housings, they are still fairly bulky. Arguably, many of the finer housings are quite ergonomic and hydrodynamic; however, they still add considerable drag to divers pulling themselves down an anchor line. In spite of these drawbacks, a housed cam-

Photo by Brian Skerry

The use of a wide angle lens in clear water will allow the photographer to capture large sections of wrecks on film.

era system is an outstanding photographic tool and with a bit of practice will yield tremendous results.

The alternative to a housed camera system is the amphibious still camera. The first commercially available camera of this genera was the Calypso, invented in part by Jacques Cousteau. The Calypso was first offered in France in 1958 by the SOS company, later produced as the Nikonos, manufactured by Nikon, Inc. Through many years and several design changes, the Nikonos is still as popular as ever as a means of taking underwater photographs. The Nikonos is a pressure proof aluminum casing, inside which a camera body is sealed with O-rings. The Nikonos also features a selection of interchangeable waterproof lenses, including 80mm, 35mm, 28mm, 20mm and 15mm, also sealed with O-rings. Although the first five Nikonos models were rangefinder type cameras, (not SLR), they gained wide acceptance for their easy to use characteristics. For the wreck diver, the Nikonos is quite attractive due to its size and simplicity. About the same size as a surface camera, a Nikonos can easily be worn around a diver's neck or carried unobtrusively on a wrist lanyard. As underwater photography equipment goes, Nikonos maintenance is minimal. Because of its aluminum body, it is also pretty rugged and will hold up to a wreck diver's standards. Aside from the non SLR features of the first five models, about the only drawback is a depth rating of 160 feet. Speaking from experience, a Nikonos can be taken considerably deeper; however, do not expect the warranty to cover a flooded camera if you just surfaced from the *Edmund Fitzgerald.*

In 1992, Nikon introduced the world's first underwater SLR, the RS. Incorporating such traditional features as interchangeable lenses with an amphibious SLR, the RS is quite attractive. For a wreck diver interested in getting his or her feet wet in shipwreck photography, a Nikonos is a wise investment. A periodic glance through the want ads will often yield numerous bargains. With their compact size, fine optics and rugged durability, you cannot go wrong.

Another option available in amphibious 35mm cameras are those manufactured by Sea&Sea. Made of a durable ABS plastic, the Motormarine I and II are viable alternatives for the wreck diver. More sophisticated of the two, the Motormarine II features TTL (through the lens) flash exposure, an in viewfinder LED display, built in flash, and automatic film advance. Unlike the Nikonos, the Motormarine features a fixed lens which cannot be removed. It can, however, be fitted with accessory lenses, such as their 20mm or 16mm. The unique feature of these accessory lenses is that they can be put on or taken off underwater, adding great versatility. Lightweight and reasonably priced, the Sea&Sea cameras will fare well in the world of wreck diving.

Lenses

Afficionados of fine music will often state that a stereo system is only as good as its speakers. A similar statement can be made in regards to a camera system being only as good as its lens. In many respects, a camera is nothing more than a box that allows light to

ABOVE: In poorer visibility the wide-angle lens allows large, identifiable objects, such as this helm on the freighter **Equipoise** *off the coast of North Carolina, to be photographed due to its great depth of field and broad-angle of coverage. RIGHT: A handwritten scale on the focusing control of a housing solves the dilemma of focusing on dark wrecks.*

enter, producing an image on the film. The lens, however, will ultimately determine the quality of that image. While good photographs can be taken without spending a fortune, it is safe to say, the better the chunk of glass, the better the image. As photographic subjects, shipwrecks present endless possibilities, but a good photo should not require a ten minute explanation. A viewer of the photo needs to be able to identify the subject quickly. Since shipwrecks are large subjects, the photograph should attempt to reveal as much of the wreck as possible. The best way to do this is with a wide-angle lens. Rarely will it be possible to capture an entire wreck in a single image; however, use of a wide-angle lens will allow the photographer to record large enough sections of a given wreck that will be quite recognizable to the viewer. If poor visibility prevents shooting large sections of a wreck, there are still options. With great depth of field, a wide angle lens will allow you to get close to single subjects, such as an anchor or helm stand, reducing the amount of dirty water between the camera and subject, producing acceptable results.

By now you may be wondering, how wide is wide angle? In underwater photography, a 35mm lens used underwater on an amphibious camera or in a housing with a flat port has the same angle of coverage as a 50mm lens above water due to refraction (50mm is considered a normal focal length, or equivalence to the human eye). Therefore, anything wider than 35mm can be considered wide angle. Lenses used in a housing with a dome port will have the same angle of coverage that they would have above water due to the fact that the dome is corrected for refraction. In this case anything wider than 50mm would be considered wide angle.

In shipwreck photography, the wider the better. One of the finest lenses for this type of work is the Nikonos 15mm lens. Corrected for underwater use, this lens offers razor sharp resolution with an angle of coverage of 94 degrees. If the Nikonos 15mm is a bit beyond your budget, consider their 20mm or one of the wide-angle lenses offered by Sea&Sea. If you are using a housing, the options are many.

In spite of the great depth of field offered by wide angle lenses, some focusing will usually be necessary when taking underwater photographs. With rangefinder cameras, like the Nikonos, focusing is achieved not with your eye, but by adjusting the focusing scale control located on the lens. With an SLR in a housing, focusing is done by looking through the lens and turning the focusing knob on the housing. In a dark environment, like the interior of a shipwreck, this can be rather difficult. On many wrecks there is rarely enough light present to properly focus the lens. One way to solve this dilemma is to create a focusing scale that can be used like the Nikonos. In clear, bright conditions, such as in a swimming pool, focus can be achieved on a fixed object at various distances. These distance settings can be marked on the focusing control of the housing, allowing quick and easy focusing when diving a dark shipwreck. Keep in mind that the lens being used should be indexed in some way so that it and your focusing scale will always line up.

Lighting

When reduced to its simplest form, photography is nothing more than capturing reflected light. When diving shipwrecks, light is not something we take for granted, since there is often so little of it present. To capture reflected light, then we must bring light with us to the wreck. Although there are plenty of shipwrecks in shallow or clear enough water for available light photography to be done, more often than not an underwater strobe will be needed for image making. The photographer's choice of a strobe must be dictated, in part, by the lens being used. The output of light must adequately illuminate the total picture area. When choosing a strobe, then the angle of coverage of light must be equal to or greater than

Photos by Brian Skerry

*Henry Keatts uses an underwater strobe when photographing the coning tower of the German submarine **U-2513** off the Dry Tortugas.*

*Gary Gentile stretches the strobe cord while hand holding his strobe to photograph a lantern globe on the wreck U.S.S. **Monitor**.*

the angle of coverage of the lens. There are numerous wide-angle strobes available on the market to meet the demands of the shipwreck photographer, any of which will do the job. Features such as recycle time, battery type and strobe size are all subject to personal preference.

A housing rigged for wreck diving with the addition of an underwater light, dome shade and lanyard.

In a world of rust particles and ever present silt, lighting can be difficult at best. To eliminate backscatter, caused from light reflecting off suspended matter, try positioning the strobe to the side of your subject. Be creative. Any angle that will not bounce the light from those floating particles directly back at the lens will be effective. Depending on conditions, exposures can vary, so bracketing is also recommended to increase the odds of success.

Cameras Rigged for Wrecks

As with most gear used in wreck diving, some customizing of photo gear is recommended before venturing forth in search of the perfect image of a sunken ship. In Chapter 7, we discussed the advantages of carrying a light on wreck dives. With your hands now full of camera gear, a dive light should be mounted to the camera tray or housing to create a compact and versatile unit. Having a light mounted to your camera system will not only allow you to see well in dark conditions, but will help you to view a scene more effectively when composing the shot.

Another important addition to a wreck diver's camera system is the attachment of a lanyard. Whether pulling yourself down the anchor line or sending up a lift bag, there will be plenty of times when your hands will need to be free. Having a lanyard around your wrist will allow you to use both hands without letting go of the camera.

Frank Nardi videotapes inside the freighter **Manuela,** *off the coast of North Carolina.*

An additional consideration in customizing camera gear for the punishing world of wreck diving is devising a means of protecting your lens or dome port. While swimming around shipwrecks, it is pretty easy to get dings and scratches in this vital area of your system. To help reduce some of this damage, a dome protector or lens shade can be added. These helpful additions can be purchased or made from available materials such as PVC.

Shipwreck Videography

Prior to the 1980's, if a diver wanted to record motion picture images of a dive, it was necessary to become proficient with underwater cinematography. This meant investing a fair amount of time learning about film stocks, how to load and unload magazines, processing film and physically editing the finished product. Also involved was considerable expense and the lugging of heavy, bulky camera housings into the deep for just a few minutes of filming.

With the rapid advancement of video technology however, things changed dramatically. Appearing on the scene was the camcorder. This small electronic camera, which could be easily housed, opened the world of motion pictures to a vastly wider audience. No longer was it necessary to enter into a serious commitment of time spent learning the intricacies and finer points of film exposure, frames per second or reading a light meter. In a nutshell, you could buy a camera and housing, go diving and be reviewing the "dailys" that evening!

For wreck divers, video capability offered exciting possibilities. With their small size and ability to record in low light situations, camcorders could easily be used to tape dramatic shipwreck footage by divers that had never before used a camera underwater. The footage could even be reviewed immediately following the dive, aboard the boat, adding a completely new dimension to diving.

Video Equipment

If there is a phrase that best describes video technology it is "continual change." With advancements always being made, it often seems as though by the time you have made a decision and purchased a state of the art unit, it is already being outperformed by a "newer" model. As frustrating as this is, one can still acquire an underwater video system that will suit his needs for a long time without feeling the need to regularly upgrade. While there are innumerable models available to choose from, the wreck diving videographer should look for a few basic features.

The size of the camera and housing is very important. In the field of still photography, the choice is somewhat limited; however, in videography, it is not. A smaller video system will naturally be easier to work with, particularly in the wreck diving environment. Housings also come in a variety of materials; however, for wreck diving, the more durable, the better. For durability, it is tough to beat a metal housing; one extruded to fit precisely around the camera. These types of housings are about as compact a unit as you can get and are quite rugged. Manufacturers of this genre include Gates Underwater Products and Amphibico, Inc.

Another consideration regarding housings is whether you prefer one that is mechanical or electronic. A mechanical housing allows for physical manipulation of functions with "through the housing" controls, while an electronic housing is controlled elec-

Photo by Brian Skerry

*Peter Hess uses the plentiful ambient light to videotape the tanker **Dixie Arrow** off Cape Hatteras, North Carolina.*

tronically with key pad controls and fewer external knobs. With fewer "through the housing" controls, the electronic housing offers a lesser number of potential leakage points but may not offer as much creative control due to lack of access to all functions.

A housing that allows the operator to easily switch from manual focus to auto focus is also an important feature. In most cases, wreck divers can get away without focusing often, due to the wide-angle lense's great depth of field. Once underwater, the diver should find an object approximately two feet away while in the auto focus mode, then lock it in by switching to the manual focus mode. With that accomplished, the diver can tour the wreck with just about everything in focus. This is especially helpful when diving deep wrecks where narcosis may prevent crisp focusing. Leaving the camera on auto focus is not recommended, since the camera will constantly be searching for the subject, particularly in low visibility or turbid water. There may be times, however, when you want to switch back to auto focus, such as inside a wreck to get a close-up of an small artifact. Having the versatility to move between modes is extremely useful.

Light levels on shipwrecks can change dramatically when trying to record both inside and outside the wreck. For this reason, it is important to have a system that allows the cameraman to switch from auto iris to manual iris. There will be times when you are inside a wreck shooting through an open hatch to the bright ambient light outside. In the auto iris mode, the camera will expose for the bright light, stopping down the aperture. In order to balance the light and capture some of the interior as well, it will be necessary to switch to manual iris.

A final feature that is very useful, is one that allows the camera to be switched from tungsten balance to daylight balance. When shooting the exterior of a brightly lit shipwreck, most often the camera will be set for daylight. Upon entering the interior it will undoubtedly become necessary to turn on video lights. Once that is done, the camera should be changed to the tungsten setting to permit proper color correction of the tape.

Video Lighting

Since we have touched on the subject of video lights, a few tips can be offered here as well. Lights that cast a nice wide beam are important for wreck diving videography. Hot spots greatly detract from the final product, so attention must be given to this feature. Two lights are preferred and, if possible, ones that allow the beam angle to be adjusted from flood to spot. Small lampheads that are lightweight and maneuverable are especially well suited. Powerful lights are best for the wreck environment; between 75 to 100 watts will do fine. It is not necessary to have extremely long arms for the lights, however. A maximum of 15" is generally more than enough distance from the camera.

One of the great advantages of video over film, is the luxury of being able to shoot much more tape on a dive than would be possible with film. The downside is that video lights use up battery power, so maximum power will be needed to allow the lights to keep up with the tape. Finding the lightest weight batteries, with the greatest output is the goal.

Taping Tips

For the beginning videographer, there are a few simple tips that, if followed, can make a great deal of difference in the final product. Perhaps the first skill to focus on is maintaining a steady picture. A moving sequence that bounces up and down is more likely to give the viewer the feeling of being on a ship that is sinking than one that is already sunk. Making a concentrated effort to maintain an even horizon and rock steady movement as you shoot, will produce a much more pleasing video. Practicing proper buoyancy control will aid tremendously in this endeavor.

Another trap to avoid is rapid movement of the camera from one object to another. If you are shooting an anchor mounted to the deck of a wreck, do not quickly pan to a winch, then to a hawsepipe, then back to the anchor. Instead, take time to allow the viewer to fully see each item before moving on to the next. When you do move, a nice slow, fluid pan will result in a pleasing sequence.

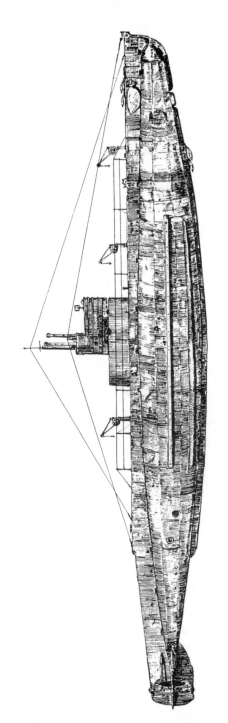

Illustration © by James L. Christley

The U.S. submarine **H-1** ran aground at the entrance to Magdalena Bay, Baja California, on March 11, 1920. She was pulled off by the U.S.S. **Vestal** but foundered in about 60 feet of water. There are unconfirmed reports that the **H-1** has been found, but several groups of divers continue their search. The first underwater images of the elusive wreck would confirm its discovery.

In still photography, it is not recommended for a diver to look at the camera since the resulting image will look staged. In video however, this is quite acceptable. If done properly it can give the illusion that the diver is communicating to another diver. Remember also to include topside footage in your tape. As we all know, much of the action on a wreck diving trip takes place on the boat. Adding in these sequences will increase interest and nicely balance out the finished tape.

Whether your tastes lean towards video, motion picture or still photography, making images of shipwrecks can provide a lifetime of satisfaction. In pursuit of shipwreck images you will learn more about ships, shipwrecks and the animals that inhabit them. On a cold winter day when the wind is blowing hard, ice is forming on the windows and wreck diving is months away, there is a pleasant feeling and sense of accomplishment that comes from glancing on the wall to see that dramatic photograph taken on the previous year's wreck diving trip. It is also possible that with that image, you just might stir someone else's emotion as well and motivate them to follow you down to the ships in the sea.

Appendix A

U.S. Research Sources of Shipwreck Information

Allen Knight Maritime Museum
550 Calle Principal
Monterey, CA 93940

Archaeological Research Division of
Historical Resources
R.A. Gray Building
Tallahassee, FL 32399

Bangor Historical Society
159 Union Street
Bangor, ME 04401

Bowers Beach Maritime Museum
Frederica, DE 19946

Brick Store Museum
117 Main Street
Kennebunk, ME 04043

Brooklyn Historical Society
128 Pierrepont Street
Brooklyn, NY 11201

Buffalo & Erie Co. Historical Society
25 Nottingham Court
Buffalo, NY 14216
(716) 873-9644

The Burton Historical Collection
Detroit Public Library
5201 Woodward Avenue
Detroit, MI 48202

Calvert Marine Museum
P.O. Box 97
Solomons, MD 20688

Cape Ann Historical Association
27 Pleasant Street
Gloucester, MA 01930

Chesapeake Bay Maritime Museum
P.O. Box 636
St. Michaels, MD 21663

Columbia River Maritime Museum
1618 Exchange St.
Astoria, OR 97103

Confederate Naval Museum
201 4th Street
Columbus, GA 31902
(404) 327-9798

Douglas County Historical Society
906 East Second Street
Superior, WI 54880
(715) 394-5712

Great Lakes Historical Society
480 Main Street
Vermilion, OH 44089

Great Lakes Maritime Institute
Dossin Great Lakes Museum
100 Strand Drive
Detroit, MI 48207
(313) 267-6440

Great Lakes Naval & Maritime Museum
Chicago, IL 60611

Great Lakes Shipwreck Historical
Museum
111 Ashmun
Sault Ste. Marie, MI 49783
(906) 635-1742

Hampton Mariners Museum
120 Turner Street
Beaufort, NC 28516
(919) 728-7317

Hart Nautical Museum
Room 5-329, MIT
Cambridge, MA 02139

Hawaii State Archives
Iolani Palace Gardens
Honolulu, HI 96813

The Howard National Steamboat
Museum
1101 East Market Street
Jeffersonville, IN 47130

Inland Rivers Library
8th & Vine Street
Cincinnati, OH 45202

Institute of Nautical Archaeology
P.O. Drawer HG
College Station, TX 77841

International Assocociation for Great
Lakes Research
c/o Institute of Science & Technology
University of Michigan
Ann Arbor, MI 48109

Lake Champlain Maritime Museum
Basin Harbor, VT 05491
(802) 475-2317

Lake Michigan Maritime Museum
P.O. Box 534
South Haven, MI 49090
(616) 637-8078

Lewes Historical Society
119 West Third Street
Lewes, DE 19958

Los Angeles Maritime Museum
Berth 84
San Pedro, CA 90731
(310) 548-7560

Mackinac Maritime Museum
P.O. Box 873
Mackinaw City, MI 49701

Maine Maritime Museum
963 Washington Street
Bath, ME 04530

Maine State Museum
State House Station 83
Augusta, ME 04333

Manitowoc Maritime Museum
809 South Eighth Street
Manitowoc, WI 54220

Marine Maritime Museum
963 Washington Street
Bath, ME 04530

Maritime Museum Assoc. of San Diego
1306 North Harbor Drive
San Diego, CA 92101

Marquette County Historical Society
213 North Front Street
Marquette, MI 49855
(906) 226-3571

M.I.T. Museum & Historic Society
Hart Nautical Collection
265 Massachusetts Avenue
Cambridge, MA 02139

Museum of History & Industry
2161 East Hamlin Street
Seattle, WA 98112

Museum of the City of New York
1220 Fifth Avenue
New York, NY 10029

National Maritime Museum of
San Francisco
Bldg. 201, Ft. Mason
San Francisco, CA 94123

Nantucket Historical Association
Old Town Building
Nantucket, MA 02554

Newark Museum
49 Washington Street
Newark, NJ 07101

North Carolina Division of Archives
& History
109 East Jones Street
Raleigh, NC 27601

North Carolina Maritime Museum
315 Front Street
Beaufort, NC 28516

Pacific Submarine Museum
Naval Submarine Base
Pearl Harbor, HI 96818
(808) 423-1341

Patriots Point Naval & Maritime
Museum
Mt. Pleasant, SC 29464

Peabody Museum of Salem
East India Square
Salem, MA 01970
(508) 745-1876

Penobscot Marine Museum
Church Street
Searsport, ME 04974
(207) 548-6634

Philadelphia Maritime Museum
321 Chestnut Street
Philadelphia, PA 19106

Portsmouth Naval Shipyard Museum
2 High Street
Portsmouth, VA 23705

Puget Sound Maritime Historical
Society
2700-24th Ave. East
Seattle, WA 98112
(206) 624-3028

San Francisco Maritime Museum
Foot of Polk Street
San Francisco, CA 94109

Society for the Preservation
of New England Antiquities
141 Cambridge Street
Boston, MA 02114
Still Photo Archives
(617) 227-3956

South Carolina Institute of
Archaeology
University of South Carolina
Columbia, SC 29208

South Street Seaport Museum
& Library
16 Fulton Street
New York, NY 10038
(212) 669-9400.

U.S. Lighthouse Society
130 St. Elmo Way
San Francisco, CA 94127

Appendix B

Research Sources Outside the United States

ANTIGUA
The Nelson Museum
Nelson's Dockyard, Antigua

ARGENTINA
Coronel de Marina Tomas Espora
Avenida Caseros 2526
Buenos Aires, Argentina

AUSTRALIA
National Library of Australia
Parkes Place
Canberra City, A.C.T. 2600, Australia

Tasmanian Maritime Museum
47 Victoria Parade
Devenport, Tasmania, Australia

BAHAMAS
Bahamas Historical Society Museum
P.O. Box N1715/Elizabeth Avenue
Nassau, Bahamas

BELGIUM
National Scheepvaartmuseum
Steenplein
200 Antwerpen, Belgium

BERMUDA
The Bermuda Maritime Museum
P.O. Box MA 273
Mangrove Bay MA BX, Bermuda
(809) 234-1333

Confederate Museum
(Blockade Runners)
Globe Hotel
King's Square, St, George's, Bermuda
(809) 297-1423

BRAZIL
Museu Naval
Rua Dom Manuel 15
Rio de Janiero, Brazil

CANADA
Canadian National Archives
Sussex Drive
Ottawa, Ontario, Canada

Vancouver Maritime Museum
1905 Ogden Street
Vancouver, B.C. V6J 3J9, Canada

Wheelhouse Maritime Museum
222 Cumberland Street
Ottawa 2, Ontario K1N 7H5, Canada

COLOMBIA
Museo Geologico Nacional
Carrera 30 No. 51-59
Apdo. Aero 4865 Bogota, Colombia

COSTA RICA
Museu Juan Santamaria
Apdo. 785
Alajvela, Costa Rica

DENMARK
Danish Admiralty Collection
Naval Museum
Royal Dockyard
Copenhagen, Denmark

Rigsarkivet
Rigsdagsgaarden 9
Copenhagen DK-1218, Denmark

DOMINICAN REPUBLIC
Comision de Rescate Arqueologico
Submarino
Museuo de Las Casas Reales
Calle Las Dames Esq. Mercedes
Santo Domingo, Dominican
Republic

FINLAND
Haapavest Museum
86600 Haapavesi, Oulu, Finland

FRANCE
Musee de la Marine
Palais de Chaillot
Paris F-75016, France

Archives National
60 Rue de Francs
Bourgeois, Paris III, France

GERMANY
Archiv Fuer Schiffbau
und Schiffahrt
2 Hamburg 1, Germany

Bundesarchiv
Postfach 320
D 5400 Koblenz, Germany

Foto Druppel
Rheinstrase 50
2940 Wilhelmshaven, Germany

Militaer Geshichteliches
Forschungsamt
Kaiser Josef Strasse 262
7800 Freiburg, Breisgau, Germany

U-Boot-Archiv
2190 Cuxhaven 12, Germany

WZ-Bilddienst (source for photos)
Postfach 644 - BorsenstraBe 27
2940 Wilhelmshaven, Germany

GREAT BRITAIN
Department Of Trade and Industry
Marine Division Library
Sunley House 90 High Holborn
London WC1V 6LP, England

Imperial War Museum
Lambeth Road
London SE1 6HZ, England
01-735 8922

Lloyds Register of Shipping
71 Fenchurch
London EC3M 4BS, England

Ministry Of Defense
Naval Historical Branch
(no photograph collection)
3-5 Great Scotland Yard, Whitehall
London SW1H 2HW, England
071-21 85454

National Maritime Museum
Park Row, Greenwich
London SE10 9NF, England
01-858 4422

Public Record Office (ship's logs &
Admiralty documents)
Ruskin Ave., Kew, Richmond
Surrey TW9 4DYU, England
01-876 3444

Royal Navy Submarine Memorial
Museum
Gosport, Hampshire, England

ICELAND
Marine Museum of Eyrarbakka
Sjominjasafn Eyrarbakka
820 Eyrarbakka, Iceland

IRELAND
National Maritime Museum
Haigh Terrace
Dun Laoghaire
Dublin, Ireland

ITALY
Collezione Istorica Cartografica
(Collection of Ancient Maps)
Via Zamboni 33
Bologna, Provincia di Bologna, Italy

JAMAICA
Old Naval Hospital Museum
Old Naval Hospital
Port Royal, Kingston, Jamaica

West India Reference Library
14-16 East Street
Kingston, Jamaica

JAPAN
Boei Kenshu jo
(National Defense College)
Senshi – Shitsu
(War History Research)
Motomura - cho 1
Ichigaya, Shinjuku-ku
Tokyo 162, Japan

MARTINIQUE
Musee Departmental
Place de la Savane 97200
Fort-De-France BP720, Martinique

MEXICO
Archivos Generales de la Nacion
Calle Soledad
Mexico D.F., Mexico

The C.E.D.A.M. Museum
Xelha
Quintana Roo, Mexico

Museo Nacional de Antropologia
Paseo de la Reforma y Ghandi
Mexico 5, D.F., Mexico

NETHERLANDS
Netherlands Royal Archives
The Hague, Netherlands

Nederlandisch Historisch
Scheepvaart Museum
Cornelius Schuytstraat 57
Amsterdam, Netherlands

NEW ZEALAND
Lyttelton Museum
Gladstone Quay
Lyttleton, Canterbury Province,
New Zealand

NORWAY
Bergen Sjofartsmuseum
Mohlenprisbakken 3
N-5010 Bergen, Norway
Norsk Sjofartsmuseum
Bygdoynesveien 37, Oslo 2, Norway

PORTUGAL
Arquivo Nacional
Largo S. Bento
Lisbon 2, Portugal

Museu de Marinha
Jeronimus, Belem
1400 Lisbon, Portugal

REPUBLIC OF THE MALDIVES
National Museum
Darvl Aasaaru
Male, Maldives

SPAIN
Archives of the Indes
Seville, Spain

Museo Naval
Calle de Montalban
Madrid, Spain

SWEDEN
Krigsarkivet
Banergatan 64
Stockholm 80, Sweden

Marinmuseum
Amiralitetsstorget
S-371 00 Karlskrona, Sweden

Statens Sjohistoriska Museum
Djurgardsbrunnsvagen 24
Stockholm S-115 27, Sweden

Bibliography

Angelucci, Enzo and Attilio Cucari. **Ships**. Greenwich House, 1993.

Bathe, Basil W. **The Visual Encyclopedia of Nautical Terms Under Sail**. Crown Publishers, Inc., 1978.

Dudley, William S. "American Naval Archaeology: Past and Prologue." **Pull Together: Newsletter of the Naval Historical Foundation and the Naval Historical Center**, Spring/Summer 1991.

Fish, John P. and Arnold Carr. **Sound Underwater Images**. Lower Cape Publishing, 1990.

Greenhill, Basil. **The Evolution of the Wooden Ship**. Facts On File, 1988.

Hansen, Robert C. **Educational Pamphlet #8: Possible Sources of Wreck Information**. NOAA, National Ocean Service, 1993.

Harrington, Steve. **Divers Guide to Michigan**. Maritime Press.

Harris, Lynn. **Underwater Archaeology Manual for South Carolina Sport Divers**. Sport Diver Archaeology Management Program, Division of Underwater Archaeology, South Carolina Institute of Archaeology & Anthropology, 1990.

Keatts, Henry C. **New England's Legacy of Shipwrecks**. American Merchant Marine Museum Press, 1988.

—**Guide to Shipwreck Diving: New York & New Jersey**. Pisces Books, 1993.

—and George C. Farr. **Dive into History Vol. 3: U-boats**. Pisces Books, 1994.

Kemp, Peter. **The History of Ships**. Orbis Publishing, 1978.

—**The Oxford Companion to Ships and the Sea**. Oxford University Press, 1976.

Luther, Jr., B. W. **Wrecks Below**. Published by the author, 1958.

Marestier, Jean Baptiste. **Memoir on Steamboats of the United States of America**. The Royal Press, 1824.

Munsey, Cecil. **Collecting Bottles**. Hawthorne Books, Inc., 1970.

Murphy, R. Joseph, & Associates. **Preservation of Artifacts Recovered from a Marine or Fresh Water Environment**. Marine Archaeological Research Services.

Nordbok, A.B. **The Lore of Ships**. Crescent Books, 1984.

Peterson, Mendel. **History Under the Sea**. Published by author, 1973.

Rowe, Alan. **Relics, Water and the Kitchen Sink: A Diver's Handbook to Underwater Archaeology**.

Singley, Katherine. **The Conservation of Archaeological Artifacts from Freshwater Environments**. Lake Michigan Maritime Museum, 1988.

Stonehouse, Frederick. **Isle Royale Shipwrecks**. Avery Color Studios, 1986.

Taylor, Poppa. "Artifacts, Fossels, & Other Things." **FSDA Bulletin**, January, 1976.

Tower, Howard B. "Conserving Metal Artifacts." **Skin Diver**, July 1989.

Turner, Ruth D. **A Survey and Illustrated Catalogue of the Teredinidae**. The Museum of Comparitive Zoology, Harvard University, 1966.

Index

National Marine Fisheries Service   74
National Ocean Service   74, 77, 78, 79, 80, 93
National Ocean Survey   78, 81, 82
National Oceanic and Atmospheric Administration (see NOAA)   74
National Ocean Service, Hydrographic Surveys Branch   80
National Weather Service   74
nautical charts   75, 77, 78, 81, 112
    foreign waters   81
Naval Historical Center   73, 86, 90, 95, 97, 233, 234
Naval Historical Center, Operational Archives Branch   95, 99
Naval History   88
Naval History Division, Museum of History & Technology   87
Naval Institute   88
Naval Review   88
Navy Department Library   85
Navy Eagle Boat   55
Navy Museum   85, 87
Navy photography   84
Navy Publications & Printing Service   84
Navy Yard   73, 84, 85, 86
Nebraska   29
New Hampshire   44
New Jersey   87
New York Public Library   72, 73
New York Times   72
Nikonos   240, 241, 242, 244
nitrogen narcosis   177, 178, 182
NOAA   16, 68, 74, 75, 81, 233, 260
North River   38
NOS Distribution Branch   81
NOS wreck charts   82

O

Office of Naval Intelligence   90
Office of Oceanic and Atmospheric Research   74
Ohio (see U.S.S. *Ohio*)   44, 196
Oregon   173, 197, 198, 206, 222
Ostfriesland   87
Owens, Michael J.   200

P

Painter, William   200
Palmer, Bill   6
penetration line   184, 185
penetration, shipwreck   180
penetration, progressive   185
Periscopes   28
photography, still   239
Piney Point   26
Pinthis   46, 47
Poling Brothers #2   100
Polo, Marco   34
pontil bottles   199
pony bottle   152, 153, 156, 157, 167
Prints and Photographs Division   82
progressive penetration   185
Public Affairs Staff   84
Public Records Office   73

Q

Quinn, Bill   7

R

range   72, 83, 104, 105, 106, 107, 108, 109, 112, 114, 116, 126, 127, 128, 132
ranges
    spatial   105
    visual   104
redundancy   151, 152, 153, 154, 155, 156, 157, 158, 160, 161
Reference Report   83
research, methodology of   90
Revere, Paul   44, 45
Rude   75
Russel, Alan   90
Ruth, Dr. Turner   7, 52

S

S-*49*   26
S-*5*   85
S-class submarine   85
S.S. *Central America*   52, 229
sacrificial metal   56
Safety Sausage   167
Sailing Ships   32
Salvage, Law of   229

Titles by Watersport Books

TECHNICAL SERIES

COMPLETE WRECK DIVING
A Guide to Diving Wrecks
by Henry Keatts and Brian Skerry

DEEP DIVING – *Revised*
An Advanced Guide to Physiology Procedures and Systems
by Bret Gilliam with Robert von Maier

DRY SUIT DIVING – *Revised*
A Guide to Diving Dry
by Steve Barsky, Dick Long, and Bob Stinton

WHEN WOMEN DIVE
A Female's Guide to Both Diving and Snorkeling
by Erin O'Neill and Ella Jean Morgan

DIVE COMPUTERS
A Consumer's Guide to History, Theory, and Performance
by Ken Loyst

MIXED GAS DIVING
The Ultimate Challenge for Technical Diving
by Tom Mount and Bret Gilliam

SOLO DIVING – *Revised*
The Art of Underwater Self-Sufficiency
by Robert von Maier

TITLES BY CARLOS EYLES

DOLPHIN BORNE

SECRET SEAS

SEA SHADOWS

THE LAST OF THE BLUE WATER HUNTERS

DIVING FREE

RECREATIONAL/TRAVEL

DIVING PIONEERS
An Oral History of Diving in America
by Eric Hanauer

THE AMBER FOREST
by Ron McPeak, Dale Glantz, and Carol Shaw

THE EGYPTIAN RED SEA
A Diver's Guide
by Eric Hanauer

HAWAI'I BELOW
Favorites, Tips and Secrets — An Island by Island Guide
by Rod Canham